Tools, Languages, Methodologies for
Representing Semantics on the Web of Things

Series Editor
Patrick Siarry

Tools, Languages, Methodologies for Representing Semantics on the Web of Things

Edited by

Shikha Mehta
Sanju Tiwari
Patrick Siarry
M.A. Jabbar

WILEY

First published 2022 in Great Britain and the United States by ISTE Ltd and John Wiley & Sons, Inc.

ISTE Ltd
27-37 St George's Road
London SW19 4EU
UK

www.iste.co.uk

John Wiley & Sons, Inc.
111 River Street
Hoboken, NJ 07030
USA

www.wiley.com

Library of Congress Control Number: 2022940900

British Library Cataloguing-in-Publication Data
A CIP record for this book is available from the British Library
ISBN 978-1-78630-764-4

Contents

Chapter 6. SciFiOnto: Modeling, Visualization and Evaluation of Science Fiction Ontologies Based on Indian Contextualization with Automatic Knowledge Acquisition   93

Gerard DEEPAK, Ayush A. KUMAR and Sheeba J. PRIYADARSHINI

Chapter 7. Semantic Web-Enabled IoT Integration for a Smart City .   123

Ronak PANCHAL and Fernando ORTIZ-RODRIGUEZ

Chapter 8. Heart Rate Monitoring Using IoT and AI   139

Kalpana MURUGAN, Cherukuri NIKHIL KUMAR, Donthu Sai SUBASH
and Sangam DEVA KISHORE REDDY

Chapter 9. IoT Security Issues and Its Defensive Methods   155

Keshavi NALLA and Seshu VARDHAN POTHABATHULA

**Chapter 10. Elucidating the Semantic Web of Things for
Making the Industry 4.0 Revolution a Success**
Deepika CHAUDHARY and Jaiteg SINGH

**Chapter 11. Semantic Web and Internet of Things
in e-Health for Covid-19**
ANURAG and Naren JEEVA

Preface

The digital revolution has led to the exponential proliferation of data across all domains. It is expected to mushroom further with the mounting utility of Internet of Things (IoT) devices. IoT is a technological revolution that provides the basic structure for next generation applications and services for routine activities, by integrating a huge number of distributed and heterogeneous devices. However, interoperability is the key challenge faced by contemporary IoT applications, due to proprietary formats and a lack of standardization. Interoperability among heterogeneous devices can be attained by developing formal semantic representations and technologies with appropriate abstraction levels. Semantic Web technologies such as ontologies, semantic web services, annotations, etc., are seen as potential solutions to solve the data interoperability issue for real-world problems.

The amalgamation of IoT with the Semantic Web has given rise to a new dimension that is the Semantic Web of Things (SWoT). The efficacy of Semantic Web technologies has already been established in diverse application domains. Developments in the field of IoT interoperability are still infant. Thus, there is immense scope for deploying the concepts, tools and technologies of the Semantic Web to handle the issues prevailing in IoT applications. The SWoT would help in the development of knowledge-based systems with enormous autonomic competence for the storage and management of information, discovery of devices, etc., for diverse applications. Semantic analytics in IoT applications is an emerging trend for discovering useful patterns to develop new business strategies.

This book focuses on the design and development of tools, technologies, frameworks, architectures and applications of the SWoT to handle the challenges posed in various applications. The objective is to accentuate the usability and performance of these techniques in dealing with problems in emerging areas. The book aims to include submissions that present innovative techniques, cutting-edge systems and novel applications supported by experimental results that reflect the current advances in these domains.

This book will serve as a research guide for graduate students and researchers in the field. The concepts, tools and technologies discussed in this book will assist practitioners in understanding the latest developments in the field. The theme of the book is in sync with the advanced technologies, systems and applications, which can be of immense benefit when solving research problems in diverse domains.

The work presented in this book is divided into 12 chapters. All of these chapters cover abundant concepts and applications from the semantic IoT perspective, such as the role of Semantic Hybrid Multi-Model Multi-Platform (SHM3P) Databases for the IoT, the role of clustering in device discovery for semantic IoT, Industry 4.0, patient monitoring, job search, ontologies in the water domain, smart cities, heart rate monitoring and security.

Chapter 1, *The Role of Semantic Hybrid Multi-Model Multi-Platform (SHM3P) Databases for IoT* provides a model for integrating DBMS (Database Management Systems) across a variety of platforms and applications. A semantic layer is glued between the platforms and subsystems to design multi-platform models. This chapter also elaborates on the need for additional computing and storage capabilities, robustness and integration with mobile applications.

Chapter 2, *A Systematic Review of Ontologies for the Water Domain* focuses on the Semantic Web technologies for water resources management. This chapter provides a systematic review of ontologies for water resources along with their features and applications.

Chapter 3, *Semantic Web Approach for Smart Health to Enhance Patient Monitoring in Resuscitation* applied Semantic Web technologies to monitor resuscitation patients. This work integrated Semantic Web tools with the IoT to automatically monitor the patients for better healthcare, reduce errors and improve patient experience. This chapter proposes a knowledge representation and reasoning framework to semantically annotate data to analyze the semantics of vital signs monitors and data that come from them.

Chapter 4, *Role of Clustering in Discovery Services for the Semantic Internet of Things* presents a detailed study of various discovery service architectures in the IoT. The discovery services are mainly categorized into three types – directory-based, directory-less and semantic-based. Semantics play an important role in building intelligent IoT systems. This chapter highlights the importance of the clustering of services and devices for designing discovery services, in order to reduce search space and look up time.

Chapter 5, *Dynamic Security Testing Techniques for the Semantic Web of Things: Market and Industry Perspective* presents the algorithms and approaches designed by researchers for dynamic security testing by including taint analysis, static analysis, etc., to improve the quality of test cases.

Chapter 6, *SciFiOnto: Modeling, Visualization and Evaluation of Science Fiction Ontologies Based on Indian Contextualization with Automatic Knowledge Acquisition* models ontologies for an interesting domain: science fiction. This model incorporates the extensive vocabulary developed by referring to science fiction literature based on Generation Z or millennials. This chapter presents an integrated framework based on a Binomial Deep Neural Network to densely populate the entities in the existing Science Fiction Ontology.

Chapter 7, *Semantic Web-Enabled IoT Integration for a Smart City* focuses on assessing the Forest Planting Ontology (FPO) using the IoT in smart cities such as New York. The performance of these ontologies has been evaluated using multiple test cases with tools such as Protégé and Apache Jena Fuseki.

Chapter 8, *Heart Rate Monitoring Using IoT and AI* applies IoT and Artificial Intelligent (AI) techniques to monitor the heart rate of patients. The chapter presents a small chip-like portable IoT device for heart patients. The device continuously monitors the temperature and heartbeat of patients and sends these signals to the cloud for timely interventions.

Chapter 9, *IoT Security Issues and Its Defensive Methods* discusses IoT security architectures for various layers. It also highlights the blockchain-based IoT security system and emphasizes its importance for IoT device management. IoT devices connected to the blockchains database would be protected by a device identification-based key mechanism. In the future, multilayer architecture for distributed and centralized IoT with blockchain technology may be developed.

Chapter 10, *Elucidating the Semantic Web of Things for Making the Industry 4.0 Revolution a Success* collates the latest developments in the SWoT that have contributed significantly in the accomplishment of Industry Revolution 4.0. It is observed that the majority of the advancements have been made in manufacturing engineering and product engineering domains.

Chapter 11, *Semantic Web and Internet of Things in e-Health for Covid-19* highlights the utility of the Semantic Web and the IoT to develop e-health applications for the prediction of Covid-19. This chapter presents an in-depth analysis of the various frameworks and architectures designed by integrating the Semantic Web with the IoT.

Chapter 12, *Development of a Semantic Web Enabled Job_Search Ontology System* presents a "SearchAJob" system using Semantic Web technologies. The job search ontology provides the benefit of executing a single query across multiple domains, in order to extract information regarding job recruitment opportunities from multiple ontologies with a single click.

Shikha MEHTA
Sanju TIWARI
Patrick SIARRY
M.A. JABBAR
May 2022

1

The Role of Semantic Hybrid Multi-Model Multi-Platform (SHM3P) Databases for IoT

To overcome the difficulties of today's zoo of data models stored and processed in companies, multi-model databases offer a simple way to access and query the data stored using different models. In contrast to other data models, the semantic model introduces an additional abstraction layer for reasoning purposes, offering superior possibilities for data integration. Hence, the semantic model is best suited to act as a glue between different data models. Today's companies are using various platforms such as mobile devices, web, desktops, servers (hardware-accelerated by GPU (Graphical Processing Unit), FPGA (Field-programmable gate array) and in the future, QPU), clouds and post-clouds (e.g. fog and edge computing) to run their applications and databases. In this chapter, we discuss the possibilities for the Internet of Things (IoT) of so called semantic hybrid multi-model multi-platform databases, which use semantic technologies as glue to integrate different data models and run on various platforms, offering the best features of the various data models and platforms.

1.1. Introduction

Today companies use data in various data formats (see Figure 1.1). Web shops are connected with relational databases containing customers and their orders. To exchange data, product catalogs of companies are serialized and transmitted in the XML, JSON or RDF data formats. Graph data is frequently processed due to the importance of social networks today. Unstructured data dominates in social media, like in wikis. Due to their simple way of retrieving the data by just using keys, key-value stores are widely used. Schema-free or schema-less databases are preferred ways to store unstructured data, because they do not require the data to stay in the inflexible corset of a schema. Document stores even support complex data formats under the absence of schemas. The data are hence stored according to and processed using different models (*multi-model data* (see Lu and Holubová (2019))). The big

Chapter written by Sven GROPPE, Jinghua GROPPE and Tobias GROTH.

challenge for today's companies are the synchronization and integration of their multi-model data into a single view of and for the customer (see Kotorov (2003)). *Multi-Model Database Management Systems* (MM-DBMSs) offer the management of different data models in one single database (see Lu and Holubová (2019)). The alternative architecture principle is polyglot persistence, where applications use several databases at the same time to handle multi-model data (Leberknight 2008). The big disadvantages are that it inherits the limitations of different databases, for example queries and rules are only optimized within one database, but not across connected Database Management Systems (DBMSs) (see Groppe and Groppe (2020) and Groppe (2021)). In Groppe (2021), we propose to use the semantic data model for unifying the other data models: the semantic data model supports ontologies as an additional abstraction layer, which best suits the data integration purposes of other data models.

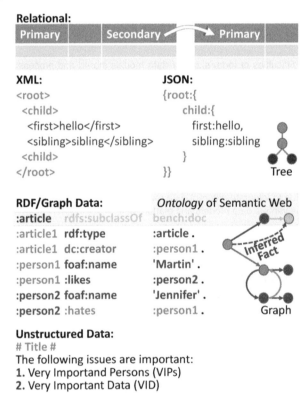

Figure 1.1. *Various data models used in today's companies. For a color version of this figure, see www.iste.co.uk/mehta/tools.zip*

Traditionally mainly running on parallel servers, today DBMSs are operating on various different platforms such as mobile devices, web, desktops, servers (maybe additionally hardware accelerated by GPUs, FPGAs and emergent technologies such as quantum computing), clouds and post-clouds (e.g. fog and edge computing) offering execution environments to run DBMSs[1].

Recent trends in programming languages like Kotlin (see JetBrains s.r.o. (2020)) include multi-platform development support to share common code between different platforms such as desktop, server, web, mobile and IoT. In this way the development costs are drastically reduced for a DBMS running on multiple platforms. For example, the Semantic Web DBMS *luposdate3000* developed in Kotlin is designed to run fast on parallel servers utilizing the Java virtual machine (JVM) (see Warnke et al. (2021)), and also offers a web app that runs completely in the web browser (see Groppe et al. (2021a,b)). Furthermore, another target platform is the IoT, where luposdate3000 is running on the edge (see Warnke (2022)) with efficient indexing schemes, as proven by experiments with the simulator SIMORA (see Warnke et al. (2022)).

By connecting all of the pieces together (M3P/HM3P/SHM3P), DBMSs are defined as follows (see Groppe (2021)):

DEFINITION 1.1 (M3P/HM3P/SHM3P DBMS).– *A multi-model multi-platform database management system (M3P DBMS) is an MM-DBMS that can be executed on different platforms. A hybrid M3P (HM3P) DBMS spans over different platforms in operation. A Semantic HM3P (SHM3P) DBMS supports a (global) semantic layer (for querying and reasoning purposes) over all platforms of an HM3P DBMS.*

Today's M3P DBMSs are usually developed for platforms of the same type (like servers running windows or linux, see Groppe and Groppe (2020) and Groppe (2021)). Only few of them support *hybrid clouds*, which integrate a (locally installed) private cloud with a public cloud[2]. In contrast, we envision SHM3P DBMSs operating over platforms of *different types* (such as IoT and hardware-accelerated parallel servers). In this way the features of different types of databases developed for different platforms can be supported (such as energy-saving on IoT devices and high throughput on servers). For Semantic DBMS, advanced global reasoning capabilities spanning over all platforms need to be developed. Hence, SHM3P databases support any data model at any platform by tightly integrating them with a semantic layer (see Groppe (2021)). For an example installation, see Figure 1.2.

---

1 Note that clients of DBMSs typically run on different platforms, but we are considering the database server here.

2 Please note that private and public clouds are platforms of the same type.

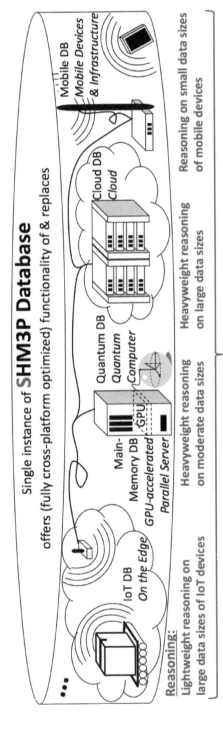

Figure 1.2. *SHM3P database spanning over multiple platforms. Here, an SHM3P database replaces an IoT database in an Industry 4.0 scenario (using edge-computing), a GPU-accelerated parallel database (on a parallel server) for archiving and generating long-term statistics of the IoT data, which is further supported by a quantum computer for query and reasoning optimization, a database in the cloud for natural language processing tasks and a mobile database (on mobile devices and infrastructure) for monitoring and controlling the production line in the company. Platforms are marked using italic font. Green text marks discussion about reasoning in these scenarios (source: Groppe (2021)). For a color version of this figure, see www.iste.co.uk/mehta/tools.zip*

1.2. Databases for multi-model data

Polyglot persistence uses different databases supporting different data models (and maybe running on different platforms) within one application (see Leberknight (2008)). There is a need for federated query languages to formulate queries over heterogeneous data stores within one single query. Examples for federated query languages include the following:

– CloudMdsQL (see Kolev et al. (2016)), which can be used to formulate queries over SQL and NoSQL databases integrated in a prototype with the support of global optimization, and push operations down to the integrated SQL and NoSQL databases as much as possible.

– Zhu and Risch (2011) propose a system to query cloud-based NoSQL such as Google's Bigtable and relational databases with the Google Bigtable query language GQL.

– Apache Drill[3] supports interactive ad hoc analysis of large-scale datasets with low-latency handling up to petabytes of data spread across thousands of servers. Drill's optimization techniques include leveraging the datastore's internal processing capabilities in query plans and considering data locality for best query performance.

The integration of diverse data sources by using database connectors (like JDBC drivers) is widely used in commercial multi-store products such as IBM BigInsights, Microsoft HDInsight and Oracle Bigdata Appliance, as well as in open source projects like PrestoDB[4]. The semantic integration is done in Tatooine (see Bonaque et al. (2016)) using a semantic layer as glue between databases for different data models. However, data processing is limited in all of these polystores, because they do not fully support the optimization of queries across the integrated, but independent data sources.

There is a long history of *federation databases* (see Hammer and McLeod (1979)) and multi-databases (see Smith et al. (1981)). Their architectures contain a mediator between different autonomous databases. This mediator integrates different databases and data sources by reformulating queries according to a global schema. The reformulated queries follow the native schemes of the integrated databases evaluating these queries. Today, some research efforts about federating databases follow the polyglot persistence approach: for example, DBMS+ (see Lim et al. (2013)) provides unified declarative processing for the integration of several processing and database platforms. Location transparency is offered by BigDAWG (see Elmore et al. (2015)), while running queries against its different integrated systems PostgreSQL, SciDB and Accumulo.

---

3 See: https://drill.apache.org/ [Accessed on 21 February 2022].
4 See: https://prestodb.io/ [Accessed on 21 February 2022].

Multi-Model Databases: A multi-model database is one single database for multiple data models, which fully integrates a backend to offer advanced performance, scalability and fault tolerance (see Lu et al. (2018)). Object-Relational DataBase Management Systems (ORDBMSs) were one of the first of this type supporting various data models such as relational, text, XML, spatial and object. ORDBMSs are based on relational databases and other data models are pressed into the relational data model for the purpose of integration. The relational model is the first-class citizen. In comparison and in general, in multi-model databases the different models can be all first-class citizens and are supported in a native way (utilizing, e.g. specialized indices for them). Holubova and Scherzinger (2020) propose the use of a semantic layer as glue between the different data models, in order to support global querying and reasoning over all data. We extend this idea to multi-platform databases integrating the technologies and features of different types of databases.

An overview of current state-of-the-art multi-model databases is provided in Groppe and Groppe (2020). Groppe (2021) contains a discussion about the importance of Semantic Web data in multi-model databases: while the support of graph data seems to be quite popular (12 from 21 MM DBMS), only five support RDF as a data model, but do not support the reasoning at all, or only in a rudimentary way. Users and applications with reasoning demands hence rely on native semantic DBMS. W3C (2001) contains a selection of 18 widely used native Semantic Web tools including triple stores and Semantic Web databases. For over half of these tools, Java is the dominating programming language (i.e. six of these tools run on any platform with Java support or four of these tools support Java language bindings). Semantic Web tools with native binaries usually run on any desktop and server computers, some only on linux operating systems. Most multi-model databases run SQL, SQL-like or extensions of SQL queries. Binaries of these databases are offered in machine code (often compiled from C/C++) or for the JVM. They usually run on all or a big subset of the major server operating systems: Linux, Windows, macOS, Unix and their variants. Few multi-model databases like IBM DB2 still operate on mainframes operating, for example z/OS. While all offer to run in the cloud, some are also enabled for the hybrid cloud.

An HM3P DBMS extends the idea of multi-model databases and supports multiple types of platforms like main-memory, cloud, IoT (with, for example, edge computing) and hardware-accelerated databases using their different advantages at runtime for database tasks such as data distribution, transaction handling and query processing. An SHM3P DBMS supports semantic layers as glue between the different data models, and supports global semantic querying and reasoning by tightly integrating local query engines and reasoners.

There is a need to integrate the data from different types of databases running on different platforms like in the following scenario: for example, we may combine the data of IoT devices (stored in an IoT database running on the edge of the network) with the accounting data containing the remaining time for charging off (stored in a main memory database). For an advanced processing of different types of data stored in different databases and other database tasks, it is indispensable to break the boundaries of the single installations of these DBMSs and run one single DBMS. Furthermore, a semantic layer between different databases helps advanced processing and reasoning capabilities and a tight integration of the different data models. This would also allow us to offer the best features of the different types of databases to applications and users "under one roof" transparently or with an intelligent integration into one query language and Application Programming Interface (API). According to Groppe (2021), this single SHM3P DBMS installation runs over all platforms at the same time, offering the advantages of all the different types of DBMSs (to the data that has been previously processed by the single installations) tightly integrated in a semantic layer, but to have, for example, a global optimization of data distribution, transaction handling and global queries and reasoning tasks with full potential by having freedom of processing down to the physical layer (e.g. index accesses)[5]. One obvious effect of developing one single SHM3P DBMS is reducing the costs of applications and periods of vocational adjustment of developers by offering one API and query language with an additional semantic layer for all different platforms. For SHM3P DBMSs it is very challenging, and also very promising to provide a global distributed reasoner integrating different types of reasoners on different platforms. The advantage of a global reasoner is global optimization for a heterogeneous environment based on a global cost model considering different costs, for example, communication, processing and lifetime of IoT devices.

1.3. Platforms

Databases have been developed for many different platforms. Please see Figure 1.3 for a taxonomy of different types of DBMS running on different types of platforms. In this section, we briefly introduce the different platforms running execution environments for different types of DBMSs.

Small- to medium-sized enterprises (SMEs) usually buy, deploy and run their own *server platforms* for their database servers. These DBMSs are typically centralized parallel databases utilizing multi-core and sometimes many-core systems, often in virtual machines. Server platforms are the dominating platforms not only for relational DBMSs, but also for most Semantic Web DBMSs and reasoners. All other types of DBMSs, including the distributed ones, usually offer a local mode to run on a single server.

---

5 Note that single installations of DBMSs can only be accessed via their offered APIs or by setting up subqueries (of the global query) to them, which hinders the full potential of the optimized processing of, for example, joins between the data of the different DBMSs.

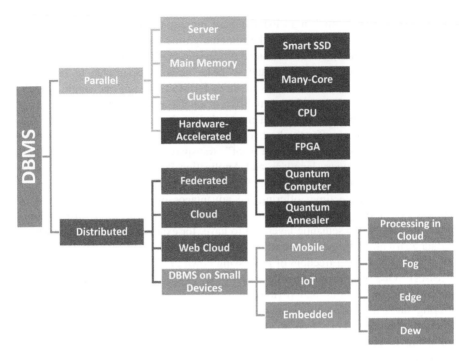

Figure 1.3. *Different types of DBMS running on different platforms and hardware technologies. For a color version of this figure, see www.iste.co.uk/mehta/tools.zip*

The massive parallelism of special hardware behind today's multi-core CPUs like many-core systems including GPUs, FPGAs and in the future quantum computers speeds up databases in *hardware-accelerated servers*. Figure 1.4 provides an overview of the different types of hardware accelerators and their properties[6]. The features of multi-core CPU are as follows:

– shared memory for all cores;

– caches in each core for faster accesses to the main memory, offering cache-coherency over all cores;

– a high single-core performance;

– threads running different code (according to the multiple-instruction multiple-data (MIMD) paradigm).

---

6 The energy consumption is according to D-Wave's quantum computing hardware, which is based on metal niobium loops acting as superconductors when cooled down to 15 millikelvin ($-273°C$). Most power is consumed by the refrigerator, which is slightly less than 25 kilowatts, see https://spectrum.ieee.org/tech-talk/computing/hardware/how-much-power-will-quantum-computing-need.

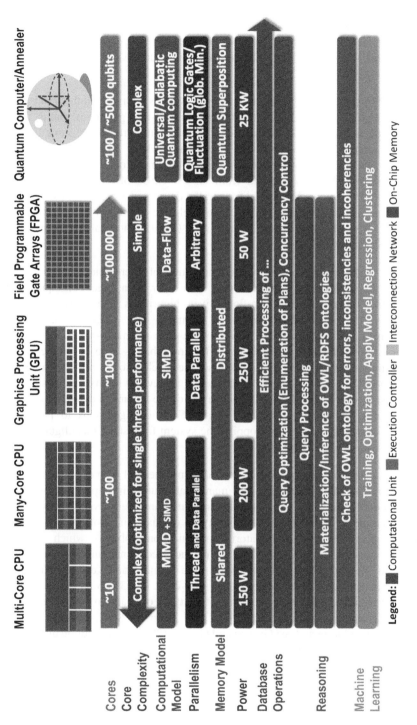

Figure 1.4. *Hardware architectures and properties. Figure is based on Groppe and Groppe (2020) and extended by the "Reasoning" and "Machine Learning" rows. For a color version of this figure, see www.iste.co.uk/mehta/tools.zip*

Many-core CPUs offer many more cores for a higher throughput, with the drawback of an increase of latency and lower single thread performance. Besides these differences, they are based on a similar architecture like that of multi-core CPUs.

Modern GPUs are a special form of many-core systems with several thousands of computing cores following the single-instruction multiple-data paradigm, that is, the same instruction is executed on different data on different cores at the same time. Hence, only certain parallel algorithms like those, where all possibilities are enumerated to find the best one (such as in query optimization and multi-version concurrency control (MVCC)), benefit from GPUs. GPUs offer a high memory bandwidth, such that they are best suited for parallel data-intensive algorithms, which process different (disjoint) subsets of data in parallel, like join algorithms especially designed for GPUs (see, for example, Zhang et al. (2019), who deal with joins for SPARQL processing on GPUs).

FPGAs offer the special feature of reconfiguration of interconnects to connect programmable logic blocks on the FPGA with each other. As a direct consequence, FPGAs are ideally suitable for data-flow-driven algorithms like processing an execution plan for evaluating queries in a streaming way without block-wise materialization of intermediate steps, which is the case for many-core CPUs and GPUs. FPGAs are so flexible that they can offer any arbitrary type of parallelism. The contribution in Werner et al. (2016) discusses the acceleration of SPARQL query processing via FPGAs, where scalable speedups are achieved with even increasingly larger datasets. Werner et al. (2016) discuss the use of the feature of dynamic partial reconfiguration to dynamically exchange the FPGAs' configurations to process different queries at runtime without stopping the system for a static reconfiguration, which is dealt with in other contributions.

Universal quantum computing tries to combine the full power of classical computers with quantum computers that manipulate qubits in super position by applying quantum logic gates. In comparison, quantum annealers – operating on up to several thousand qubits – only run special types of quantum algorithms to solve adiabatic (as special form of combinatorial) optimization problems, which is, for example, the case for traffic control[7], selecting the execution plan with the best estimated costs (from a set of enumerated plans) (see Trummer and Koch (2016)) and concurrency control between transactions (see Roy et al. (2013)). Some algorithms for optimizing databases have been studied for both types of quantum computers like optimizing transaction schedules (see Bittner and Groppe (2020a, 2020b) for a quantum annealer solution and see Groppe and Groppe (2021) for a solution utilizing universal quantum computers).

---

7 Investigated by Volkswagen, see https://www.volkswagenag.com/en/news/stories/2019/11/where-is-the-electron-and-how-many-of-them.html [Accessed on 28 February 2022].

Clouds are designed for dynamical allocation of resources like storage and computing according to users' demands. *Cloud databases* are especially developed for the cloud environment. Because of the dynamic allocation of resources (for storing and computing), nodes are frequently joining and leaving, which must be dealt with in cloud databases, including the redistribution of data (in the case of joining or leaving storage nodes) and ways to manage processing jobs on leaving nodes. In contrast to servers typically running on high-end hardware with redundant components, commodity hardware is usually used for the (up to several thousand) nodes in clouds with the drawback of more frequent hardware and communication failures. The design of cloud computing architectures considers these failures by applying simple fault-tolerance mechanisms to repeat crashed jobs. Typical queries in databases are one-time queries, which are also supported by cloud systems such as Apache Spark and Apache Flink. In addition, they support data streams and continuous queries of *stream databases*. Many Semantic Web databases are built on top of the different cloud technologies (see Groppe et al. (2014b) (HBase, Pig), Graux et al. (2016) (Spark) and Azzam et al. (2018) (Flink)). Few other contributions neglect well-known technologies (see Groppe et al. (2014a)) for the benefit of supporting more local joins without the huge redistribution of data for each new join.

New forms of clouds include the web cloud (see Groppe and Reimer (2019)), which supports easy and more ad hoc deployments of nodes to the web cloud: a user can just use their web browser to visit a certain web page, in order to connect their computer to the web cloud. This promises a much larger number of potential nodes, as any computer running a browser may connect to and be integrated in the web cloud by any user worldwide. On the other hand, the nodes may be disconnected more often, which poses new challenges to the technologies for processing jobs in web clouds. As a consequence, data are processed within the browser and browser technologies must be used for data management purposes in so-called *web cloud databases*. New technologies for the browser can be utilized for data management purposes like WebAssembly (see Rossberg (2019)), which introduces a virtual machine for the browser, promising speed ups for tasks processed in the browser in contrast to running JavaScript. Grall et al. (2017) deal with the first approaches to distribute SPARQL queries in some kind of web clouds.

Mobile databases (see Kumar (2006)) are a special form of databases, which involve the technical infrastructure of mobile providers like base stations (being near-by to their connected mobile devices) for their tasks to be processed. Approaches tailored to the technical infrastructure of mobile providers try to overcome limitations of the mobile devices and promise to lower communication (and hence also energy) costs and increase availability and durability (by logging at the base stations instead on mobile devices). Although some RDF stores, like in Le-Phuoc et al. (2010), are especially designed to run on mobile devices, they do not utilize the backend of mobile providers for advanced mobile processing so far.

Graffi et al. (2010) and Mietz et al. (2013) propose *P2P databases*, which utilize the features of peer-to-peer (P2P) networks to master a frequent joining and leaving of nodes for data storing and processing. P2P networks are designed for a very frequent change in their topology and do not differentiate master and slave nodes for an equal distribution of functionality. In comparison to cloud databases and because of the frequent changes in the underlying topology due to the frequent disconnections of nodes, P2P databases apply a high redundancy in data storing and processing. Furthermore, the connected nodes are highly heterogeneous, which must be especially dealt with in P2P databases. Many approaches, like in Mietz et al. (2013), already propose semantic data processing in P2P networks. However, these approaches only address ontology inference on a very rudimentary basis at most, and not at all for trigger and continuous queries (see Groppe (2020)).

The IoT often comes along with a large-scale installation of IoT devices together with a sufficient backend infrastructure to handle this large-scale installation. *IoT databases* (see, for example, ObjectBox Limited (2019)) are especially designed to offer data management functionalities in IoT environments. IoT databases often run in the cloud, and require a high bandwidth from the IoT devices to the cloud resources. Otherwise, there is a communication bottleneck hindering a good scalability of large-scale IoT environments with high velocity of data.

Fog computing (see Abdelshkour (2015)) aims to save communication by avoiding the route over the Internet backbone. For this purpose, fog computing utilizes near-things edge devices with higher capabilities for storing data and processing application logic. One possible drawback is that the near-things edge devices do not increase in number and capabilities in the same way as the IoT devices, because one near-things edge device typically handles a large number of IoT devices. Therefore, fog computing is not really scalable in the number of connected things.

Edge computing (see Garcia Lopez et al. (2015)) tackles the scalability issue by additionally utilizing all IoT devices for the storage of data and processing of application logic: with a larger deployment of IoT devices, more data needs to be stored and processed, which can be compensated with the larger number of available IoT devices.

Dew computing (see Skala et al. (2015) and Wang (2016)) addresses availability problems due to disconnections between cloud and IoT devices. In their proposed architecture, an additional local server is placed near to the IoT devices responsible for tasks during downtimes and for synchronization with the cloud at uptimes.

When studying relevant literature, one may recognize that there are many contributions (see, for example, Mishra and Jain (2020)) introducing corresponding ontologies and targeting on interoperability issues (see Cimmino et al. (2020)), but there are still only a few contributions to semantic IoT databases. It seems to be natural that IoT databases (especially those running on the fog or edge) are often organized as P2P databases. Another obvious choice is to apply dew computing principles. Hence, contributions to P2P networks processing Semantic Web data, like in Mietz et al. (2013), can be run as a kind of semantic IoT database. The distribution of data and processing tasks between cloud and IoT infrastructures, including the IoT devices, becomes one of the major challenges in this area. New challenges also arise when considering the requirements of processing data streams in an efficient way, especially when offering reasoning capabilities, which demand for a high processing capacity. Furthermore, especially in high velocity environments, it may be difficult to find the right trade-off between storing not all data, but enough for future analysis in case of failures.

1.4. Variations of SHM3P DBMS

Figure 1.5 introduces a taxonomy of different types of DBMS, considering if they are multi-platform, multi-model, hybrid in operation spanning over multiple platforms and supporting semantic layers.

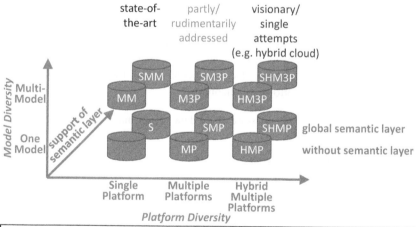

Figure 1.5. *Taxonomy of different types of databases toward SHM3P databases. For a color version of this figure, see www.iste.co.uk/mehta/tools.zip*

We can classify various DBMSs according to this taxonomy: for example, according to Groppe and Groppe (2020), MySQL is an M3P database running on different platforms (server and cloud, but not on completely different platforms like IoT) supporting the relational, key/value and object data models. In contrast, luposdate3000 (see Warnke et al. (2021) and Groppe et al. (2021a,b)) is an SMP database running on parallel servers, in the browser and soon in IoT platforms supporting only the semantic data model. We have plans to develop luposdate3000 further to a full-fledged SHM3P DBMS in our future work.

It is obvious that transforming databases in any of the directions from support of a single platform over multiple platforms to hybrid support of platforms, from single to multiple data models and from without to with the support of a semantic layer is challenging and needs huge development efforts, but will offer many more possibilities for installations (after supporting more platforms) and for the user (especially after the support of more data models, and also of more platforms when considering additional platform features).

1.5. What are the benefits of SHM3P databases for IoT?

We identify benefits of future SHM3P databases for IoT in the areas of data storage and placement, data processing and applications.

1.5.1. *Data storage and placement*

In current state-of-the-art systems, the data of IoT devices and applications are typically either completely stored in the cloud (for large-scale processing) or in the edge and/or fog layer (for processing close to where the data are generated). Hybrid solutions storing data at storage locations best suited for the specific tasks of processing and their applications are uncommon.

SHM3P DBMSs promise to store their data at optimal locations according to criteria such as:

– high throughput of transactions;

– low latencies of IoT applications;

– balanced input data for parallel processing to avoid variance in parallel tasks;

– data replication for resilient processing in case of system crashes, empty batteries, network partitions, etc.;

– suitability for efficient fault-tolerance methods.

It is often the case that not only one of the criteria is the dominating one to be primarily considered, but a mixture of these criteria. One obvious way is to give each of these sub-criteria a weight and build one overall metric for optimizing an overall function, which sums up the ratings of all sub-criteria for a candidate data placement.

While traditional DBMSs stay in the boundary of their platform, SHM3P DBMSs consider storage locations at different platforms. In contrast to hybrid IoT solutions,

SHM3P DBMSs cannot only consider a connected cloud and the IoT network of its devices and backend infrastructure like routers, but also other platforms like hardware-accelerated servers and mobile platforms. This allows us to look at the specific processing tasks and choose the best platforms for their processing. For example, quantum computers promise huge speedups and maybe even the so called quantum advantage (i.e. solving problems that are no longer possible for classical computers due to enormous processing times), but only for certain data and processing tasks. If these kinds of tasks have to be processed often, then data placement strategies have to adapt accordingly.

1.5.2. *Data processing*

While data placement is critical for the processing times of tasks, we also have different possibilities of processing. IoT data can be processed by the IoT devices themselves, but can also be processed by backend infrastructure in the fog layer like routers. Clouds are also often utilized for processing large-scale data, but would be underutilized for simple tasks and are not the optimal choice for frequently changing data. Hardware-accelerated servers are the first choice for medium-sized datasets with a lot of dependencies within these datasets, which hinder the partition of data into datasets to be independently processed in parallel and distributed like in the cloud. Specialized computing tasks like mathematical optimizations are the first choice for processing tasks via quantum computers. Also, quantum machine learning has its benefits compared to classical machine learning, promising a quantum advantage for certain datasets and tasks (see Huang et al. (2021)). Mobile devices may be considered for mobile applications, as well as those taking the current location into account for their tasks.

1.5.3. *IoT applications*

IoT applications are often not only running on IoT devices, but need additional computing capabilities or information not stored in the connected IoT devices. One typical example is the processing of spoken natural language, which is recorded by IoT devices, but processed in the cloud by retrieving the answer from a knowledge graph.

Hence, we classify IoT applications in those:

– running only on IoT devices, like simple requests for the status of IoT devices and triggering actions, for example switching on lights and heating, and changing music;

– which need additional processing capabilities in the cloud or on hardware-accelerated servers for the processing of spoken natural language and training of machine learning models;

– which work on huge datasets like Internet searches and retrieve facts from knowledge graphs to answer user questions;

– based on location-aware functionalities and data like the personalized advertisement of local shops, or access control by checking bought tickets.

Overall, IoT applications today already span over IoT devices, the IoT backend and cloud, as well as hardware-accelerated devices and mobile devices. Utilizing SHM3P DBMSs can help IoT applications to offer a smoother user experience in terms of latencies, better handling of failures and crashes, and quality and completeness of results of user requests in comparison to relying only on the IoT platform.

1.6. Summary and conclusions

M3P DBMSs provide the infrastructure to handle not only the zoo of data models deployed in today's companies (which is the focus of pure *multi-model databases*), but also integrate a variety of platforms and inherit their various features for the benefit of users and their applications. We call M3P DBMSs spanning over different platforms at run-time *Hybrid M3P* (HM3P) *DBMSs*. We discuss the variant to add a semantic layer as glue between each platform and subsystems for the simple integration of the DBMS technologies, calling it *Semantic HM3P* (SHM3P) *DBMSs*. We extensively discuss the possibilities of SHM3P DBMSs for IoT applications and categorize IoT applications according to their needs for additional computing and storage capabilities, as well as robustness and integration with mobile applications.

In our future work, we will develop luposdate3000 further to a fully-fledged SHM3P DBMS, with a focus on the support of IoT scenarios. We are especially interested in the efficient processing of data and queries in large-scale networks with frequent changes in the network topology, and the smooth interplay of various platforms and their technologies for the benefit of users and their applications.

1.7. References

Abdelshkour, M. (2015). IoT, from cloud to fog computing. Cisco Blogs [Online]. Available at: http://blogs.cisco.com/perspectives/iot-from-cloud-to-fog-computing [Accessed 29 April 2022].

Azzam, A., Kirrane, S., Polleres, A. (2018). Towards making distributed RDF processing FLINKer. *4th International Conference on Big Data Innovations and Applications (Innovate-Data)*, 9–16. IEEE, Barcelona.

Bittner, T. and Groppe, S. (2020a). Avoiding blocking by scheduling transactions using quantum annealing. *24th Symposium on International Database Engineering & Applications (IDEAS)*, 21, 1–10. Association for Computing Machinery, Seoul.

Bittner, T. and Groppe, S. (2020b). Hardware accelerating the optimization of transaction schedules via quantum annealing by avoiding blocking. *Open Journal of Cloud Computing (OJCC)*, 7(1), 1–21 [Online]. Available at: http://nbn-resolving.de/urn:nbn:de:101:1-20201122183332015343957 [Accessed 29 April 2022].

Bonaque, R., Cao, T.D., Cautis, B., Goasdoué, F., Letelier, J., Manolescu, I., Mendoza, O., Ribeiro, S., Tannier, X., Thomazo, M. (2016). Mixed-instance querying: A lightweight integration architecture for data journalism. *PVLDB*, 9(13), 1513–1516.

Cimmino, A., Poveda-Villalón, M., García-Castro, R. (2020). EWOT: A semantic interoperability approach for heterogeneous IoT ecosystems based on the web of things. *Sensors*, 20(3), 822.

Elmore, A., Duggan, J., Stonebraker, M., Balazinska, M., Cetintemel, U., Gadepally, V., Heer, J., Howe, B., Kepner, J., Kraska, T. et al. (2015). A demonstration of the bigdawg polystore system. *Proc. VLDB Endow.*, 8(12), 1908–1911.

Garcia Lopez, P., Montresor, A., Epema, D., Datta, A., Higashino, T., Iamnitchi, A., Barcellos, M., Felber, P., Riviere, E. (2015). Edge-centric computing: Vision and challenges. *SIGCOMM Comput. Commun. Rev.*, 45(5), 37–42.

Graffi, K., Stingl, D., Gross, C., Nguyen, H., Kovacevic, A., Steinmetz, R. (2010). Towards a P2P cloud: Reliable resource reservations in unreliable P2P systems. *16th International Conference on Parallel and Distributed Systems (ICPADS)*. IEEE Computer Society Press, Shanghai.

Grall, A., Folz, P., Montoya, G., Skaf-Molli, H., Molli, P., Vander Sande, M., Verborgh, R. (2017). Ladda: SPARQL queries in the fog of browsers. *European Semantic Web Conference*, 10577, 126–131. Springer, Portoroz.

Graux, D., Jachiet, L., Geneves, P., Layaïda, N. (2016). Sparqlgx: Efficient distributed evaluation of SPARQL with apache spark, *ISWC*, Springer, Kobe.

Groppe, S. (2020). Emergent models, frameworks, and hardware technologies for big data analytics. *The Journal of Supercomputing*, 76, 1800–1827.

Groppe, S. (2021). Semantic hybrid multi-model multi-platform (SHM3P) databases. *Proceedings of the International Semantic Intelligence Conference (ISIC'21)*, February 25–27, New Delhi [Online]. Available at: http://ceur-ws.org/Vol-2786/Paper2.pdf [Accessed 29 April 2022].

Groppe, S. and Groppe, J. (2020). Hybrid multi-model multi-platform (HM3P) databases. *Proceedings of the 9th International Conference on Data Science, Technology and Applications (DATA)*. SciTePress.

Groppe, S. and Groppe, J. (2021). Optimizing transaction schedules on universal quantum computers via code generation for Grover's search algorithm. *Proceedings of the 25th International Database Engineering & Applications Symposium (IDEAS)*, 149–156. Association for Computing Machinery, Montreal [Online]. Available at: https://doi.org/10.1145/3472163.3472164.

Groppe, S. and Reimer, N. (2019). Code generation for big data processing in the web using WebAssembly. *Open Journal of Cloud Computing (OJCC)*, 6(1), 1–15.

Groppe, S., Blume, J., Heinrich, D., Werner, S. (2014a). A self-optimizing cloud computing system for distributed storage and processing of semantic web data. *Open Journal of Cloud Computing (OJCC)*, 1(2), 1–14.

Groppe, S., Kiencke, T., Werner, S., Heinrich, D., Stelzner, M., Gruenwald, L. (2014b). P-luposdate: Using precomputed bloom filters to speed up SPAQRL processing in the cloud. *Open Journal of Semantic Web (OJSW)*, 1(2), 25–55.

Groppe, S., Klinckenberg, R., Warnke, B. (2021a). Generating sound from the processing in semantic web databases. *Open Journal of Semantic Web (OJSW)*, 8(1), 1–27 [Online]. Available at: https://nbn-resolving.org/urn:nbn:de:101:1-2022011618330544843704.

Groppe, S., Klinckenberg, R., Warnke, B. (2021b). Sound of databases: Sonification of a semantic web database engine. *Proc. VLDB Endow.*, 14(12), 2695–2698 [Online]. Available at: https://doi.org/10.14778/3476311.3476322.

Hammer, M. and McLeod, D. (1979). On database management system architecture. Technical report, MIT, Cambridge Laboratory for Computer Science.

Holubova, I. and Scherzinger, S. (2020). Nextgen multi-model databases in semantic big data architectures. *Open Journal of Semantic Web (OJSW)*, 7(1), 1–16.

Huang, H.-Y., Broughton, M., Mohseni, M., Babbush, R., Boixo, S., Neven, H., McClean, J.R. (2021). Power of data in quantum machine learning. *Nature Communications*, 12(1) [Online]. Available at: https://doi.org/10.1038/s41467-021-22539-9.

JetBrains s.r.o. (2020). FAQ - Kotlin Programming Language [Online]. Available at: https://kotlinlang.org/docs/reference/faq.html [Accessed 29 April 2022].

Kolev, B., Valduriez, P., Bondiombouy, C., Jiménez-Peris, R., Pau, R., Pereira, J. (2016). CloudMdsQL: Querying heterogeneous cloud data stores with a common language. *Distributed and Parallel Databases*, 34(4), 463–503.

Kotorov, R. (2003). Customer relationship management: Strategic lessons and future directions. *Business Process Management Journal*, 9(5), 566–571.

Kumar, V. (2006). *Mobile Database Systems*. Wiley Online Library.

Le-Phuoc, D., Parreira, J.X., Reynolds, V., Hauswirth, M. (2010). RDF on the go: An RDF storage and query processor for mobile devices. *ISWC*, Springer, Shanghai.

Leberknight, S. (2008). Polyglot persistence. Scott Leberknight's Weblog [Online]. Available at: http://www.sleberknight.com/blog/sleberkn/entry/polyglot_persistence [Accessed 29 April 2022].

Lim, H., Han, Y., Babu, S. (2013). How to fit when no one size fits. *CIDR*, Asilomar, California.

Lu, J. and Holubová, I. (2019). Multi-model databases: A new journey to handle the variety of data. *ACM Computing Surveys (CSUR)*, 52(3), 1–38.

Lu, J., Liu, Z.H., Xu, P., Zhang, C. (2018). UDBMS: Road to unification for multi-model data management. *ER Workshops*, Springer, Xi'an.

Mietz, R., Groppe, S., Kleine, O., Bimschas, D., Fischer, S., Römer, K., Pfisterer, D. (2013). A P2P semantic query framework for the internet of things. *PIK-Praxis der Informationsverarbeitung und Kommunikation*, 36(2), 73–79.

Mishra, S. and Jain, S. (2020). Ontologies as a semantic model in IoT. *International Journal of Computers and Applications*, 42(3), 233–243.

ObjectBox Limited (2019). The best IoT Databases for the Edge – An overview and compact guide [Online]. Available at: https://objectbox.io/the-best-iot-databases-for-the-edge-an-overview-and-compact-guide/ [Accessed 29 April 2022].

Rossberg, A. (2019). WebAssembly Core Specification. *W3C Proposed Recommendation* [Online]. Available at: https://www.w3.org/TR/wasm-core-1/ [Accessed 29 April 2022].

Roy, S., Kot, L., Koch, C. (2013). Quantum databases. *CIDR*, Asilomar, California.

Skala, K., Davidovic, D., Afgan, E., Sovic, I., Sojat, Z. (2015). Scalable distributed computing hierarchy: Cloud, fog and dew computing. *Open Journal of Cloud Computing (OJCC)*, 2(1), 16–24.

Smith, J.M., Bernstein, P.A., Dayal, U., Goodman, N., Landers, T., Lin, K.W.T., Wong, E. (1981). Multibase: Integrating heterogeneous distributed database systems. *AFIPS National Computer Conference*, Association for Computing Machinery, Chicago.

Trummer, I. and Koch, C. (2016). Multiple query optimization on the d-wave 2x adiabatic quantum computer. *Proc. VLDB Endow.*, 9(9), 648–659.

W3C (2001). Semantic web development tools [Online]. Available at: https://www.w3.org/2001/sw/wiki/Tools [Accessed 23 April 2020].

Wang, Y. (2016). Definition and categorization of dew computing. *Open Journal of Cloud Computing (OJCC)*, 3(1), 1–7.

Warnke, B. (2022). Github [Online]. Available at: https://github.com/luposdate3000/luposdate3000 [Accessed 21 February 2022].

Warnke, B., Rehan, M.W., Fischer, S., Groppe, S. (2021). Flexible data partitioning schemes for parallel merge joins in semantic web queries. *Datenbanksysteme für Business, Technologie und Web (BTW)*, 19. Fachtagung des GI-Fachbereichs "Datenbanken und Informationssysteme", Dresden [Online]. Available at: https://doi.org/10.18420/btw2021-12.

Warnke, B., Sehgelmeble, Y.C., Mantler, J., Groppe, S., Fischer, S. (2022). Simora: Simulating open routing protocols for application interoperability on edge devices. *6th IEEE International Conference on Fog and Edge Computing (ICFEC)*, IEEE Computer Society Press, Messina.

Werner, S., Heinrich, D., Groppe, S., Blochwitz, C., Pionteck, T. (2016). Runtime adaptive hybrid query engine based on FPGAS. *Open Journal of Databases (OJDB)*, 3(1), 21–41.

Zhang, X., Zhang, M., Peng, P., Song, J., Feng, Z., Zou, L. (2019). A scalable sparse matrix-based join for SPARQL query processing. *International Conference on Database Systems for Advanced Applications*, Springer, Chiang Mai.

Zhu, M. and Risch, T. (2011). Querying combined cloud-based and relational databases. *International Conference on Cloud and Service Computing*, IEEE Computer Society Press, Hong Kong.

A Systematic Review of Ontologies for the Water Domain

Current water research integrates Semantic Web technologies for effective water resources management. Various semantic models have been designed to describe water resources, such as water body, water type, water pipe, water meter, reservoir, catchment, pump and sensor. It is challenging to find the water-related ontologies in one place as recent studies are primarily focused on water resources management by developing different water ontologies. However, no-one has presented a literature review to provide all information on existing ontologies. This chapter presents a systematic literature survey to discuss different existing ontologies for water resources and explore their features and applications. A three-step research methodology has been followed to conduct the detailed systematic literature review, ontology characterization and ontology selection from existing sources. As a survey finding, several resources and repositories have been deeply analyzed, and 25 related studies are found. Further more, 14 ontologies are extracted from the related studies. The main finding is that only seven of them are available online to be reused or guide the development of new water ontologies. A detailed review is presented in the chapter with different parameters of existing water-related ontologies and short descriptions of all these ontologies. This chapter also highlights the application of ontologies in different water domains to analyze the existing concepts that can be reused in any proposed water ontology.

2.1. Introduction

Water is precious for human life, in regular activities like recreation and transportation, and in different areas, such as climate, health, agriculture and energy. The information related to water features, such as water quality, water distribution, wastewater management and flooding, can be acquired by water sensors. Water quality monitoring is also an essential issue as it is time-consuming and expensive to collect water samples manually. Recently, several pieces of research have been focused on the semantic representation of the water domain by representing

Chapter written by Sanju TIWARI and Raúl GARCÍA-CASTRO.

hydrological concepts, such as water body, water quality and wastewater. Ontologies are considered a semantic model with intense expressivity to capture the knowledge in different water domains. They play a significant role in describing the characteristics and relations among the concepts included in water domains.

Ontologies are efficient in structuring the knowledge and information with a common representation and language to provide a shared vocabulary for presenting different domains' different classes, properties and other attributes. Ontologies are built to describe the concepts, relationships, restrictions and data properties within a domain and to provide machine readability. In general, ontologies promote accessibility, extensibility and reusability (Howell et al. 2018) and have been successfully applied in different domains, such as buildings, agriculture, energy and transport. Several water ontologies are proposed to organize and specify the concepts and terminologies applied in different water domains, generally composed of hydraulic and hydrological components as a semantic model. Semantic modeling promoted the interoperability between shared information and domain knowledge by developing ontologies. Ontologies are designed to provide interoperability between different water domains. These domains are growing daily to integrate the enormous variety of water-related data. Internet of Things (IoT) technologies play a significant role in dealing with smart water data by using sensing devices. Ontologies have been designed by acquiring the sensor and observation data collected with the help of sensing devices to organize the huge amount of water data and data formats and measurement tasks. Semantic models are developed using OWL and further extend the SSN (Haller et al. 2019) and SAREF (Daniele et al. 2015) to deal with smart water management or frameworks. The SSN ontology facilitates different knowledge management for wireless sensor networks (WSNs) (Katsiri and Makropoulos 2016), while the SAREF ontology models the concepts of sensors and control in smart applications. This chapter has presented a comprehensive literature review of existing ontologies for heterogeneous water domains. A systematic review has been conducted to analyze the existing water ontologies. This review will be helpful to extract the ontologies for reuse in various applications. There are several projects that follow ontology-based approaches to present the information of water domains, such as WatERP (Anzaldi 2015), Hydro Ontology (Brodaric and Hahmann 2014) for water data interoperability, DiHydro Ontology (Katsiri and Makropoulos 2016), SWIM (Reynolds 2014), WISDOM (Zarli et al. 2014), WDTF (Walker et al. 2009), ICT4Water (Curry et al. 2014), Waste Water Treatment Plant (WWTP) Ontology (Ceccaroni et al. 2000), CUAHSI (Kadlec et al. 2015) Hydrologic Information System and many more. To our best knowledge, no-one has covered a comprehensive literature review on water ontologies to extract the features of existing ontologies that can be reused in future ontology development. Our findings suggest reusing the existing ontologies while constructing a new ontology for water domains.

The rest of the chapter is structured as follows. Section 2.2 presents a literature review to conduct a detailed characterization of existing water ontologies. A three-step methodology has been followed to conduct the review. Section 2.3 discusses the different applications of ontologies in the water domain. Finally, section 2.4 presents the discussion and concludes the chapter.

2.2. Literature review

In general, ontologies are reused to integrate with different ontologies and speed up the ontology construction process, thus enabling reuse of the concepts and properties with their definitions that are already evaluated, and providing robustness and consistency to new ontologies (Gómez-Pérez and Rojas-Amaya 1999). It is recommended to reuse ontologies following ontology development guidelines and methodologies by Gómez-Pérez and Rojas-Amaya (1999) as this reduces the cost of ontology construction and engineering tasks such as verification and validation. Reusing ontologies advances application interoperability on the semantic and syntactic level (Bontas et al. 2005). An upper ontology such as BFO (Arp et al. 2015) and SUMO (Pease et al. 2002) also guides the newly developed ontologies as their formalization describes the association between non-material and material concepts along with their attributes, such as Roles, Processes and Qualities.

This section will discuss existing work to show the importance of semantic representation in the water domain. Several studies have been presented to deal with water management by applying Semantic Web technologies and IoT to promote the water domains. This section will cover the comprehensive literature of existing water ontologies and features of water that need to be modeled along with the semantic models for water domains.

2.2.1. *Features in the water domain*

A feature represents entities (building, building space, rivers and aquifers), qualities (weight, shape, color, dimension, etc.) and amount of materials (Sanfilippo and Borgo 2016). Water features play an important role in several individual activities that are mostly related to climate, health, energy, agriculture, transportation and recreation. Various sensors are used to collect the information of water features by measurements and provide a considerable amount of dynamic data. Brodaric and Hahmann (2014) have presented significant water feature aspects, such as container, supporter, water object, water matter amount and flow. These features are considered under the physical entities category that contains water and other objects. They can be found above, below or on the planetary surface with representative examples, such as puddles, rivers, aquifers and clouds, reservoirs, canals and catchments. Different properties always express these features with an estimated value captured by the sensing devices. For example, a river can have the properties level, velocity, pH, temperature and turbidity with an estimated value, and a lake can have the properties volume, level and temperature (Taylor 2014).

2.2.2. *Semantic models in the water domain*

Recently, semantic representation in the water domain has been recognized as a significant challenge. With the incremental growth of the IoT in several domains, such as agriculture, building and transportation, attention is being paid to the water domain with ICT techniques. Several semantic models are presented to show the importance of semantics in specific domains. Semantic models promote accessibility, extensibility and reusability (IAB 2015) in the form of ontologies to share and exchange the data in different formats and provide machine understanding to model domain knowledge. Several water resources are presented as a semantic model to design the concepts of water resources and water-related devices, such as actuators, sensors, pumps, valves and reservoirs. Several existing water ontologies that have been discussed in the literature are presented with their different parameters in Table 2.2.

2.2.3. *A comprehensive review of ontologies in the water domain*

The information about water availability and water consumption will make a solid impact to enhance the quality aspects of water management as it is not easy to find the solution to water resources problems (Blodgett et al. 2016). This section presents a comprehensive review of existing work in ontology-based water management. A three-step methodology (Kitchenham and Charters 2007) has been followed to conduct the systematic literature review of existing water-related ontologies. Deep analysis has been done to analyze the related research deeply and the authors have applied a selection criterion to select relevant papers. Several sources, such as Google Scholar, Scopus, Web of Science, Semantic Web Journal and Vocabularies, are analyzed for collecting related research as discussed in Table 2.1. As a finding, 25 relevant papers are considered to present the comprehensive review in Table 2.2.

The selection of relevant sources is essential for preparing a systematic literature review. This chapter has analyzed several sources to prepare a comprehensive review of any specific domain. Water ontologies are selected after conducting a complete review by following the prepared methodology (Kitchenham and Charters 2007, Espinoza-Arias et al. 2019). Figure 2.1 shows the methodology to conduct the review of existing ontologies in water domains.

This methodology has been categorized in three steps: a systematic review is conducted to acquire the water ontologies related papers in step 1; step 2 characterizes water ontologies with their different features. Finally, ontology selection is discussed in step 3. A comprehensive review is presented in Table 2.2, ontology characterization is discussed in Table 2.3 and finally selected ontologies are presented in Table 2.4.

Source	Type	URL
Google Scholar (GS)	Database	https://scholar.google.com/
Scopus	Database	https://www.scopus.com/
Web of Science (WoS)	Database	https://apps.webofknowledge.com/
Semantic Web Journal (SWJ)	Journal	https://content.iospress.com/journals/
Linked Open Vocabularies (LOVs)	Ontology Index	https://lov.linkeddata.es
Linked Open Vocabularies for Internet of Things (LOV4IoT)	Ontology Catalog	http://lov4iot.appspot.com/

Table 2.1. *Sources to collect the related research*

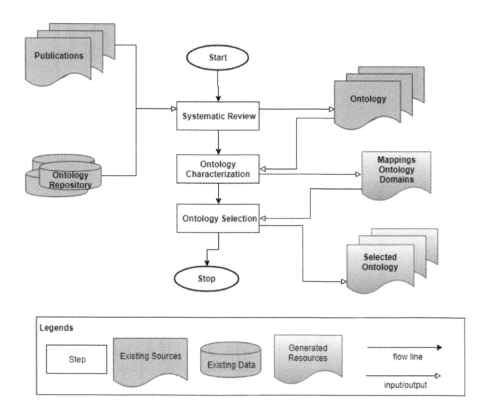

Figure 2.1. *Three-step methodologies to conduct systematic review (source: Espinoza-Arias et al. (2019))*

Ref.	Major techniques	Reasoning type	Representation language	Informative	Features covered	Reused ontologies	Ontology available	Ontology evaluation	Status
García-Castro (2020)	Ontologies, Sensor, Actuator	SPARQL	OWL, RDFs	Yes	Modeling, generating, publishing and exploiting datasets	SAREF, S4CITY, Time, GeoSparql	Yes	Protégé, OOPs, SPARQL	Consider
Escobar et al. (2020)	Ontologies, Linked Data	SPARQL	OWL, RDF	No	Modeling, generating, publishing and exploiting datasets	GeoNames	No	SPARQL	Reject
Wang et al. (2020)	Ontologies, Sensor, Actuator	SWRL	OWL	Yes	Modeling, generating	SSN, DOLCE	No	Protégé	Reject
Corchero (2019)	Ontologies, Sensor	NA	OWL, RDFs	Yes	Modeling, generating, publishing and exploiting datasets	SAREF, time, GeoSparql, time, om	Yes	Protégé	Consider
Howell et al. (2018)	Ontologies, Sensor	SPARQL, SWRL	OWL	Yes	Modeling, generating	GIS schema	No	SPARQL	Reject
Hahmann and Stephen (2018)	Ontologies	NA	FOL	Yes	Extending HyFO with groundwater concepts	HyFO, DOLCE	No	NA	Reject
Poveda-Villalon et al. (2018)	Ontologies	SPARQL	OWL, RDF	Yes	Modeling	SOSA, SAREF	No	NA	Reject

Ref.	Major techniques	Reasoning type	Representation language	Informative	Features covered	Reused ontologies	Ontology available	Ontology evaluation	Status
Goel et al. (2017)	Ontologies, Sensors	Dynamic Bayesian network based probabilistic reasoning	OWL, RDF	No	NA	NA	No	NA	Reject
Howell et al. (2017)	Ontologies, Sensors	SPARQL	OWL, RDF	Yes	Modeling, generating	SSN	No	By domain expert with SPARQL	Reject
Stephen and Hahmann (2017)	Ontologies	SWRL	NA	No	Taxonomy	HyFO	NA	NA	Reject
Sánchez-de Rivera et al. (2017)	Ontologies, Sensors	SPARQL	NA	No	NA	NA	NA	NA	Reject
Wang et al. (2017)	Ontologies, Sensors	SPARQL, SWRL	OWL	Yes	Modeling	SSN/SOSA, geo, DUL, time, space	NA	Protégé, SPARQL	Reject
Xiaomin et al. (2016)	Ontologies	SPARQL	OWL, RDFs	No	Modeling	NA	NA	Protégé, SPARQL	Reject
Kontopoulos et al. (2016)	Ontologies	SPARQL	OWL	Yes	Modeling	Ontology 1405430314	Yes DSHWS	Protégé, SPARQL, OOPs	Consider
Rahman (2015)	Ontologies	NA	OWL, RDFs	No	Modeling	NA	Yes EUWEF	Protégé	Consider
Varanka and Usery (2015)	Ontologies	NA	OWL, RDFs	Yes	Modeling	Geo	Surface water	Protégé	Consider

Ref.	Major techniques	Reasoning type	Representation language	Informative	Features covered	Reused ontologies	Ontology available	Ontology evaluation	Status
Sinha et al. (2014)	Ontologies	SPARQL	OWL, RDFs	Yes	Modeling	GeoSparql	NA	Protégé	Reject
Agresta et al. (2014)	Ontologies, Sensors	SWRL	OWL, RDFs	Yes	Modeling	SSN	NA	Protégé	Reject
Kämpgen et al. (2014)	Ontologies	NA	OWL, RDF	No	Modeling	NA	NA	NA	Reject
Brodaric and Hahmann (2014)	Ontologies	NA	NA	No	Modeling	NA	NA	NA	Reject
Elag and Goodall (2013)	Ontologies	NA	OWL, RDFs	No	Modeling	NA	NA	Protégé	Reject
Scheuer et al. (2013)	Ontologies	NA	OWL, RDFs	No	Modeling	NA	NA	NA	Reject
Ahmedi et al. (2013)	Ontologies, Sensor	SWRL	OWL, RDFs	Yes	Modeling	SSN/SOSA, geo, DUL, time	Yes InWaterSense	Protégé	Consider
Ceccaroni et al. (2000)	Ontologies	Case-Based, Rule-Based	OWL, RDFs	No	Modeling	NA	Yes OntoWAWO	Protégé	Consider
Kinceler et al. (2011)	Ontologies	SPARQL	OWL, RDFs	Yes	Modeling	NA	NA	Protégé	Reject

Table 2.2. A comprehensive review of existing research

Ontologies	Reused ontologies	Concept	Year	Online	Published
SAREF4WATR	SAREF, S4CITY, Time, Geosp	71	2020	Yes	Yes
WaterNexus Ontology	SAREF (Measurements, UnitOfMeasure, Property), GeoSparql, time, om	30	2019	Yes	Yes
DSHWS	Ontology1405430314	25	2016	Yes	No
EUWEFNexus	No	157	2015	Yes	No
SurfaceWater	Geo	93	2015	Yes	No
OntoWAWO	No	223	2013	Yes	No
xLMINWS.owl	dbpedia, time, **SSN**	31	2013	Yes	No

Table 2.3. *Selected ontologies for the water domain*

2.2.3.1. *Step 1: A systematic review*

A systematic approach has been followed to conduct a complete review. We have analyzed different sources to collect the relevant papers and prepared a descriptive review of 25 related studies in Table 2.1. Different keywords are used to search water ontology-related research, such as "water ontologies", "semantics in smart water", "flood ontologies" and "ontology in hydrology". In total, 11 parameters are examined for all collected sources that explore existing papers' findings. These parameters extracted primary techniques, reasoning, representation language, metadata, coverage of features, reused and imported ontologies, online availability of ontologies, ontology evaluation and status of ontologies in existing studies. Only sources from the 10 years from 2010 to 2020 are taken into account to conduct the review.

In total, 25 relevant studies are taken into account after conducting a systematic review of existing literature from different sources. Table 2.1 analyzes several features of existing work, such as Major Techniques, Reasoning Type, Representation Language, Informative, Features Covered, Reused Ontologies, Ontology Available, Ontology Evaluation and Status. It is found that 25 studies have used ontologies as major techniques and 22 studies used OWL, RDFs and FOL as representation language. For reasoning, SPARQL is used in 11 studies, six used SWRL, one study used case-based and rule-based reasoning while one study used probabilistic reasoning. In the Informative parameter, 14 studies have complete metadata information of proposed ontologies. In Features Covered, 21 studies have completely covered the modeling feature. It is also analyzed that 15 studies have reused existing ontologies, such as SSN/SOSA, SAREF, om, time, geo and GeoSparql; 7 ontologies are available online; 17 studies show that ontologies are evaluated with different evaluation tools; and the last parameter shows that only 7 studies are further considered as only 7 ontologies are available online for reuse in future development.

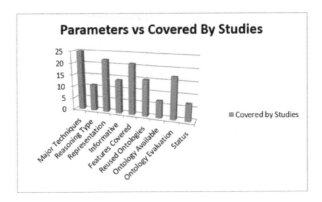

Figure 2.2. *Parameters covered by conducted studies*

Figure 2.2 shows the analysis of parameters covered by studies. According to the status of all existing studies from Table 2.2, a total of 13 studies are considered for ontology characterization due to solid coverage of parameters such as their Description, Owner, Concepts, Year, Published, Online and Sources in Table 2.3.

2.2.3.2. *Step 2: Characterization of water ontologies*

Ontology characterization is a basic idea to provide the characteristics (Howell et al. 2017, 2020) of existing ontologies. In this section, 13 ontologies are characterized to explore their different features, such as Name attribute to recognize the name of the ontology; the Description of Domain attribute presents the description of the ontology; Owner presents the name of the responsible organization; Entities presents the number of ontology classes and properties; Year presents the creation year of the ontology; and the Published attribute presents that the ontology is published on its web page with ontology documentation. Ontology publication provides (1) a human-interpretable HTML page for navigation and browsing with the help of embedded links; (2) different formats of the ontology, such as Turtle, JSON, RDF/XML and N-Triples. On the other hand, the Online attribute tells us that the ontology is available to download from different sources like GitHub or others but not published. The Sources attribute presents the ontology source to download and reuse in future applications.

2.2.3.3. *Step 3: Ontology selection for water management*

Step 3 performed the ontology selection approach from the conducted review of existing work. This section focuses on available online ontologies for the water domain. As per our findings, there are seven ontologies online, but only two ontologies are published, and the remaining five are unpublished. Table 2.4 presents those available online with their different dimensions and also explores the reused ontologies.

Table 2.4 shows that only seven ontologies are available online and can be reused in any new proposed water ontology. These ontologies are significant for water domains as they are designed for different purposes and analyzed with their features. The SAREF4WATR ontology, as an extension of the SAREF series, is designed to manage the flow, storage and characteristics of water with different concepts, such as *WaterAsset, WaterInfraStructure, WaterMeter, Tariff* and their subclasses. The WaterNexus ontology is designed to harmonize the policies and game data to deal with different concepts, such as the *NexusComponent* concept which represents nexus elements (water, element, food, energy, land-use) as subclasses.

The DSHWS ontology is designed to represent the Domestic Hot Solar Water System that dealt with different concepts, such as *AverageDailyUse, AverageOccupancy* manages the consumption of water, while *System* manages Domestic Solar Hot Water system (DSHWS) and *SystemComponent* manages different aspects like *Aperture, Collector, Hydraulics, Installation* and *Tank*. The DSHWS ontology has the *Capacity* and *Size* concepts as a subclass of the *PhysicalProperty* concept to measure the capacity and size of *SystemComponent*. The EUFNexus ontology presents the legal ontology for nexus and deals with different activities, such as *ConsumptionActivity, ProductionActivity* and *DistributionOfWater*, to monitor the activities.

The SurfaceWater ontology presents classes and properties based on attributes of the National Hydrography Dataset, such as *TerrainFeatureType* to support body of water as an earth feature type, and *WaterBody* to manage different water resources such as *Bay, Lake, Sea and Waterfall*. This ontology also presents spatial features such as *SpatialExtent, SpatialMeasurement, SpatialMeasurementUnit* and *SpatialRelation* to manage the qualities of continuants. The WAWO ontology presents wastewater management features, such as WaterComposition to manage the *CleanWaterComposition* and *WWComposition*; *WaterFeatures* to handle the *ChemicalFeatures, IndicatorParameters, Microbiological, Radioactivity* features of water; WaterMass to manage Flow_water_mass and Static_water_mass of water; *WaterProducer, WaterQualityParameters, WWMass* for Wastewater, *WWTP* for Waste Water Treatment Plant, *WWTreatmentUnit*. The InWaterSense (xLMINWS.owl) ontology provides rule-based reasoning over sensor data with different concepts, such as *ConductivitySensor, TemperatureSensor, pHSensor* and *DissolvedOxygenSensor*.

This ontology also represents different situations, such as Calibration, Evaluation, Maintenance, Monitoring, Observation and Reporting. This review analyzed the existing water ontologies with their features that can reuse and also analyze reused concepts in existing water ontologies. Table 2.5 discusses the analysis of reused concepts in existing water ontologies. It is observed in Table 2.5 that the top four ontologies, *WaterNexus, xLMINWS, SAREF4WATR and DSHWS* have reused maximum concepts as recommended by the methodologies and guidelines. However, the next three, *SurfaceWater*, *EUWEFNexus and OntoWAWO* ontologies, did not reuse existing ontology, and all concepts are defined in themselves. The *SurfaceWater* ontology reuses only one concept point from the *geo* ontology, it has created several existing concepts, such as *FeatureObjects* and *Waterbody* while these concepts are already available in the *OntoWAWO* ontology. The *EUWEFNexus* ontology has created 157 new concepts, such as Value, Waste, Animal, Human, while these concepts are also already available in the *OntoWAWO* ontology.

As it is analyzed that the last three ontologies did not follow the suggested guidelines and methodologies for ontology construction, the proposed literature review of existing water ontology will help reduce the construction costs and time by reusing the existing concepts of water ontologies rather than to creating a new one. Section 2.3 will discuss the applications of these ontologies.

2.3. Applications of ontologies in the water domain

Ontologies are an important tool used to overcome the semantic aspects of several challenges by enabling digital representations of intended meanings to be associated with data and other resources. Several water ontologies are developed for different purposes, such as SAREF4WATR, WaterNexus Ontology, DSHWS, EUWEFNexus, SurfaceWater, OntoWAWO, xLMINWS, SWIM, WISDOM, WatERP, WaterML2 and WDTF. In this section, we focus on different purposes to explore the ontology usage in water domains.

Table 2.4 discusses different parameters such as purposes, coverage, advantage and the major component of the existing ontologies. These features show water ontologies' applications for different purposes along with different features and advantages. The purpose parameter discussed the aim of the design of the ontology. The coverage parameter shows the features covered by the proposed ontology. The advantage parameter shows the primary significance of ontology. The main component presents the significant concepts that fulfill the ontology coverage. It is analyzed from Table 2.4 that reusability is the main application of all ontologies while flexibility, sustainability, extensibility, operationally, adequacy and rule-based reasoning are other applications of existing water ontologies. The SAREF4WATR, SWIM and xLMINWS ontologies are designed with sensing devices for monitoring quality and measuring water consumption dynamically. SurfaceWater is the only ontology developed to organize the geographical features, while OntoWAWO is significant for wastewater management. The DSHWS ontology can be reused to manage the domestic solar hot water system in buildings. WaterML2 and WDTF are significant in managing time-series data, while others (WaterNexus, EUWEFNexus, WISDOM and WatERP) can be used in general water management.

Ontology	Purposes	Coverage	Advantages	Main component
SAREF4WATR	Ontology is designed to manage the water infrastructure, asset, billing and remote monitoring by smart devices	To acquire the information of Water Asset, Infrastructure, Property, Devices and Tariff	Reusability, Sustainability	Water asset, Water infrastructure, Tariff, Property, Water meter, Water device
WaterNexus	Ontology associates water nexus variables according to different regions	To assimilate information from various data sources referring water, land use, energy, climate change	Reusability	Scale, PhysicalObject, Model, Region, PolicyGoal
DSHWS	Ontology-based decision support tool designed to promote the usage of domestic solar hot water systems in building	Computes number of occupants, need of daily hot water and location	Sustainability, Adaptability, Flexibility	Household, System, Aperture, Tank, Collector, Hydraulics
EUWEFNexus	Nexus aspect involves dealing with water, energy and food with EU laws and policies. The legal ontology has been developed for nexus	Legal knowledge acquisition for nexus	Adequacy, Reusability, Operationality	Living Organism, Energy, Authority, Quality, Material, Resource
SurfaceWater	Designed to model the semantic concepts of National Hydrology Datasets with GIS information such as points, areas and lines as feature objects	Hydrographic, geographical and terrain features	Reusability, Flexibility	WaterBody, Event, Feature, SpatialExtent, SpatialMeasurement
OntoWAWO	WAWO harmonizes the knowledge about WWTP management	WAWO capture chemical, physical and microbiological knowledge of a WWTP	Reusability	LandUse, WaterFeatures, WWTP, WWTreatmentUnit

Ontology	Purposes	Coverage	Advantages	Main component
xLMINWS	Ontology developed for water quality monitoring with the help of sensing devices and making observations	Captures the pH, temperature, water-relevant contaminants, bodies of water and amount of ammonia	Reusability, Rule-based Reasoning	PersonDevice, SensorNode, pHSensor, TemperatureSensor
SWIM	Presented as an IoT-based semantic model for water interoperability	Provides the description for water sector devices	Not Applicable	Pumps, Sensors, Valves and Reservoirs
WISDOM	Captures domestic knowledge and integrates water data value chain to contextualize smart meter and behavioral data	Physical element types (storage, transfer, etc.) and types of actors (bulk water suppliers, consumers, regulators and water utilities)	Reusability, Extensibility	WaterPipe, WaterType, WaterTariff, WaterBill
WatERP	Ontology developed to present the water supply domain and demand knowledge	Provides a new way of association and improves the water resource management domain knowledge	Reusability	WaterResourceManagement, Regulators, Water Utilities, and Water Bulk Suppliers
WaterML2	Developed to provide a common format for time series data and constructed on existing standards such as GML	Used to exchange several hydro-meteorological observation and measurements	Reusability	Measurement, MeasurementTimeseries
WDTF	Presented as precursor of WaterML2 as a transferring format for forecasting data and flood warnings	Not Applicable	Not Applicable	HydroCollection, TimeSeriesObservation

Table 2.4. *Ontology applications in water domains*

Ontology	New concepts	Reused concepts	Total concepts	Reused (%)
WaterNexus	19	11	30	37
xLMINWS.owl	21	10	31	36
SAREF4WATR	47	24	71	33
DSHWS	17	8	25	32
SurfaceWater	92	1	93	1
EUWEFNexus	157	0	157	0
OntoWAWO	223	0	223	0

Table 2.5. *Reused concepts in existing water ontology*

2.4. Discussion and conclusion

The main contribution presented is to highlight the reusable ontologies for the water domain. It is always suggested that one should not reinvent the wheel and reuse existing concepts rather than design from scratch. In this chapter, a systematic literature review has been conducted to explore the knowledge from shallow to deep analysis of existing ontologies in the water domain. The main advantages of the proposed work are: (1) acquiring existing water ontologies in one place; (2) exposing the semantic richness of existing water ontologies; (3) extracting online available ontologies for reuse; and (4) applicability of existing water ontologies. A three-step methodology has been followed to conduct the systematic literature review, characterize existing ontologies and select available online ontologies.

The key contribution is to analyze the different sources such as Scopus, Google Scholar, WoS, Journals and Repositories to acquire and select related studies, hence characterizing the related ontologies with water domains and finally extracting only online available water domain ontologies. One of the significant benefits of the systematic review is exploring existing water domain ontologies for reusing with domain-specific requirements. Domain experts can easily reuse the existing ontologies to reduce the construction efforts and cost. It supports the reuse of the modeled knowledge within multiple domains. As a finding, 14 ontologies are taken into account and categorized based on different features that are covered by conducted studies, but only seven ontologies (SAREF4WATR, WaterNexus, DSHWS, EUWEFNexus, SurfaceWater, OntoWAWO and xLMINWS) are available online to reuse; hence the other seven (SWIM, WISDOM, WatERP, WaterML2, WDTF, Utility Network Schemas and Hydrologic Ontology) ontologies were discarded.

Although these ontologies are designed for real application and have significant features to reuse in new development, they are lacking reusability in general as users need approval from the owners to reuse these models. Online available ontologies have used different reasoning types, for example the DSHWS ontology used

SPARQL for reasoning, the xLMINWS (InWaterSense) ontology used SWRL rules and the OntoWAWO ontology used case-based and rule-based reasoning. In contrast, reasoning information is not available in the other three ontologies (WaterNexus, EUWEFNexus and SurfaceWater). It is also analyzed that these ontologies reused several existing ontologies, such as SAREF (Measurements, UnitOfMeasure, Property), GeoSparql, time, om, dbpedia and SSN. Existing ontologies, SAREF4WATR, WaterNexus, xLMINWS and DSHWS, have reused a maximum of concepts to reduce construction cost, effort and time.

To our best knowledge, no such study has been previously conducted to present a comprehensive study of semantic water resources models. As a future scope, this review will help identify the existing work and ontologies for reuse to propose a new water ontology.

2.5. References

Agresta, A., Fattoruso, G., Pollino, M., Pasanisi, F., Tebano, C., De Vito, S., Di Francia, G. (2014). An ontology framework for flooding forecasting. In *International Conference on Computational Science and Its Applications – ICCSA 2014*. Springer, Cham.

Ahmedi, L., Jajaga, E., Ahmedi, F. (2013). An ontology framework for water quality management. *SSN ISWC*, 35–50.

Anzaldi, G. (2015). *Generic Ontology for Water Supply Distribution Chain*. Eurecat Technology Center, Barcelona.

Arp, R., Smith, B., Spear, A.D. (2015). *Building Ontologies with Basic Formal Ontology*. MIT Press, London [Online]. Available at: https://scholar.google.co.in/scholar?hl=en&as_sdt=0%2C5&q=Building+Ontologies+with+Basic+Formal+Ontology.+MIT+Press.&btnG.

Blodgett, D., Read, E., Lucido, J., Slawecki, T., Young, D. (2016). An analysis of water data systems to inform the open water data initiative. *JAWRA Journal of the American Water Resources Association*, 52(4), 845–858.

Bontas, E.P., Mochol, M., Tolksdorf, R. (2005). Case studies on ontology reuse. *Proceedings of the IKNOW05 International Conference on Knowledge Management*, 74, 345.

Brodaric, B. and Hahmann, T. (2014). *Toward A Foundational Hydro Ontology For Water Data Interoperability*). CUNY Academic Works, New York [Online]. Available at: https://academicworks.cuny.edu/cc_conf_hic/424.

Ceccaroni, L., Cortes, C., Sànchez-Marrè, M. (2000). WaWO: An ontology embedded into an environmental decision-support system for wastewater treatment plant management, LSI-00-37-R [Online]. Available at: http://hdl.handle.net/2117/96412.

Corchero, A., Westerhof, E., Echeverria, L. (2019). Water Nexus Ontology to support generation of policies [Online]. Available at: https://rioter-project.github.io/rioter-nexus-variables-ontology [Accessed 10 October 2021].

Curry, E., Derguech, W., Hasan, S., Maali, F., Reforgiato, D., Stasiewicz, A., Hassan, U.U., Bortoluzzi, D. (2014). D3. 1.1 linked water dataspace. *Work*, 3, 1–1.

Daniele, L., den Hartog, F., Roes, J. (2015). Created in close interaction with the industry: The smart appliances reference (SAREF) ontology. In *International Workshop Formal Ontologies Meet Industries*, Cuel, R., Young, R. (eds). Springer, Cham.

Elag, M. and Goodall, J.L. (2013). An ontology for component-based models of water resource systems. *Water Resources Research*, 49(8), 5077–5091.

Escobar, P., Roldán-García, M.D.M., Peral, J., Candela, G., García-Nieto, J. (2020). An ontology-based framework for publishing and exploiting linked open data: A use case on water resources management. *Applied Sciences*, 10(3), 779.

Espinoza-Arias, P., Poveda-Villalón, M., García-Castro, R., Corcho, O. (2019). Ontological representation of smart city data: From devices to cities. *Applied Sciences*, 9(1), 32.

García-Castro, R. (2020). SAREF extension for water [Online]. Available: https://saref.etsi.org/saref4watr/v1.1.1 [Accessed 10 October 2021].

Goel, D., Chaudhury, S., Ghosh, H. (2017). Smart water management: An ontology-driven context-aware IoT application. In *International Conference on Pattern Recognition and Machine Intelligence*, Shankar, B., Ghosh, K., Mandal, D., Ray, S., Zhang, D., Pal, S. (eds). Springer, Cham.

Gómez-Pérez, A. and Rojas-Amaya, M.D. (1999). Ontological reengineering for reuse. *International Conference on Knowledge Engineering and Knowledge Management*, Springer, Berlin, Heidelberg.

Hahmann, T. and Stephen, S. (2018). Using a hydro-reference ontology to provide improved computer-interpretable semantics for the groundwater markup language (GWML2). *International Journal of Geographical Information Science*, 32(6), 1138–1171.

Haller, A., Janowicz, K., Cox, S.J., Lefrançois, M., Taylor, K., Le Phuoc, D., Lieberman, J., García-Castro, R., Atkinson, R., Stadler, C. (2019). The SOSA/SSN ontology: A joint W3C and OGC standard specifying the semantics of sensors, observations, actuation, and sampling. *Semantic Web-Interoperability, Usability, Applicability an IOS Press Journal*, 56, 1–19.

Howell, S., Rezgui, Y., Beach, T. (2018). Water utility decision support through the semantic web of things. *Environmental Modelling & Software*, 102, 94–114.

Howell, S., Beach, T., Rezgui, Y. (2020). Robust requirements gathering for ontologies in smart water systems. *Requirements Engineering*, 1–18.

Howell, S., Beach, T., Rezgui, Y. (2021). Robust requirements gathering for ontologies in smart water systems. *Requirements Engineering*, 26(1), 97–114.

IAB (2015). AIOT Standardisation. Semantic interoperability [Online]. Available at: https://www.iab.org/wp-content/IAB-uploads/2016/03/AIOTIWG03Report2015-Semantic Interoperability.pdf [Accessed 10 October 2021].

Kadlec, J., StClair, B., Ames, D.P., Gill, R.A. (2015). WaterML R package for managing ecological experiment data on a CUAHSI hydroserver. *Ecological Informatics*, 28, 19–28.

Kämpgen, B., Riepl, D., Klinger, J. (2014). Smart research using linked data-sharing research data for integrated water resources management in the lower Jordan valley. *CEUR Workshop Proceedings*, 1155.

Katsiri, E. and Makropoulos, C. (2016). An ontology framework for decentralized water management and analytics using wireless sensor networks. *Desalination and Water Treatment*, 57(54), 26355–26368.

Kinceler, L.M., Massignam, A.M., Todesco, J.L. (2011). An ontology for a hydro-meteorological observation network. *KEOD*, 26–29 October, Paris.

Kitchenham, B. and Charters, S. (2007). Guidelines for performing systematic literature reviews in software engineering. *Software Engineering Group*, 2, 1–57.

Kontopoulos, E., Martinopoulos, G., Lazarou, D., Bassiliades, N. (2016). An ontology-based decision support tool for optimizing domestic solar hot water system selection. *Journal of Cleaner Production*, 112, 4636–4646.

Pease, A., Niles, I., Li, J. (2002). The suggested upper merged ontology: A large ontology for the semantic web and its applications. *Working Notes of the AAAI-2002 Workshop on Ontologies and the Semantic Web*, 28, 7–10.

Poveda-Villalon, M., Nguyen, Q.D., Roussey, C., de Vaulx, C., Chanet, J.P. (2018). Ontological requirement specification for smart irrigation systems: A SOSA/SSN and SAREF comparison. *9th International Semantic Sensor Networks Workshop (SSN 2018)*, CEUR Workshop Proceedings, 2213, 16.

Rahman, M. (2015). WEFNexus [Online]. Available at: https://github.com/mizanur3/WEFNexus/blob/master/EUDefBiofuels.owl [Accessed 10 October 2021].

Reynolds. (2014). Swim a semantic ontology for interoperability [Online]. Available at: https://www.swig.org.uk/wp-content/uploads/2014/01/Laurie-Reynolds-2014.pdf [Accessed 10 October 2021].

Sánchez-de Rivera, D., Robles, T., López, J.A., de Miguel, A.S., De La Cruz, M.N., Gómez, M.S.I., Martínez, J.A., Skarmeta, A.F. (2017). Adaptation of ontology sets for water related scenarios management with IoT systems for more productive and sustainable agriculture systems. *SEMANTiCS 2017 Workshops Proceedings: SIS-IoT*, 1–8.

Sanfilippo, E.M. and Borgo, S. (2016). What are features? An ontology-based review of the literature. *Computer-Aided Design*, 80, 9–18.

Scheuer, S., Haase, D., Meyer, V. (2013). Towards a flood risk assessment ontology–knowledge integration into a multi-criteria risk assessment approach. *Computers, Environment and Urban Systems*, 37, 82–94.

Sinha, G., Mark, D., Kolas, D., Varanka, D., Romero, B.E., Feng, C.-C., Usery, E.L., Liebermann, J., Sorokine, A. (2014). An ontology design pattern for surface water features. In *Geographic Information Science. GIScience 2014. Lecture Notes in Computer Science*, Duckham, M., Pebesma, E., Stewart, K., Frank, A.U. (eds). Springer, Cham.

Stephen, S. and Hahmann, T. (2017). An ontological framework for characterizing hydrological flow processes. *13th International Conference on Spatial Information Theory (COSIT 2017)*. Schloss Dagstuhl-Leibniz-Zentrum fuer Informatik, Wadern.

Taylor, P. (ed.) (2014). OGC® WaterML 2.0: Part 1- Timeseries, Version 2.0.1. Open Geospatial Consortium (OGC 10-S126r4), Maryland [Online]. Available at: http://dx.doi.org/10.25607/OBP-611.

Varanka, D.E. and Usery, E.L. (2015). An applied ontology for semantics associated with surface water features. In *Land Use and Land Cover Semantics: Principles, Best Practices, and Prospects*, Ahlqvist, O., Varanka, D., Fritz, S., Janowicz, K. (eds). CRC Press, Boca Raton.

Walker, G., Taylor, P., Cox, S., Sheahan, P., Anderssen, R., Braddock, R., Newham, L. (2009). Water Data Transfer Format (WDTF): Guiding principles, technical challenges and the future. *Proceedings of the 18th World IMACS Congress and the MODSIM09 International Congress on Modelling and Simulation*, 4381–4387.

Wang, C., Wang, W., Chen, N. (2017). Building an ontology for hydrologic monitoring. *IEEE International Geoscience and Remote Sensing Symposium (IGARSS)*, IEEE, 6232–6234.

Wang, X., Wei, H., Chen, N., He, X., Tian, Z. (2020). An observational process ontology-based modeling approach for water quality monitoring. *Water*, 12(3), 715.

Xiaomin, Z., Jianjun, Y., Xiaoci, H., Shaoli, C. (2016). An ontology-based knowledge modelling approach for river water quality monitoring and assessment. *Procedia Computer Science*, 96(C), 335–344.

Zarli, A., Rezgui, Y., Belziti, D., Duce, E. (2014). Water analytics and intelligent sensing for demand optimised management: The wisdom vision and approach. *Procedia Engineering*, 89, 1050–1057.

3

Semantic Web Approach for Smart Health to Enhance Patient Monitoring in Resuscitation

The monitoring of resuscitation patients is one of the most critical healthcare tasks. The Internet of Things medical devices enable healthcare providers to continuously monitor patients by providing them with vital signs data. However, where hospitals and resuscitation rooms are overcrowded, and medical staff is in short supply, detecting critical patients during pandemics is complex, and prompt intervention is impossible. To make these tasks easier, data analytics, using Smart Health Internet of Things applications, provide a boost for automatically monitoring patients to ameliorate healthcare, reduce errors and improve the patient experience. However, it is impossible without understanding data semantics due to the various and heterogeneous sources that provide raw data. To address this, one could provide semantic interoperability for medical monitoring devices in resuscitation and data generated using Semantic Web technologies to transform raw data into harmonized data to build innovative e-Health applications to enhance the monitoring of intensive care patients and help resuscitation personnel make accurate and timely decisions. Hence, this chapter proposes a knowledge representation and reasoning framework to semantically annotate data for analyzing the semantics of vital signs monitors and data that come from them. The authors also infer and discover new information and address complex queries on semantically annotated data. Finally, the datasets will be published as Linked Data, which will allow querying data streams and enriching them with other datasets to obtain additional information.

Chapter written by Fatima Zahra AMARA, Mounir HEMAM, Meriem DJEZZAR and Moufida MAIMOUR.

3.1. Introduction

The concept of the Internet of Things (IoT) refers to millions of connected real-world things involved in intelligent interactive objects that communicate between themselves and sense their surroundings. The advancement of remote sensing technologies and the enhancement of the Internet have allowed the IoT to reach many areas. Smart Health is an IoT application. The current healthcare system has realized the benefits of employing technology to improve healthcare quality. Using IoT in healthcare has prompted researchers worldwide to create potential frameworks and technologies that can give comfortable medical support to everyone (Sundaravadivel et al. 2017) by transforming traditional healthcare into smart healthcare.

Intensive healthcare units (ICU) provide treatment and monitoring for people who are very ill. Sophisticated medical smart devices monitor patients continuously in resuscitation, such as with the vital signs monitor that represents the primary data source. This anticipates healthcare providers with vital signs data to indicate the status of the patients and show progress toward recovery and so that they can intervene in critical cases. The intensive care unit contains many patients with different conditions and situations that require critical care, such as serious accidents, severe short-term conditions including heart attack or stroke, serious infections and major surgery. Patients in resuscitation will be looked after closely by medical staff and will be connected to equipment. Typically, there will be at most one nurse for every two patients.

These conditions cannot be met in pandemics like that experienced with Covid-19 and disasters where hospitals and resuscitations are congested, and medical personnel is in low supply and overburdened. Hence, the IoT has connected devices that can be used by Smart Health applications, which help monitor patients automatically and analyze data and improve healthcare, reduce errors and improve the patient experience. However, the raw data transmitted is not processable by machines due to their different formats and types that give rise to scalability, heterogeneity and several interoperability issues. In particular, semantic interoperability among things on the IoT is one of the foremost necessities to hold up object addressing, tracking, discovery and also information representation, storage and exchange (Barnaghi et al. 2012). Semantic Web technologies have increasingly been deployed to handle the challenge of heterogeneity and the lack of semantic interoperability. Semantic Web technologies are also used in the IoT domains for other intentions, such as the description and search of things and IoT services, the composition of services, models, and reasoning upon IoT resources (Andročec et al. 2018). The proposed approach could have several advantages to overcome this, improving the quality of care in resuscitation and ensuring effective monitoring, allowing the medical staff to make an almost complete analysis of the patient's physiological conditions by reading the signs correctly and discovering the causes. So, they can act quickly, efficiently and timely.

This chapter proposes a knowledge representation and reasoning framework to represent data for analyzing resuscitation monitors' semantics and their generated data. The formal model of knowledge makes it possible to automate various processing operations on this information. Semantically enriched data provide semantic interoperability for analyzing the semantics of vital signs monitors and data derived from them. First, to represent knowledge, several ontologies exist such as SSN (Compton et al. 2012), BOT (Rasmussen et al. 2021), SAREF (Daniele et al. 2015), etc., which can be reused to build the ontology. An ontological model will be developed extending the W3C SSN ontology, the most popular one to describe sensors and observations by adding specific knowledge for patient monitoring, spatial, temporal and thematic concepts appropriate for the application domain. Queries and semantics reasoning rules to infer and discover new knowledge and answer complex queries will then be applied. Finally, the structured datasets will be published as Linked Data to be reused, allow querying the data streams and enriching them with other datasets to obtain additional information.

The remainder of the chapter is organized as follows: a background study of our research is given in section 3.2. Section 3.3 presents work that used the IoT in healthcare applications and applies semantic in smart health. Section 3.4 provides the detail and implementation of our proposed approach to enhance the monitoring of patients in intensive healthcare units. Conclusion and future works are given in section 3.5.

3.2. Background

3.2.1. *Semantic Web*

The Semantic Web (SW), coined for the first time by Tim Berners-Lee (Berners-Lee et al. 2001), aims to make web content machines comprehensible by allowing agents and applications to access a wide range of heterogeneous resources, analyze and integrate the contents and generate additional value output for consumers. Semantic Web technologies enable the creation of data stores, build vocabularies and write rules for handling data. In this light, a variety of languages have been created.

Resource Description Framework (RDF) (World Wide Web Consortium 2014), RDFs (RDF Schemas) (Brickley, et al., 2014) and Web Ontology Language (OWL) (World Wide Web Consortium 2012) are representation languages developed by the W3C. RDF is a simple language that expresses data models and refers to objects and relations between them. RDFs extend RDF, a vocabulary for describing properties and classes of RDF-based resources. OWL is intended to represent complex and rich knowledge about things, groups of things and their relationships.

SPARQL (W3C SPARQL Working Group and Others 2013) is the standard query language and protocol for Linked Open Data and RDF triple-stores. It was designed by the W3C for process data to enable users to query data and extract information from datasets.

To enable the updating of the RDF triples-store with new additional triples and new knowledge, the W3C proposed SWRL (Semantic Web Rule Language) (Horrocks et al. 2004), a language for the Semantic Web to express rules for reasoning and which infers new knowledge from existing data. It exploits the idea of Linked Rules.

Linked Data is a W3C initiative aimed at promoting the publication of structured data on the web. It was described by Tim Berners-Lee (2006) as follows: "The Semantic Web is not just about putting data on the web that a person or machine can explore the data network. With Linked Data, when you have a part of it, you can find other related data". This refers to a method of publishing and linking data from heterogeneous data sources that can be connected and shared. Semantic Web technologies such as RDF, SPARQL and OWL allow Linked Data.

3.2.2. *SSN (Semantic Sensor Network) ontology*

The W3C Semantic Sensor Network Incubator Group developed the SSN ontology (Compton et al. 2012). One of the primary goals of this group is to create an ontology that defines sensors and sensor networks for use in web applications. The SSN ontology is an ontology for describing sensors and their observations. The development of SSN was resolutely influenced by the SSNX ontology (Lefort et al. 2011) and models from the OGC's Sensor Web Enablement initiative (SWE) (Botts et al. 2006).

Sensor technology, network technology and computer technology are all advancing concurrently. Methods for connecting information systems to the physical world are in high demand. The OGC's SWE initiative enables developers to make various sensors, transducers and sensor data repositories discoverable, accessible and usable over the web. The key OGC (Open Geospatial Consortium) standards that have been adopted under the SWE framework are as follows:

– O&M (Observations & Measurements) are the general models and XML encodings for observations and measurements.

– SensorML (Sensor Model Language) is a standard model and XML Schema for describing the processes that occur within sensors and observation processing systems.

– SOS (Sensor Observation Service) represents an open interface for a web service to get observations, sensor and platform descriptions from one or more sensors through a web service.

The SSN is a high-level ontology that describes generic concepts extended in several domains. It is used extensively as an ontological model for removing semantic barriers in sensor networks (Ruta et al. 2013; Wang et al. 2018) since it allows for flexible and consistent representations of the entities, relationships and activities involved in sensing, sampling and actuation.

3.3. IoT Smart Health applications and semantics

In recent years, Smart applications have gained exceptional attention. IoT interconnected devices bring significant advantages to the development and have been widely employed in all aspects of smart health and IoT-based medical solutions. Mahmud et al. (2018) demonstrated IoT-enabled universal medical applications with cloud-based data management and processing. The prototype that was implemented gathers patient data from IoT devices and sends it to the cloud for analysis. The work in Chen et al. (2018) introduces UH-BigDataSys urban. The big data system for urban healthcare was created by combining air quality data from multiple sources and implementing air quality-conscious health applications. This offers health advice for city residents on respiratory diseases, sleep quality, etc. Muneer et al. (2020) built a smart mirror linked to smart devices to give advanced functionality such as tracking its users' health to help in the construction of a platform for users to monitor their health and fitness condition with self-adapting features utilizing smart wireless sensors and computer vision.

In addition to the presented works that integrated IoT in healthcare, several other works use semantics. In Abatal et al. (2018), a healthcare-specific intelligent semantic system has been created. It combines the Semantic Web and cloud computing to enable the visualization, transmission and exchange of medical records and reports via the cloud, as well as real-time data acquisition and ontology modeling. In Sharma et al. (2021), a framework is presented that provides updated information on Covid-19 patients nearby. The model is an IoT-based remote access and alarm-enabled bio wearable sensor system for early detection of Covid-19 based on an ontology model. Alti and Laouamer (2021) proposed a novel autonomous and agent-based semantic contextual, a software platform for disease detection and intelligent health monitoring using the Semantic Web, the Cloud and the Kalimucho middleware. In Shahzad et al. (2021), a conceptual framework for integrated healthcare services is designed to combine methods for constructing an integrated platform with knowledge of smart healthcare services. In Zgheib et al. (2020), a new scalable semantic framework for IoT healthcare applications has been presented. It is based on reasoning techniques that are delivered through semantic middleware.

Also, there are several IoT-based ontologies developed in healthcare. For example, Health IoT (Rhayem et al. 2017) introduced the Health IoT ontology to express the semantic interoperability of medical interconnected objects and data to assist a doctor in analyzing the signs observed and prescribing the best medication for the patient. In Moreira et al. (2018), the authors extended the Smart Appliances REFerence framework (SAREF) and built the SAREF4 health ontology. The ontology is implemented in RDF with Protégé to evaluate it. Reda et al. (2018) developed an IoT fitness ontology (IFO), an ontology-based eHealth system for transforming low-level health and fitness data from heterogeneous IoT devices into an enhanced information model encoded in RDF. A healthcare system based on IoT for continuous monitoring of chronically unwell elderly people has been proposed by Sondes et al. (2019). They developed an ontology-based context model for the modeling of health and environmental data. The ontology was created by combining various ontologies related to the IoT and health domains. The Smart HealthCare Ontology models patient health for remote monitoring (Tiwari and Abraham 2020). This ontology is a formal description model produced by health knowledge extracted to monitor doctors and patients pervasively.

3.4. Proposed approach and implementation

This section details the approach proposal, which permits knowledge representation and reasoning using Semantic Web technologies. On the one hand, defining and conceptualizing an ontological model, and on the other hand reasoning and querying the developed ontology, allow us to provide a well-defined sense of the vital signs sensors and the transmitted data. The datasets are then published as Linked Data, as shown in Figure 3.1 that depicts an overview of the proposed approach.

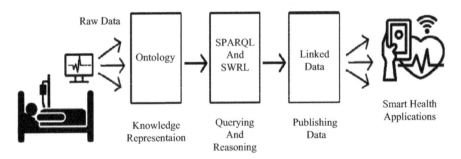

Figure 3.1. *An overview of proposed approach*

The developed ontology was implemented with version 5.5.0 of Protégé. The querying sentences were written with SPARQL and executed by the Protégé SPARQL Plugin (version 3.0.0). HermiT (version 1.4.3 456) is used as a reasoner. The reasoning rules were edited with SWRL and implemented in SWRLTab Protégé 5.0+ Plugin (version 2.0.6) in Protégé. The detailed activities of our study are represented in the following sections.

3.4.1. *Knowledge representation*

Knowledge representation refers to a collection of tools and procedures designed to represent, give a consistent interpretation and organize human knowledge to be used and shared readily. More formal techniques for representing complex knowledge are available. The approach of the Semantic Web has renovated the discipline by introducing the contentious ontology concept. Ontologies are useful for representing shared domain knowledge and enabling semantic interoperability (Mishra and Jain 2019, 2020; Panchal et al. 2021) and are increasingly being used in a variety of sectors nowadays. They are regarded as a key paradigm in semantic interoperability, data integration and knowledge exchange among humans, but especially among machines. A detailed needs analysis was performed for our application domain. The results of this analysis allowed us to classify the modeling needs of the different concepts and their relationships. The proposed ontology is designed by extending the SSN ontology that had many successful applications, as shown previously (section 3.2), integrating with its concepts of the application domain of monitoring patients in intensive healthcare units. To represent the knowledge and achieve our goal to well-defined meaning and offer semantic interoperability to develop innovative smart health applications, the ontology is built by going through the following stages.

3.4.1.1. *Ontology modeling procedure*

Developing the ontology must be created in a standard process to identify the tasks to be accomplished when constructing it (planning, supervision, quality assurance, specification, acquisition of knowledge, conceptualization, integration, formalization and implementation) with METHONTOLOGY (Fernandez-Lopez et al. 1997). It is a method developed by the artificial intelligence laboratory of Madrid University. It allows going from raw data to an ontological model represented in the OWL language.

3.4.1.2. *Domain of the ontology*

The representation of vital signs monitors, their sensors and data gathered was determined as a domain that can determine the following scopes: monitor, sensor, observation, patient, future of interest, etc.

3.4.1.3. *List of important terms in ontology*

The main terms of our domain application ontology are described and used in the class definition. The general terms required for this domain application are sensor, observations sensor, situation, patient and knowledge for modeling temporal and spatial location.

3.4.1.4. *Classes and their relation*

The precedent cited terms allowed the creation of a set of classes like patient, unit_of_measurement, time, location, physiological_qualities, etc., in addition to subclasses of SSN ontology. Figure 3.2 represents the essential terms of the developed ontological model.

Figure 3.2. *Ontology class hierarchy. For a color version of this figure, see www.iste.co.uk/mehta/tools.zip*

3.4.1.5. Object/data properties of classes

Object properties of classes were defined with OWL to define relationships between already presented classes. The related object properties were inherited from the SSN ontology. Data properties connect individuals with literals to specify the type of the value of data. For example, the value of property has_name has a data type string and reel for property has_value.

3.4.1.6. Create instances

The last step of creation is to define individual instances of classes. In the developed ontology, the instances refer to sensors, observations data and patients' data. Figure 3.3 represents the main ontological elements classes, data/objects properties and a part of instances.

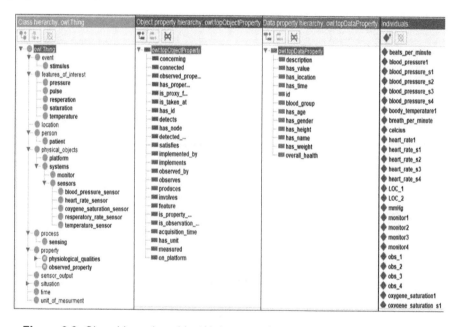

Figure 3.3. *Class hierarchy, object/data properties and individuals of developed ontology. For a color version of this figure, see www.iste.co.uk/mehta/tools.zip*

3.4.1.7. Construction of binary relations diagram

As demonstrated in Figure 3.4(a), part of the developed ontology is represented graphically by the different binary relations and the classes hierarchy of the various ontology concepts, with VOWL Plugin for Protégé, which is focused on visualizing the ontology schema.

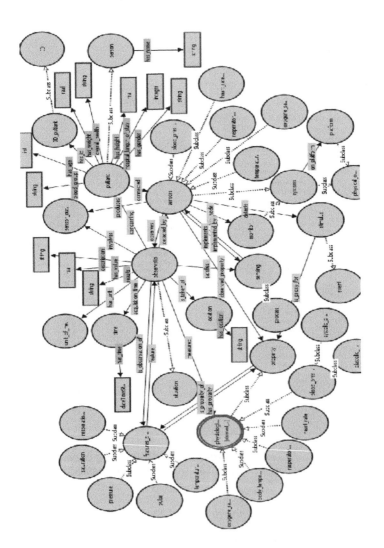

Figure 3.4. *Binary relationships diagram. For a color version of this figure, see www.iste.co.uk/mehta/tools.zip*

3.4.2. *Ontology evaluation*

The next stage in ontological modeling is the evaluation. While the real-world domain ontology, particularly complicated domain ontologies like medicine, might include thousands of concepts, the validation of a large ontology is a dominant problem since ontologies are used as reference models.

Supporting the reasoning of OWL ontologies is essential to ensure the validity and correctness of ontologies and to deduce implicit knowledge. In addition, integrity determines whether the topic of interest has been adequately addressed or not. The HermiT reasoner is used to evaluate the ontological model to assess whether or not the ontology is consistent, identify subsumption relationships between classes and represent any taxonomic errors or redundancy anomalies.

The ontology evaluation is guaranteed from two crucial perspectives (Hlomani and Stacey 2014) – quality and correctness. That addresses a set of criteria such as accuracy, completeness, conciseness, adaptability, clarity, computational efficiency and consistency (Raad and Cruz 2015). The developed ontology satisfies the presented criteria:

– Accuracy: all definitions, descriptions of classes, properties and individuals in the proposed ontology are correct.

– Completeness: the domain of interest (resuscitation monitoring) is appropriately covered in the proposed ontology.

– Conciseness: is evaluated by comparing the developed ontology to a text corpus to see if it includes irrelevant elements regarding the covered domain and check if every concept in the ontology is available.

– Adaptability: the proposed ontological model offers a conceptual foundation for a range of anticipated tasks.

– Clarity: defined terms in the developed ontology are objective and independent of the context.

– Computational efficiency: the ability of the used tools and the speed of reasoners are provided in the ontological model.

– Consistency: the proposed ontology does not include any contradictions.

3.4.3. *Reasoning and querying*

The use of ontologies in information retrieval systems allows query types to be defined based on Semantic Web languages. Several inference engines can be integrated into the system to query the knowledge base.

Semantic reasoning is the ability to derive logical consequences from a set of asserted facts or axioms. The concept of a semantic reasoner generates inference engines, resulting in a more diverse set of mechanisms to work with. An ontological language is typically used to specify inference rules.

3.4.3.1. *Semantic query using developed ontology*

The SPARQL language was developed to query the properties and concepts defined in the developed ontology. The sensors, observations or patients can be accessed with any of their attributes. So, to evaluate the ontology, a set of semantic queries were intended. The querying language was encoded with SPARQL, executed in Protégé with the SPARQL Query tab.

For example, an example of a query and its results are shown in Figure 3.5. The query asks for a list of patients older than 60 years and who have been in intensive healthcare for more than one week (7 days).

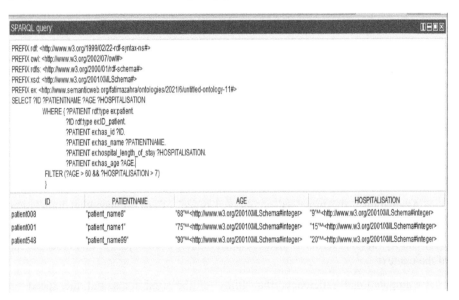

Figure 3.5. *Query all patients who are older than 60 years and have hospital length of stay more than a week. For a color version of this figure, see www.iste.co.uk/mehta/tools.zip*

EXAMPLE OF SPARQL QUERY.–

PREFIX xsd: http://www.w3.org/2001/XMLSchema#
PREFIXex:<http://www.semanticweb.org/fatimazahra/ontologies/2021/6/untitled-ontology-11#>
SELECT ?ID ?PATIENTNAME ?AGE ?HOSPITALISATION
WHERE { ?PATIENTrdf:typeex:patient.
?IDrdf:typeex:ID_patient.
?PATIENTex:has_id ?ID.
?PATIENTex:has_name ?PATIENTNAME.
?PATIENTex:hospital_length_of_stay ?HOSPITALISATION.
?PATIENTex:has_age ?AGE.
FILTER (?AGE> 60 && ?HOSPITALISATION > 7 }

3.4.3.2. Semantic reasoning

The rules were defined with SWRL and implemented in Protégé to provide rule-based reasoning. In the context of our application, rule-based reasoning is used to answer complex queries to discover and infer new knowledge. SWRL is a proposed Semantic Web language for expressing rules as well as logic, integrating OWL DL or OWL Lite with a subset of the Rule Markup Language. So, the rules are expressed in "antecedent→ consequent" form.

A part of created rules for the developed ontology are presented below.

Rule 1: If the value of body temperature of a patient, given by temperature sensor from defined monitor location, is greater than 37°C, a rule-based reasoning infers new knowledge: give an antipyretic.

RULE 1 IS WRITTEN IN SWRL AS FOLLOWS.–

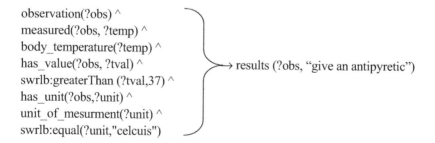

```
observation(?obs) ^
measured(?obs, ?temp) ^
body_temperature(?temp) ^
has_value(?obs, ?tval) ^          → results (?obs, "give an antipyretic")
swrlb:greaterThan (?tval,37) ^
has_unit(?obs,?unit) ^
unit_of_mesurment(?unit) ^
swrlb:equal(?unit,"celcuis")
```

Rule 2: If the value of saturation of the oxygen in the blood of the patient is lower than 80%, and the value of respiratory rate is greater than 25 breath_per_munit, then a rule-based reasoning infers new knowledge: give corticoid and oxygen therapy.

RULE 2 IS WRITTEN IN SWRL AS FOLLOWS.–

observation(?obs1) ^
measured(?obs1, ?satoxy) ^
oxygen_saturation(?satoxy) ^
has_value(?obs1, ?oxyval) ^
swrlb:lessThan(?oxyval,80) ^   →   results (?obs1, "give corticoid and
measured(?obs1, ?resrat) ^   oxygen therapy")
respiratory_rate(?resrat) ^
has_value(?obs1, ?resratval) ^
swrlb:GreaterThan(?resratval,25)

Rule 3: If the value of the diastolic blood pressure of the patient is lower than 80 mmHg and the systolic lower than 120 mmHg, a rule-based reasoning infers new knowledge: give catecholamine and blood transfusion.

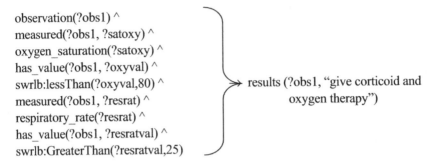

Figure 3.6. *Rules editor*

Figure 3.6 showed the rules editor of the SWRLTab and Figure 3.7 represents the SWRLTab and executed rules.

RULE 3 IS WRITTEN IN SWRL AS FOLLOWS.–

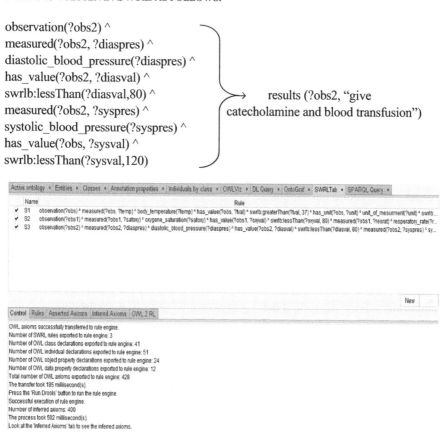

observation(?obs2) ∧
measured(?obs2, ?diaspres) ∧
diastolic_blood_pressure(?diaspres) ∧
has_value(?obs2, ?diasval) ∧
swrlb:lessThan(?diasval,80) ∧
measured(?obs2, ?syspres) ∧
systolic_blood_pressure(?syspres) ∧
has_value(?obs, ?sysval) ∧
swrlb:lessThan(?sysval,120)

→   results (?obs2, "give catecholamine and blood transfusion")

Figure 3.7. *SWRLTab and Rules execution*

3.4.4. *Linked Data*

Linked Data refers to structured data interlinked with other kinds of data to become more valuable through semantic queries. The World Wide Web is transformed into a worldwide dataset through Linked Data, which is called the Web of Data. Developers query Linked Data from numerous sources simultaneously and integrate it on the fly, which is difficult or impossible with traditional data-management solutions.

Linked Data is a collection of design principles for exchanging machine-readable, interconnected data over the Internet. It enables the enrichment of the datasets with links between data from different data sources to get additional information.

Data integration and fusion are attained by linking sensor descriptions and sensor data such as type, future of interest and observation to other types of data that already exist (Djezzar et al. 2018). So, we suggest to publish our dataset as Linked Data to be enriched and reused. It then becomes more useful through semantic queries and achieves the primary goal of the Semantic Web, large-scale integration of data and reasoning on data on the web.

To publish the structured data RDF/XML on the web, it should be on the RDF data model (subject → predicate → object). For example:

– patient → connected → sensor.

– feature_of_interest → feature → observation.

– observation → measured → physiological_quality.

Therefore, users can sail between various sources of data by ensuing RDF links in Linked Data browsers. The user can start with a single data source and traverse a theoretically infinite network of data sources connected by RDF connectors.

3.5. Conclusion

This part of our research work is mainly motivated by the intensifying use of IoT devices in all application areas of our daily lives and the massive amount of raw data gathered. In Smart Health, connected devices are widely deployed to monitor health conditions and provide medical staff with data. Then, to allow machines and humans to collaborate, it is necessary to make IoT data processing interoperable, because it requires a high level of expressiveness and complex reasoning tasks. The semantic approach proposed is based on Semantic Web technologies to enhance the monitoring of patients in ICU to permit the development of innovative Smart Health applications to help healthcare providers give better care to patients.

The chapter proposed to represent knowledge through the development of an ontology extended to the SSN ontology and adding the core concepts of the application domain. A set of queries and reasoning rules is then applied to infer new knowledge. In the end, the dataset will be published as Linked Data to be reused and enriched by the semantic engine.

There are many extensions of our presented work in the future, such as ameliorating the developed ontology by adding new concepts and semantic rules to enrich additive knowledge. Also, innovative Smart Health applications are built to allow end-users to interrogate and make semantic reasoning on the already presented ontology. Finally, the proposed approach is applied to other IoT applications domains to ensure semantic interoperability amonsg the IoT data transmitted to the web.

DATA AVAILABILITY.– The developed ontology file is available from the first author.

3.6. References

Abatal, A., Khallouki, H., Bahaj, M. (2018). A semantic smart interconnected healthcare system using ontology and cloud computing. *2018 4th International Conference on Optimization and Applications (ICOA)*, 26 April.

Alti, A. and Laouamer, L. (2021). Autonomic semantic agent-based platform for dynamic diseases detection with optimal services selection and deployment. *CCF Transactions on Pervasive Computing and Interaction*, 3(3), 270–283.

Andročec, D., Novak, M., Oreški., D. (2018). Using semantic web for Internet of Things interoperability: A systematic review. *International Journal on Semantic Web and Information Systems (IJSWIS)*, 14(4), 147–171.

Barnaghi, P., Wang, W., Henson, C., Taylor, K. (2012). Semantics for the Internet of Things: Early Progress and Back to the Future. *International Journal on Semantic Web and Information Systems (IJSWIS)*, 8(1), 1–21.

Berners-Lee, T. (2006). Linked data [Online]. Available at: http://www.w3.org/DesignIssues. LinkedData.html [Accessed 20 August 2021].

Berners-Lee, T., Hendler, J., Lassila, O. (2001). The semantic web. *Scientific American*, 284(5), 34–43.

Botts, M., Percivall, G., Reed, C., Davidson, J. (2006). *OGC Sensor Web Enablement: Overview and High Level Architecture*. Springer, Berlin, Heidelberg.

Brickley, D., Guha, R.V., McBride, B. (2014). RDF Schema 1.1. *W3C Recommendation*, 25, 2004–2014.

Chen, M., Yang, J., Hu, L., Hossain, M.S., Muhammad, G. (2018). Urban healthcare big data system based on crowdsourced and cloud-based air quality indicators. *IEEE Communications Magazine*, 56(11), 14–20.

Compton, M., Barnaghi, P., Bermudez, L., Garcia-Castro, R., Corcho, O., Cox, S., Graybeal, J., Hauswirth, M., Henson, C., Herzog, A. et al. (2012). The SSN ontology of the W3C semantic sensor network incubator group. *Journal of Web Semantics*, 17, 25–32.

Daniele, L., Hartog, F.D., Roes, J. (2015). Created in close interaction with the industry: The smart appliances reference (SAREF) ontology. *International Workshop on Formal Ontologies Meet Industry*, Springer, Cham.

Djezzar, M., Hemam, M., Maimour, M., Amara, F.Z., Falek, K., Seghir, Z.A. (2018). An approach for semantic enrichment of sensor data. *IEEE*, 1–7.

Fernandez-Lopez, M., Gomez-Perez, A., Juristo, N. (1997). Methontology: From ontological art towards ontological engineering, AAAI Technical Report SS-97-06.

Hlomani, H. and Stacey, D. (2014). Approaches, methods, metrics, measures, and subjectivity in ontology evaluation: A survey. *Semantic Web Journal*, 1(5), 1–11.

Horrocks, I., Patel-Schneider, P.F., Boley, H., Tabet, S., Grosof, B., Dean, M. (2004). SWRL: A semantic web rule language combining OWL and RuleML. *W3C Member Submission*, 21(79), 1–31.

Lefort, L., Henson, C., Taylor, K., Barnaghi, P., Compton, M., Corcho, O., García-Castro, R., Graybeal, J., Herzog, A., Janowicz, K. et al. (2011). Semantic sensor network xg. Final report, W3C Incubator Group.

Mahmud, R., Koch, F.L., Buyya, R. (2018). Cloud-fog interoperability in IoT-enabled healthcare solutions. *Proceedings of the 19th International Conference on Distributed Computing and Networking*, 1–10.

Mishra, S. and Jain, S. (2019). Towards a semantic knowledge treasure for military intelligence. In *Emerging Technologies in Data Mining and Information Security*, Ella Hassanien, A., Bhattacharyya, S., Chakrabati, S., Bhattacharya, A., Dutta, S. (eds). Springer, Singapore.

Mishra, S. and Jain, S. (2020). Ontologies as a semantic model in IoT. *International Journal of Computers and Applications*, 42, 233–243.

Moreira, J., Pires, L.F., van Sinderen, M., Daniele, L. (2018). SAREF4health: IoT standard-based ontology-driven healthcare systems. *FOIS*, 239–252.

Muneer, A., Fati, S.M., Fuddah, S. (2020). Smart health monitoring system using IoT based smart fitness mirror. *Telkomnika*, 18(1), 317–331.

Panchal, R., Swaminarayan, P., Tiwari, S., Ortiz-Rodriguez, F. (2021). AISHE-Onto: A semantic model for public higher education universities. *DG. O2021: The 22nd Annual International Conference on Digital Government Research*, 545–547.

Raad, J. and Cruz, C. (2015). A survey on ontology evaluation methods. *Proceedings of the International Conference on Knowledge Engineering and Ontology Development, Part of the 7th International Joint Conference on Knowledge Discovery, Knowledge Engineering and Knowledge Management*, November.

Rasmussen, M.H., Maxime, L., Schneider, G.F., Pauwels, P. (2021). BOT: The building topology ontology of the W3C linked building data group. *Semantic Web*, 12(1), 143–161.

Reda, R., Piccinini, F., Carbonaro, A. (2018). Towards consistent data representation in the IoT healthcare landscape. *Proceedings of the 2018 International Conference on Digital Health*, 5–10.

Rhayem, A., Mhiri, M.B.A., Gargouri, F. (2017). HealthIoT ontology for data semantic representation and interpretation obtained from medical connected objects. *IEEE/ACS 14th International Conference on Computer Systems and Applications (AICCSA)*, 30 October.

Ruta, M., Scioscia, F., Pinto, A., Di Sciascio, E., Gramegna, F., Ieva, S., Loseto, G. (2013). Resource annotation, dissemination and discovery in the Semantic Web of Things: A CoAP-based framework. *IEEE International Conference on Green Computing and Communications and IEEE Internet of Things and IEEE Cyber, Physical and Social Computing*, 20 August.

Shahzad, S.K., Ahmed, D., Naqvi, M.R., Mushtaq, M.T., Iqbal, M.W., Munir, F. (2021). Ontology driven Smart Health service integration. *Computer Methods and Programs in Biomedicine*, 207, 106146.

Sharma, N., Mangla, M., Mohanty, S.N., Gupta, D., Tiwari, P., Shorfuzzaman, M., Rawashdeh, M. (2021). A smart ontology-based IoT framework for remote patient monitoring. *Biomedical Signal Processing and Control*, 68, 102717.

Sondes, T., Elhadj, H.B., Chaari, L. (2019). An ontology-based healthcare monitoring system in the Internet of Things. *IEEE*, 319–324.

Sundaravadivel, P., Kougianos, E., Mohanty, S.P., Ganapathiraju, M.K. (2017). Everything you wanted to know about smart health care: Evaluating the different technologies and components of the Internet of Things for better health. *IEEE Consumer Electronics Magazine*, 7(1), 18–28.

Tiwari, S. and Abraham, A. (2020). Semantic assessment of smart healthcare ontology. *International Journal of Web Information Systems*. doi: 10.1108/IJWIS-05-2020-0027.

W3C SPARQL Working Group and Others (2013). SPARQL 1.1 overview. World Wide Web Consortium.

Wang, C., Chen, N., Wang, W., Chen, Z. (2018). A hydrological sensor web ontology based on the SSN ontology: A case study for a flood. *ISPRS International Journal of Geo-Information*, 7(1), 2.

World Wide Web Consortium (2012). OWL 2 web ontology language document overview [Online]. Available at: https://www.w3.org/TR/owl2-overview/ [Accessed 20 June 2021].

World Wide Web Consortium (2014). RDF 1.1 concepts and abstract syntax [Online]. Available at: https://www.w3.org/TR/rdf11-concepts/ [Accessed 29 May 2021].

Zgheib, R., Stein, K., Conchon, E., Plageman, T., Goebel, V., Bastide, R. (2020). A scalable semantic framework for IoT healthcare applications. *Journal of Ambient Intelligence and Humanized Computing*, 1–9.

4

Role of Clustering in Discovery Services for the Semantic Internet of Things

In the evolving field of the Internet of Things (IoT), one of the prime requirements is to empower heterogeneous devices with the capability of searching, identifying and communicating with each other. Standardization body ITU-T too has recognized the importance of cross-technology communication among diverse devices and recommended the inclusion of the directory service function in IMT-2020 architecture. In order to cater to the complex requirements, such as huge number of devices, heterogeneity, various protocols, constrained resources and dynamicity in the IoT domain, discovery services have been proposed in the literature. The chapter presents a comprehensive review of this literature and also explores how clustering algorithms can address some of the prevalent issues like scalability, while designing and developing discovery services, particularly, semantic-based discovery services.

4.1. Introduction

In recent years, the number of connected devices and objects has increased enormously (Al-Fuqaha et al. 2015) and this trend is expected to continue in the future. It is forecasted that more than 1.25 billion devices will be connected to the Internet by 2030 (Marletta 2019), primarily because the importance of IoT has been realized in diverse fields ranging from healthcare, logistics, smart transportation, smart education and connected cars to smart grids (Al-Sarawi et al. 2020). Almost all aspects of life are expected to transform with the use of the IoT. The prime objective of the IoT is to connect all things in the physical world to the Internet. The terms "things", "objects" and "devices" are used interchangeably in IoT literature. Connectivity of all things to the Internet gives rise to many challenges, such as heterogeneity, scalability and dynamicity (Atzori et al. 2010). Among these problems, heterogeneity of devices and protocols restricts interoperability. The lack of adoption of a global standard further adds to the problem.

Chapter written by Shachi SHARMA.

One of the possible approaches to solve the problem of heterogeneity and interoperability in the IoT domain is by building discovery services. The prime task of discovery services is to locate a device offering a specified service in the network. The very idea of discovery services is not new and has its origin in the web. However, traditional web-based discovery service solutions cannot be applied to the IoT network because of its very nature of connecting diverse objects in dynamic environments, as well as the presence of a wide range of protocols and technologies (Sharma 2019). The simplest approach for implementing a discovery service is to create a single centralized repository or directory of all the devices and the services offered by them. Any device discovery or service discovery request is then processed at the repository. This not a feasible solution for IoT as it is envisioned to connect billions of devices. Moreover, the dynamic nature of the IoT devices is also a hindrance. Hence, distributed discovery services are expected to provide a better solution.

The directory-based discovery service function has also been included in the IMT-2020 architecture by standardization body ITU-T for heterogeneous devices management (ITU-T 2019). A usecase from ITU-T (2019) is shown in Figure 4.1, where a car (Car A) reaching a traffic crossing prepares a message consisting of its position, speed, direction, etc., and sends it to another car (Car B). This is to alert Car B about the arrival of Car A at the crossing so that it can apply the required safety measures and any occurrence of an accident can be avoided. Car B then validates the message from Car A using the directory-based discovery service function. Such directory services are deployed near intersections to reduce delays. The directory service stores the records of all approaching vehicles. Car B queries the directory service, which in turn authenticates the identity of Car A and sends a response back to Car B. Upon successful authentication of Car A, Car B takes safety action such as stopping at the intersection. This usecase also highlights some key requirements of IoT directory-based discovery services. The two cars can be of any make or manufacturer and hence are heterogeneous objects. The two cars may support different communication technologies and protocols. The usecase also represents a dynamic environment, as vehicles approaching the intersection appear and disappear frequently, hence the directory needs to be updated continuously.

There are various types of discovery services presented in the literature. Some authors have classified them into two broad categories, namely, directory-based and directory-less (Marino et al. 2019), while others have grouped them into six, namely, distributed and P2P discovery services, centralized architecture for resource discovery, Constrained Application Protocol (CoAP) based service discovery, semantic-based discovery, search engine for resource discovery and utilization of ONS (Object Naming Service) and DNS (Domain Name System) (Datta et al. 2015). In a recent work, Zorgati et al. (2019) have categorized discovery services in the IoT into two, namely, protocol-based and semantic-based. Irrespective of the categorization of discovery services, their role in achieving cross-technology communication and thus interoperability cannot be overlooked.

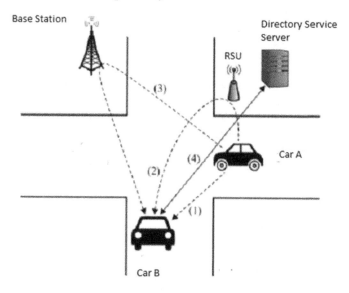

Figure 4.1. *Usecase highlighting the importance of directory-based discovery services for connected vehicles in IMT-2020 architecture (source: adapted from ITU-T (2019))*

In this context, efforts have been made to apply Semantic Web technologies (SWT) to the IoT, leading to the emergence of the Semantic IoT (SIoT) (Rhayem and Gargouri 2020). It is expected that SWT can solve the problem of heterogeneity and interoperability. While designing new discovery services of any type, another issue relates to the handling of an enormous number of devices, services or resources in the IoT. The importance of clustering in the IoT was first recognized by Sharma et al. (2011). Later on, Kapoor and Sharma (2019) have shown how clustering can reduce the search time in directory-based discovery services for the IoT. Chirila et al. (2016) also propose a recommendation system for device discovery, where they have utilized clustering methods to reduce search space.

This chapter presents a detailed discussion on various types of discovery services in the IoT and the role of clustering therein. The chapter is organized into six sections. Section 4.2 provides an overview of various basic categories of discovery services in the IoT. An alternate method to implement discovery services is through ontologies and semantics, which is discussed in section 4.3. The role of clustering methods in improving the search of discovery services is outlined in section 4.4. The IoT specific requirements from clustering methods and a comparative analysis of some of the popular clustering methods in fulfilling these requirements is presented in section 4.5. Finally, section 4.6 contains the conclusion and future directions on improving the efficiency of discovery services in the IoT.

4.2. Discovery services in IoT

In this section, various classes of discovery services in the IoT are described. Typically, discovery services can be centralized or distributed. Because of the dynamicity and scalability requirements of the IoT, distributed discovery service architectures are being investigated more. A point worth mentioning is that the Internet Engineering Task Force (IETF) has standardized Service Location Protocol (SLP) for locating a service in both directory-based and directory-less discovery architectures (Veizades et al. 1999).

4.2.1. *Directory-based architectures*

In this architecture, information about devices and services is kept in a repository, called a directory. The devices and service providers register to the directory whereas service consumers interrogate it. Even though centralized directory-based discovery service architectures are not very suitable for the IoT, for completeness, a brief discussion on them is provided in the following subsection.

4.2.1.1. *Centralized directory*

A single directory of all devices and services is created in centralized directory architecture. Owing to the simplicity and ease of implementation, there is interest from researchers in exploring centralized directory architecture in the context of the IoT.

Jini (2016) allows devices supporting Java to discover each other through a centralized discovery service architecture. The service provider devices in Jini architecture publish services to a lookup server, which can be interrogated by the service consumer devices. The Jini discovery services architecture can be applied in a local network. However, there are global directory-based discovery service architectures as well, such as ONS (ONS 2013). It is a DNS-based network that allows us to search and obtain information about Electronic Product Code (EPC) enabled devices. The standard DNS query can be initiated by encoding EPC into a proper Fully Qualified Domain Name (FQDM). An implementation of ONS service directory is by GS1. Another notable work is Digcovery by Jara et al. (2014) for smart cities, allowing devices supporting heterogeneous technologies to discover and communicate using its centralized global discovery service architecture. It provides a REST API interface for its lookup service. A search engine like discovery framework has been proposed in Datta and Bonnet (2015) using a CoAP resource discovery mechanism. It is worth highlighting here that CoAP allows devices to find resources via a centralized resource repository (Shelby et al. 2014). A CoAP resource directory server provides a common entry by a specific URI "well-known/core". It replies with the details of hosted resources in the CoRE Link Format (Shelby 2010). In Datta and Bonnet (2015), a new URI "well-known/servers" has been introduced to retrieve the list of CoAP servers that are reachable, so that a hierarchy of linked CoAP servers can be created and the global discovery of resources and services can be enabled.

Since the centralized directory discovery service architectures fail to provide required scalability for IoT and are also prone to failure, distributed directory-based discovery service architecture is discussed next.

4.2.1.2. Distributed directories

A novel distributed discovery service architecture has been proposed by Sharma (2019), which is presented in Figure 4.2. The distributed directories (called DSN in this work) are constructed based on logical attributes characterizing devices. The service provided by a device is also its one such attribute. Thus, this architecture is capable of handling heterogeneity. The DSNs are responsible for establishing communication with the devices under control following protocols supported by them. The DSNs can be connected to each other over the Internet or any other wireline or wireless network. The devices are required to know the identity of the nearest DSN. A service consumer device sends a query consisting of the required service to the nearest DSN, which in turn makes an intelligent decision by sending the query to the most probable DSN if the queried service is not available with it. A probabilistic flood search algorithm is implemented in all DSNs to resolve the queries intelligently. The details of the architecture and algorithm can be found in Sharma (2019).

An altogether different mechanism of distributed directory-based discovery service is proposed in Kozat and Tassiulas (2002), where a network of directory nodes is created using a Minimum Dominating Set (MDS) algorithm. Service provider devices advertise services to backbone nodes. The backbone node that receives a query forwards it to others in case the query cannot be satisfied locally.

Liu et al. (2016a) discuss many distributed discovery architectures, also mentioning the limitation of distributed architecture as it leads to a high volume of network traffic when compared to centralized architectures.

4.2.1.3. Distributed P2P directories

Distributed Hash Table (DHT)-based directories are also studied in the literature. DHT is a distributed hash table data structure (Balakrishnan et al. 2003) with its origination in computer networks, and is widely used in P2P networks for the dissemination of information. In DHT-based architectures, gateways act as directory nodes, tracking devices entering and leaving the network.

Paganelli and Parlanti (2012) have presented a DHT-based P2P discovery service architecture. In DHT, the key space is partitioned among nodes thus requiring knowledge of the key a priori. If there is a change in the key set then the whole hash table needs to be reconstructed. This is a major limitation in dynamic IoT environments as whenever a new device is introduced in the network, the hash table needs to be reconstructed. A distributed resource discovery (DRD) architecture is proposed in Liu et al. (2013), where peers are responsible for both service or resource registration and discovery. There are three components in a peer – the resource registration component is responsible for registering devices resources by storing their IP address, resource path, resource type, content type, etc.; the resource discovery component performs the task of look-up based on the description in the request; and a proxy layer handles CoAP and HTTP messages.

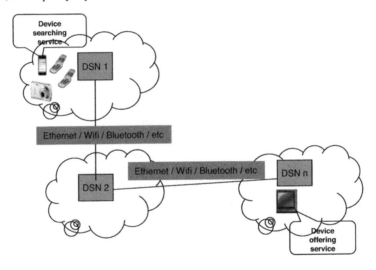

Figure 4.2. *Attributed-based distributed directory discovery service architecture (source: adapted from Sharma (2019)). For a color version of this figure, see www.iste.co.uk/mehta/tools.zip*

4.2.2. *Directory-less architectures*

The directory-less discovery service architectures are much simpler than directory-based architectures as they do not require dedicated directory nodes. The service provider devices simply advertise their services, while the service consumer devices broadcast the requests. Universal Plug and Play (UPnP) is a well-known industry standard of directory-less architecture (Balakrishnan et al. 1989). Another example is Bluetooth SDP by BluetoothSIG (1988), in which a service is represented by a set of attribute-value pairs. A query consisting of attributes is broadcasted. The devices with matching descriptions respond.

The main challenge in directory-less architectures is that a lot of bandwidth and energy of the devices get wasted in finding the appropriate frequency of the advertisements. Several solutions are proposed in the literature to reduce this wastage (Ratsimor et al. 2002; Gao et al. 2004; Chakraborty et al. 2006; Lee et al. 2006; Nguyen and Aggarwal 2018).

4.3. Semantic-based architectures

An alternate method to implement directories is using ontology and semantics. This has become an integral part of the SIoT.

Zhou and Ma (2012) present a proof of concept of vehicular sensors ontology and an algorithm to find appropriate web services by computing matching degree using semantic similarity and relativity. Alam and Noll (2010) propose a semantic-based framework using service advertisements by IoT devices to accelerate the service registration. The advertisement contains service metadata such as name, identifier, endpoint, location and semantic annotation link. A Semantic Web based service discovery middleware is proposed in Liu et al. (2016b), which uses sensor data. A semantic-based discovery service, called DiscoWoT, is proposed in Mayer and Guinard (2011) for the Web of Things (WoT). DiscoWoT applies a mapping scheme internally to semantically discover services. It uses JSON to represent services semantically. This ensures interoperability between devices. Gomes et al. (2019) developed an ontology-based multi-repository system, QoDisco, that can handle queries spanned over multiple attributes and range. Many optimizations are also discussed to reduce the time of semantic search in this work.

The literature on semantic-based discovery service architectures in the IoT can be broadly divided into two classes – search engine based and ONS DNS based.

4.3.1. *Search engine-based*

The search engine utilizes a lot of semantic matching algorithms and the same idea can be used in designing discovery services in the IoT. In Ding et al. (2012), a hybrid three layer search engine is proposed that supports spatio-temporal, value and keyword searches. This search engine enables data generated by IoT devices to be searched for. Hence, it has a sensor and device monitoring layer that connects to physical devices and collects data, a storage layer that is responsible for storing data and an index layer that allows searching on the three criteria mentioned above. It is shown in this work that keyword search gives the best performance when searching real-time sensor data. This work does not provide device or service searches. However, it shows the possibility of using search engines for device and service discovery.

4.3.2. *ONS DNS-based*

ONS stands for object name service and it takes advantage of DNS to find information or locate a service, usually for EPC devices.

A distributed information system using ONS is presented in Minbo et al. (2013). The ONS-based lookup service provides a mapping between a product code and IoT system resource address, whereas DNS stores the related data. The system is shown to have application in agricultural products.

The focus of most of the proposed discovery service architectures is on improving the performance by reducing the search time, handling heterogeneity and interoperability and returning quality results. The issue of scalability is not much addressed in the literature of discovery services. The next section discusses some studies that suggest using clustering to develop scalable architectures.

4.4. Discovery services and clustering

The very idea of applying clustering methods in the IoT was proposed by Sharma et al. (2011). In the context of discovery services, the idea of forming clusters of services based on physical and semantic closeness is used in Klein et al. (2003). Each cluster has a Service Access Point (SAP) that handles registration and queries for that cluster. The advantage of organizing services in clusters is that a query can be quickly narrowed down and answered by search space reduction. In Schiele et al. (2004), clusters are created based on the mobility pattern of the devices. A cluster head is chosen periodically and handles queries. Chirila et al. (2016) proposed a broker-based service discovery and recommendation system for IoT devices. A new service clustering algorithm is used in the recommendation system. The clustering method basis is a new similarity metric.

Noting that the IoT is a dynamic environment and service discovery is not a trivial task there, Fredj et al. (2014) emphasize the need for re-clustering. They also propose an approach based on the hierarchy of semantic gateways to fasten the discovery of IoT Semantic Web services. An incremental clustering algorithm is used to group similar services. An optimized clustering-based framework for discovering services is presented in Bharti and Jinal (2021) using Web Ontology Language (OWL) for efficient semantic matching.

The following section illustrates some IoT specific requirements for clustering methods and provides an overview of the HiCHO clustering method.

Clustering Methods	Attribute Based	Hierarchical	Supports Numeric and Categorical Value Set	Applies to a Dynamic Environment	Incremental	Online	Attribute and Value Based both
HiCHO Sharma et al. Mobiquitous, (2011)	✓	✓	✓	✓	✓	✓	✓
Friedman et al. J. R. Statist. Soc. B (2004) 66, Part 4, pp. 815–849	✓	Distance Based ✗	Numeric only ✗	✗	✗	✗	✓
Pratipta Maji, IEEE Transactions On Knowledge And Data Engineering, 2010	✓	✗	Numeric only ✗	✗	✗	✗	✗
OPTICS Mihael Ankerst et al. ACM SIGMOD, pp. 49–60, 1999	✗	Density Based ✗	Numeric only ✗	✗	✗	✗	✗
Real Time OPTICS Fei Shao et al. Journal of Information & Computational Science 7: 10 (2010), pp. 2110–2121	✗	Density Based ✗	Numeric only ✗	✓	✓	✓	✗
Squeezer, Zengyou et al. Journal of Computer Science and Technology, Volume 17 (5), 2002	✓	✗	Categorical only ✗	✗	✗	✗	✓
Shuyun Wang et al. Seventh IEEE/ACIS International Conference on Computer and Information Science, pp 140-145, 2008	✓	Divide and Co ✓	✓	✗	✗	✗	✓
Gibson et al. The VLDB Journal (2000) 8: 222–236	✓	Iterative ✗	Categorical only ✗	✗	✗	✗	✓
Chen et al. The VLDB Journal (2009) 18: 502-506	✗	✗	Categorical only ✗	✓	✓	✓	✗

Figure 4.3. *Requirements for designing clustering methods in the IoT and comparative analysis of some existing algorithms (source: adapted from Kapoor et al. (2014)). For a color version of this figure, see www.iste.co.uk/mehta/tools.zip*

4.5. Clustering methods in IoT

Heterogeneity, dynamicity and scalability are the key requirements in the IoT domain. Considering them, an attribute-based clustering method for IoT devices was first proposed in Sharma et al. (2011). Using the logical attributes of devices makes the method independent of any technology. As noted by Sharma et al. (2011), the set of logical attributes may change over time and the classification mechanism must allow the modification of attributes.

The following definitions are given in Sharma et al. (2011):

DEFINITION 4.1.– *An Attribute characterizes a device and can be used to classify it. Attributes can be physical (e.g. serial id) or logical (e.g. color).*

DEFINITION 4.2.– *A Value represents a specific instantiation of the device's attribute. For example, red is an instantiation of attribute color.*

Both attributes and values are strings and form an attribute-value or av-pair together.

DEFINITION 4.3.– *A set of possible av-pairs characterizes a device completely and is referred to as a Characteristics Set (CS). For example, a smart camera may have its CS as (manufacturer, "Nikon"); (model, "S20"); (color, "silver"); (wifi, "yes"); (camera, "yes"); (owner, "Mary").*

Using these definitions, a hierarchical, incremental, online clustering algorithm HiCHO was developed in Sharma et al. (2011) with two levels – Level 0 clustering based on attributes and Level 1 clustering based on attribute-values. The performance of this algorithm has also been analyzed in detail, and both the feasibility and accuracy are ascertained.

There are some requirements specific to clustering in the IoT domain, which are discussed in Kapoor et al. (2014). The same are shown in Figure 4.3. Some existing clustering methods are also compared and analyzed against these requirements. According to the discussion in Sharma et al. (2011) and Kapoor et al. (2014), these requirements are as follows:

– **Online**: in order to support the dynamicity of the IoT environment, it is essential that the clustering method is online. Particularly, as the clustering has to be performed using logical attributes to address the issue of heterogeneity and the value of these attributes may change with time, also, in the worst case even the attribute may change.

– **Incremental**: the majority of the IoT devices in the future will be mobile. The future devices are not known; hence, the clustering should be incremental in nature. This is in contrast to traditional data mining where the complete dataset is known.

– **Attributes and their values based**: as the clustering is to be used in discovery services, the devices should be classified in groups such that the search time gets minimized. The devices or services can be looked up by specifying complete or partial CS. If the clustering is performed in multiple levels, that is hierarchy, first by using attributes and then by using av-pairs, then the search domain gets reduced quickly at the first level itself. This leads to a faster discovery of service or device.

– **Capable of working with numeric as well as categorical data**: attributes are categorical, however, values can be numeric or categorical. The clustering method then should be capable of handling both types of data.

The current literature on clustering does not fulfill the above requirements collectively. For instance, the work of Friedman (2004) is based on attributes, but is an offline algorithm and only deals with numeric data. The real-time clustering algorithm (real-time OPTICS) by Shao et al. (2010) and data stream clustering by Wang et al. (2008) require training before they can be deployed. Real-time OPTICS is density-based clustering, that is, clusters are built around core objects using core-distances, and thus only work with numeric data. Stream data clustering (Wang et al. 2008) uses entropy measures to create micro-clusters that are later updated in the online process when data arrives as a stream. It should be noted that entropy is a measure of uncertainty. A cluster with less entropy is more dense compared to one with more entropy. The goal of entropy-based clustering algorithms is to divide the dataset into groups, such that the entropy of entire system (i.e. collection of all the clusters) gets minimized. There are also many clustering algorithms for categorical data (Li et al. 2004), but they are mostly not incremental and are not online.

These requirements can be treated as guidelines to design new clustering algorithms in the IoT.

4.6. Conclusion

The chapter presents an extensive discussion of various discovery service architectures in the IoT. The existing literature on discovery services can be broadly divided into three types – directory-based, directory-less and semantic-based. Semantics play a pivotal role in the IoT leading to the SIoT, and help in building more intelligent systems. It has been realized that the introduction of the clustering of services, devices, as well as other resources while designing discovery services can reduce search space and thereby lookup time. A set of guidelines while designing new clustering algorithms for the IoT are also discussed.

The future research on discovery services must also include new clustering algorithms considering the discussed guidelines to improve their performance.

4.7. References

Al-Fuqaha, A., Guizani, M., Mohammadi, M., Aledhari, M., Ayyash, M. (2015). Internet of things: A survey on enabling technologies, protocols, and applications. *IEEE Communication Surveys & Tutorials*, 17(4), 2347–2376.

Al-Sarawi, S., Anbar, M., Abdullah, R., Al Hawari, A.B. (2020). Internet of Things market analysis forecasts, 2020–2030. *4th World Conference on Smart Trends in Systems, Security and Sustainability (WorldS4)*, London.

Alam, S. and Noll, J. (2010). A semantic enhanced service proxy framework for internet of things. *IEEE/ACM International Conference on Green Computing and Communications & International Conference on Cyber, Physical and Social Computing*, Hangzhou.

Atzori, L., Antonio, I., Morabito, G. (2010). The Internet of Things: A survey. *Computer Networks*, 54(15), 2787–2805.

Apache River (2016). DJ – JiniTM Discovery & Join Specification [Online]. Available at: https://river.apache.org/release-doc/current/specs/html/discovery-spec.html [Accessed 28th November 2021].

Balakrishnan, H., Kaashoek, M.F., Karger, D., Morris, R., Stoica, I. (1989). Universal plug and play: Background [Online]. Available at: http://www.upnp-hacks.org/upnp.html [Accessed 1st November 2021].

Balakrishnan, H., Kaashoek, M.F., Karger, D., Morris, R., Stoica, I. (2003). Looking up data in P2P systems. *Communications of ACM*, 46(2), 43–48.

Bharti, M. and Jinal, H. (2021). Optimized clustering–based discovery framework on Internet of Things. *The Journal of Supercomputing*, 77, 1739–1778.

Bluetooth (2020). Bluetooth Core Specifications Version 5.2 Feature Overview [Online]. Available: https://www.bluetooth.com/wp-content/uploads/2020/01/Bluetooth_5.2_Feature _Overview.pdf [Accessed 15th November 2021].

Chakraborty, D., Joshi, A., Yesha, Y., Finin, T. (2006). Toward distributed service discovery in pervasive computing environments. *IEEE Transactions on Mobile Computing*, 5(2), 97–112.

Chirila, S., Lemnaru, C., Dinsoreanu, M. (2016). Semantic-based IoT device discovery and recommendation mechanism. *IEEE 12th International Conference on Intelligent Computer Communication and Processing (ICCP)*, Cluj-Napoca.

Datta, S.K. and Bonnet, C. (2015). Search engine based resource discovery framework for Internet of Things. *IEEE Global Conference on Consumer Electronics*, Osaka.

Datta, S.K., Costa, R., Bonnet, C. (2015). Resource discovery in Internet of Things: Current trends and future standardization aspects. *IEEE 2nd World Forum on Internet of Things (WF-IoT)*, Milan.

Ding, Z., Xu, G., Guo, L., Yang, Q. (2012). A hybrid search engine framework for the internet of things based on spatial-temporal value-based and keyword-based conditions. *IEEE International Conference on Green Computing and Communications (GreenCom)*, Besançon.

Fredj, S.B., Boussard, M., Kofman, D., Noirie, L. (2014). Efficient semantic-based IoT service discovery mechanism for dynamic environments. *IEEE 25th Annual International Symposium on Personal, Indoor, and Mobile Radio Communication (PIMRC)*, Washington, DC.

Friedman, J.H. (2004). Clustering objects on subsets of attributes. *Journal of Royal Statistical Society*, 66(4), 815–849.

Gao, Z., Yang, X., Ma, T., Cai, S. (2004). RICFFP: An efficient service discovery protocol for manets. *Embedded and Ubiquitous Computing EUC 2004*, 3207, Springer, Berlin, Heidelberg.

Gomes, P., Cavalcante, E., Batista, T., Taconet, C., Conan, D., Chabridon, S., Delicato, F.C., Pires, P.F. (2019). A semantic-based discovery service for the Internet of Things. *Journal of Internet Services and Applications*, 10 [Online]. Available at: https://doi.org/ 10.1186/s13174-019-0109-8.

ITU-T (2019). ITU-TY.3074 framework for directory service management of large numbers of heterogeneously-named objects in IMT-2020.

Jara, A.J., Lopez, P., Fernandez, D., Castillo, J.F., Zamora, M.A., Skarmeta, A.F. (2014). Mobile digcovery: Discovering and interacting with the world through the Internet of Things. *Pervasive and Ubiquitous Computing*, 18, 323–338.

Kapoor, S. and Sharma, S. (2019). Dynamic directory of objects using based on logical attributes. US Patent, US010423608B2.

Kapoor, S., Sharma, S., Srinivasan, B. (2014). Clustering devices in an Internet of Things. US Patent, USOO8671099B2.

Klein, M., Konig-Ries, B., Obreiter, P. (2003). Service rings – A semantic overlay for service discovery in ad hoc networks. *International Workshop on Database and Expert Systems Applications*, Prague.

Kozat, U.C. and Tassiulas, L. (2002). Service discovery in mobile ad hoc networks: An overall perspective on architectural choices and network layer support issues. *Adhoc Network*, 2, 2–44.

Lee, C., Helal, S., Lee, W. (2006). Gossip-based service discovery in mobile ad hoc networks. *IEICE Transactions on Communications*, E89-B, 2621–2624.

Li, T., Ma, S., Ogihara, M. (2004). Entropy-based criterion in categorical clustering. *Proceedings of the 12th International Conference on Machine Learning*, Association for Computing Machinery, New York.

Liu, M., Leppanen, T., Harjula, E., Ou, Z., Ylianttila, M., Ojala, T. (2013). Distributed resource discovery in the machine-to-machine applications. *International Conference on Mobile Ad-Hoc and Sensor Systems*, Hangzhou.

Liu, L., Antonopoulos, N., Zheng, M., Zhan, Y., Ding, Z. (2016a). A socio ecological model for advanced service discovery in machine-to-machine communication networks. *ACM Transactions on Embedded Computing Systems*, 15(2), 1–28.

Liu, M., Yang, X., Hu, H., Mohammed, A. (2016b). Semantic agent-based service middleware and simulation for smart cities. *Sensor*, 16(12) [Online]. Available at: https://doi.org/10.3390/s16122200.

Marino, F., Moiso, C., Petraccaa, M. (2019). Automatic contract negotiation, service discovery and mutual authentication solutions: A survey on the enabling technologies of the forthcoming IoT ecosystem. *Computer Networks*, 148, 176–195.

Marletta, M. (2019). Life after graduation: Iot: Forecasts, challenges and opportunities. *IEEE Instrumentation & Measurement Magazine*, 22(6), 76–77.

Mayer, S. and Guinard, D. (2011). An extensible discovery service for smart things. *WoT '11: Proceedings of the 2nd International Workshop on Web of Things*, Association for Computing Machinery, New York.

Minbo, L., Zhu, Z., Guangyu, C. (2013). Information service system of agriculture IoT. *Automatika-Journal for Control Measurement Electronics Computing and Communications*, 54(4), 415–426.

Nguyen, P.T. and Aggarwal, A. (2018). Enhanced DNS-based service discovery in an Internet of Things (IoT) environment. US Patent, 9906605.

Object Name Service (2013). Object Name Service (ONS) [Online]. Available at: https://www.gs1.org/standards/epcis/ epcis-ons/2-0-1 [Accessed 2nd December 2021].

Paganelli, F. and Parlanti, D. (2012). A DHT-based discovery service for the Internet of Things. *Journal of Computer Networks and Communications* [Online]. Available at: https://doi.org/10.1155/2012/107041.

Ratsimor, O., Chakraborty, D., Joshi, A., Finin, T. (2002). Allia: Alliance-based service discovery for ad-hoc environments. *International Workshop on Mobile Commerce*, Atlanta.

Rhayem, A., Mhiri, M.B.R., Gargouri, F. (2020). Semantic Web technologies for the Internet of Things: Systematic literature review. *Internet of Things*, 14 [Online]. Available at: https://doi.org/10.1016/j.iot.2020.100206.

Schiele, G., Becker, C., Rothermel, K. (2004). Energy-efficient cluster-based service discovery for ubiquitous computing. *EW 11: Proceedings of the 11th Workshop on ACM SIGOPS European Workshop*, Association for Computing Machinery, New York.

Shao, F., Cao, Y., Gu, J., Wang, Y. (2010). A new real-time clustering algorithm. *Journal of Information and Computational Science*, 7(10), 2110–2121.

Sharma, S. (2019). Attribute based discovery architecture for devices in Internet of things (IoT). *International Conference for Convergence of Technology (I2CT)*, Mumbai.

Sharma, S., Kapoor, S., Srinivasan, B.R., Narula, M.S. (2011). HiCHO: Attributes based classification of ubiquitous devices. *MobiQuitous 2011*, 104, 113–125.

Shelby, Z. (2010). Core link format. IEFT [Online]. Available at: https://datatracker.ietf.org/doc/html/draft-shelby-core-link-format [Accessed 13th November 2021].

Shelby, Z., Hartke, K., Bormann, C. (2014). Constrained application protocol (CoAP). Memo, RFC 7252 Internet Engineering Task Force.

Veizades, J., Guttman, E., Perkins, C., KaplanGuttman, S. (1999). Service location protocol [Online]. Available at: https://www.ietf.org/rfc/rfc2608.txt [Accessed 27th November 2021].

Wang, S., Fan, Y., Zhang, C., Xu, H., Hao, X., Hu, Y. (2008). Entropy based clustering of data streams with mixed numericand categorical values. *IEEE/ACIS International Conference on Computer and Information Science*, Portland.

Zhou, M. and Ma, Y. (2012). A web service discovery computational method for IoT system. *IEEE 2nd International Conference on Cloud Computing and Intelligence Systems*, Hangzhou.

Zorgati, H., Djemaa, R.B., Amor, I.K.B. (2019). Service discovery techniques in internet of things: A survey. *IEEE International Conference on Systems, Man and Cybernetics (SMC)*, Bari.

Dynamic Security Testing Techniques for the Semantic Web of Things: Market and Industry Perspective

As businesses are moving toward digitalization, their essential operation on Web Applications is also increased. The complexity and the size of Web Applications are growing, and so is the concern of Web Application Security. The dynamic nature of Web Applications calls for a dynamic and robust testing methodology, a Dynamic Web Application testing, which tests the dynamic nature of the Web App and discovers vulnerabilities in run time or a dynamic state of Web Application. But as Web Applications grow faster, there is a need for dynamic testing to grow simultaneously. This chapter presents insights into methodologies and techniques that various researchers devise. These techniques include the use of static analysis with dynamic testing to increase the coverage of dynamic analysis, use of Tainted Mode Model to surplus the dynamic testing, and use of user session data to generate test cases that are effective in finding vulnerabilities in Web Application at run time by using dynamic testing. We have also presented a roadmap for research directions.

5.1. Introduction

Dynamic Application Security Testing (DAST) is defined as a type of Black Box testing, where the tester has no access to the internal working of the Web Application, and the tester tries to test the working of a Web Application by targeting scripts or actual attacks on the Web Application to find out about the existence of various kinds of vulnerabilities discussed by Sönmez and Kiliç (2021) and Huang et al. (2003). Dynamic testing is the phase of testing that is conducted on the Web Application when the application is in a production environment or in a running state. Most Dynamic Web Application testing is automated and performed by tools.

Chapter written by Dhananjay SINGH CHAUHAN, Gaurav CHOUDHARY, Shishir Kumar SHANDILYA and Vikas SIHAG.

DAST has the benefit that it can be used to find vulnerabilities with less coverage of the Web Application but with more accuracy in comparison to other techniques like SAST (Static Application Security Testing) as discussed in Petukhov and Kozlov (2008a). Dynamic Web Application testing is used increasingly by independent testers as it requires no prior working knowledge of the workings of the internals of the Web Application. Dynamic testing has its merits as it can be applied to production-ready applications and can be used to find vulnerabilities that exist in the run time behavior of the Web Application.

Dynamic Web Application testing uses the tester's knowledge to devise the test cases that may discover potential vulnerabilities. However, sometimes this may be a huge job, as the size of the Web Application is so large, so the generation of test cases must be automated, and not only automated but the test cases must also address the specific type of functionality that they are targeting, as covered in Curphey and Arawo (2006). Another situation that arises is that dynamic testing has a good rate of confirming the presence of a vulnerability in run time, but lacks the high coverage to cover the entire Web Application. This weakness of dynamic testing can also be added. Another advantage of dynamic testing of Web Application is that testing is done against a running Web Application, so flaws that exist in logic are easily discovered.

Dynamic Web Application testing has many uses in the field of testing and automated testing, but the power of dynamic testing can be increased by mixing dynamic testing with other forms of testing and information gathering techniques as explained by Benedikt et al. (2002). Many kinds of research in the field have proved that combining DAST with other techniques increases the accuracy of DAST testing. One such technique is the coupling of DAST with static analysis. This technique increases the power of dynamic analysis greatly by providing the static analysis data to the dynamic analysis phase. Another most famous technique is to use test cases generated by the user session data itself to perform dynamic testing on the Web Application, as these test cases are more effective as they are derived by real-time user experience from the Web Application, so when these test cases are used in the dynamic testing of Web Applications, they yield results that contain fewer false positives and more vulnerabilities or anomalies, as discussed by Zou et al. (2014), You et al. (2018a) and Sharma et al. (2018). Another technique that also turns the tables when combined with dynamic testing is the coupling of dynamic testing with tainted analysis, where the tainted analysis helps build a model known as the Tainted Mode Model, which assumes certain assumptions, and marks the data as tainted or non-tainted and tracks the data throughout the Web Application with the help of dynamic analysis, and stops the tainted data from being used in sensitive operations or sensitive functionality.

Dynamic Web Application Security testing is a growing paradigm and necessary to cope up with the size of the growing Web Applications. DAST testing is testing that finds vulnerabilities in the behavior and functionality of the running Web Application. Currently, the testing industry is trying to push DAST testing toward more automated testing and less manual involvement, the push is toward to further automating the process by building test cases to craft inputs automatically according to the functionality being tested. But another trend is to make DAST testing more suitable by learning from the user experience data and incorporating that into the generation of test cases. Moreover, the surveys in the field of Dynamic Web Application testing mostly show the working of web testing and all the trends currently on the rise, like in the paper by Doğan et al. (2014). Another review paper by Lakshmi and Mallika (2017) discusses how money efficiency can be achieved while testing and the frameworks that are used in testing and the techniques, but it does not lay emphasis upon techniques that are related to dynamic testing. In this chapter, we discuss how techniques and information gathering methodologies from other testing areas can be added to dynamic testing and how they can increase the power of dynamic testing or analysis by aiding or fusing the dynamic testing with another type of testing such as static analysis and utilizing the power of one to benefit the other. Furthermore, the scope of research can be extended to include the power of machine learning to incorporate dynamic analysis and increase its accuracy by great factors.

5.2. Related studies

As the complexity of Web Applications increases with the increase in the use of Dynamic Web Pages, fast testing and covering a large part of the Web Application is needed. For such needs, a variant of Black Box testing comes in with Dynamic Web Application testing, also known as DAST. It is a tool or collection of scripts that communicate with the Web Application's front end and try to find various vulnerabilities that can persist like SQL, Cross-Site Scripting (XSS) and Non-Validation of the Input. There are various tools that have been developed to perform DAST on Web Applications, tools that exist in both Open Source and Proprietary. Various methodologies and techniques have been developed to perform DAST effectively, several in the paper by Imran et al. (2016) Agent Technology basically combines the static analysis with the dynamic analysis to increase the detection capability of the tool. Followed, another technique or strategy proposed by Alshahwan and Harman (2011) DAST using search-based software engineering, this technique is implemented by the tool named SWAT (Search-Based Web Application Tester). As proposed by Artzi et al. (2010), it is a test generation technique that supplements the working of DAST, this technique utilizes the input on the test generated and collects the logical constraints generated.

The DAST technique as mentioned in Imran et al. (2016) uses the flavor of both static analysis and dynamic analysis, static analysis is used in the technique to approximate the presence of a vulnerability in the source code, which is followed by the dynamic analysis, where the various test inputs are passed to the running Web Application to confirm the presence of the vulnerability, the whole technique comprised in the tool named as Java Web Application Security Tester (JWAST). As the paper presents a great technique but only takes into account the Java-Based Web Apps, which limits the scope of wide effectiveness of the methodology. Following, this trail, another paper by Vogt et al. (2007) demonstrated the combination of dynamic and static analysis of Web Application, this paper proposes a technique under dynamic analysis where it marks the data as sensitive and tracks the data under the Web Application as it flows, and whenever a cross-domain request is made using that marked sensitive data, the technique raises an alert to the user, this technique is used in stopping XSS attack in Web Application. This technique also uses static analysis, where the data that are changed in the flow of Web Application are also required to be marked using static analysis and are tracked to block any cross-domain request. This paper demonstrates a good technique to stop XSS attacks in Web Application, but the technique only stops the XSS that diverts the user toward other domain but does not block the redirect or XSS directing in a sub-domain.

Other techniques that leverage DAST of Web Application involve using the data generated by user session in Web Application, one such methodology is demonstrated in a paper by Elbaum et al. (2005), this paper demonstrates that how data generated by the user sessions in the Web Application can be used to generate test cases for the Web Application that are more effective in comparison to the test cases that are generated by the White Box testing alone. This paper uses methodology of storing user request and responses with the server in a database, along with the sessions data generated by the user. The step that this approach misses is that it does not have any mechanism to decrease the number of sessions that it captures that results in an increase in execution time. Another paper (Zhongsheng 2010) that leverages the data generated by the user and also solves the previous paper problem, demonstrates a technique that collects all the user sessions and then removes the redundant sessions, further the techniques divide the sessions into clusters and prioritize these clusters and sessions within them, further the technique uses genetic algorithm to prioritize the sessions of the users. The technique presented in the paper is highly effective in the scenarios where the user generates an ample amount of sessions, but where the user does not produce many sessions the technique is less effective.

The major DAST challenge for Web Application is the input provided by the user, the input could be malicious and affect the Web Application in drastic ways. The solution to the problem is tainted analysis of the data, one such technique is provided in a paper by Pandikumar and Eshetu (2016), this paper proposes a technique where it uses Tainted Mode Model in compliance to dynamic analysis and then uses that obtain data from dynamic analysis in the penetration testing phase to more effectively find vulnerabilities in the Web Application, the tainted approach in this paper handles the inter-module vulnerabilities that are overlooked by other approaches based on the tainted analysis. Another approach is mentioned by Petukhov and Kozlov (2008b), this paper shows another approach using Tainted Mode Model, in this approach an enhanced Tainted Mode Model is prepared that covers the deficiency to detect inter-module data flow to discover vulnerabilities. But the technique in the paper does not support the input of data from several sources or stored procedures.

Author	Year	P1	P2	P3	P4	P5	P6
Imran et al. (2016)	2016	Yes	No	No	No	Yes	No
Alshahwan and Harman (2011)	2011	Yes	No	No	No	Yes	No
Artzi et al. (2010)	2010	No	No	No	No	Yes	Yes
Vogt et al. (2007)	2007	Yes	Yes	No	No	Yes	No
Elbaum et al. (2005)	2005	No	No	No	Yes	Yes	Yes
Zhongsheng (2010)	2010	No	No	No	Yes	Yes	Yes
Pandikumar and Eshetu (2016)	2016	No	Yes	Yes	No	Yes	No
Petukhov and Kozlov (2008b)	2008	No	Yes	Yes	No	Yes	No
Balzarotti et al. (2008)	2008	Yes	Yes	No	No	Yes	No
Halfond and Orso (2005)	2005	Yes	Yes	No	No	Yes	No
Sampath et al. (2008)	2008	No	No	No	Yes	Yes	Yes
Maung (2014)	2014	No	No	No	Yes	Yes	Yes
Sreenivasa Rao and Kumar (2012)	2012	No	Yes	Yes	No	Yes	No

Table 5.1. *The state-of-the-art comparison of existing works. P1: static analysis, P2: tainted analysis, P3: penetration testing, P4: user session data gathering, P5: dynamic analysis, P6: test case generation*

5.3. Background of dynamic security testing techniques

Black Box testing: It is defined as the testing methodology where the tester has no knowledge of the internal working of the Web Application or does not have the source code. Black Box testing in contrast to White Box testing may lead to the discovery of vulnerabilities that exist in the run time logic of the Web Application and are hidden or may not exist in the static analysis. As Black Box testing does not require any knowledge of the internal working of the Web Application, it is widely used by independent security researchers and throughout the security community. An overview of how Black Box testing works is shown in Figure 5.1.

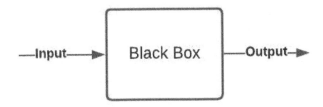

Figure 5.1. *Black Box testing*

5.3.1. *Black Box testing techniques*

1) *Syntax-driven technique*: the Syntax-driven technique is a Black Box technique that checks the input to a system; basically, it checks the syntax and grammar of the input, and this type of testing is automated as an increased amount of data is generated.

2) *Equivalence partitioning*: in this type of testing, the tester divides the inputs into sets or classes. As a similar type of input generates a similar type of output, all these similar types of input are clubbed together into classes of input. When these classes are used in the input, if even just one input from that class results in a type of error then it is concluded that every other input from that particular class will yield the same result.

3) *Boundary value analysis*: in this type of technique, the tester tests the Application for values that are on the edge and may be valid or invalid. These boundary values predict or analyze the nature of how a Web Application may behave if a boundary value is given or tested for; will the Application handle the boundary value or will it show an error or some other anomaly.

4) *Cause-effect graphing*: the cause-effect graphing technique is a Black Box technique where the input is categorized as a cause and the particular action of the input is categorized as an effect of the cause. The bond between the cause and effect is shown using Boolean graphs.

5) *Requirement-based testing*: requirement-based testing is a Black Box technique where the tester uses the Software Requirement Specification (SRS) document to understand the requirements of the Application, and according to these requirements test cases are formed, conditions are made and data are collected. This type of testing is specific to the Application and is not conducted under any generalization.

6) *Compatibility Testing*: compatibility testing is a type of Black Box testing where the test case designed by the tester is designed in such a way that they not only test the functionality of the Application but also test the infrastructure upon which the Application or the functionality is running.

7) *DAST (Dynamic Application Security Testing)*: DAST is defined as a tool or set of instructions which communicates with the front end of the running Web Application and executes an attack on the Web Application in real-time to check for the presence of any vulnerability in the Web Application. After the attack is executed, the DAST technique analyzes the output generated by the Web Application to check whether the executed attack was successful or not. DAST is a type of Black Box testing where the DAST does not know the internal working of the Application or have any access to the code base. DAST methodology is very heavily used by testers to find the vulnerabilities in running Web Applications. DAST also helps in establishing the Proof of Concept for the vulnerabilities discovered in a real-time environment where the Web Application is running. DAST is defined as dynamic as the state of the Web Application when DAST is performed is dynamic, in contrast to SAST which has a Web Application static state when the SAST is performed. Due to the dynamic state, the DAST technique can determine run time flaws and anomalies in the Web Application. DAST has its advantages over other types of testing as it is not dependent upon the technology underlying the Web Application because it does not work upon the codebase or with the code directly, instead, it deals with the running functionality. DAST also has a minor drawback of speed. As the DAST technique is applied on the entire running Web Application, it takes time to cover the entire application for testing and also the test cases for a different part of the Web Application have to be written by the tester, so the DAST technique can become a bit slow. The pros and cons of DAST are shown in Figure 5.2.

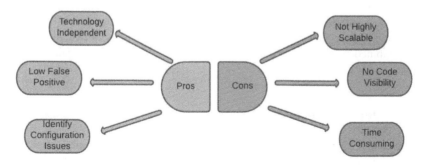

Figure 5.2. *Pro and cons of Dynamic Application Security Testing*

8) *Model-based testing*: model-based testing is defined as the testing of an application in which the run time behavior of the Application is predicted by a model.

A model is defined as a set of behaviors that an Application might show. This behavior could be anything such as to how an application behaves when a specific type of input is provided or how an application behaves when a specific trigger is triggered or functionality is set.

9) *Crawling*: the crawling technique is defined as a tool known as a Crawler that crawls the given Web Application, crawling from one hyperlink to another hyperlink, and marking the domain of the Web Application, and excluding everything beyond the domain. The Crawler tool that follows the crawling technique gathers the point of communication that the DAST tool can use while performing the attack. The crawling technique is widely used in dynamic analysis of Web Applications.

10) *Tainted analysis*: tainted analysis is defined as the analysis technique where the data that enter the Web Application from a non-trusted source are tracked through the Web Application. To protect Web Application from malicious or crafted data, these data are sanitized before being included in the code in the Web Application or are saved into the database. Most of the vulnerabilities that exist over non-sensitization of input like XSS and SQL Injection can be traced and found using this technique.

5.4. DAST using static analysis

DAST using static analysis is an effective technique using DAST techniques. It enhances or couples the power of DAST testing. As static analysis works upon the application when it is in static state, the code covered by the static analysis is increased, but the accuracy by which the static analysis determines the presence of a vulnerability is low. On the other hand, dynamic analysis or DAST acts upon the application when it is in dynamic state or running application, so the coverage of application is low but the accuracy by which the dynamic analysis confirms the presence of a vulnerability is a lot higher. So the high coverage property of static analysis and high accuracy of detection of vulnerability property of dynamic analysis when combined results in a technique that is more efficient and advantageous for testing.

5.4.1. *Current implementation*

In the paper by Imran et al. (2016), the main focus is to develop an approach that includes the combination of dynamic analysis and static analysis, to devise an approach that can increase the vulnerability detecting capability and also enable the prevention of attacks from happening at run time. The paper offers a tool that implements the above DAST and SAST integrated approach. The approach in the paper starts with static analysis of the code, where the static analysis marks the vulnerabilities present in the code based on a set of rules that define the knowledge base for static analysis. Upon completion of the static analysis, the approach moves toward the dynamic analysis, in which the approach uses an instrumentation technique, which creates instrumentation templates that can stop any vulnerability that occurs due to non-proper sanitization of input. These instrumentation templates are applied in the dynamic application to stop these types of vulnerabilities. So the dynamic analysis stage uses the knowledge from the static analysis and confirms the presence of a vulnerability and also stops the vulnerabilities that happen due to non-sanitization of the input.

Another paper by Vogt et al. (2007) demonstrates the application of integration of dynamic analysis and static analysis for stopping XSS in Web Applications. The approach uses dynamic analysis to track and stop tainted data from making any changes in run time and on the second part the static analysis is used to analyze the source to mark all the variables that may accept new values at the run time, and all those variables that are under tainted analysis in the run time of the Web Application. The code that is analyzed in the static analysis is the code that the server sends to the user side, and this user side code is analyzed in this approach. The authors demonstrate the use of static analysis to aid dynamic analysis. This helps in detecting the XSS and decreases the number of false positives. This is shown in Figure 5.3.

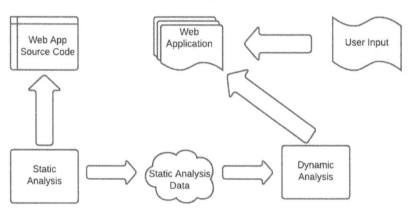

Figure 5.3. *How SAST works with DAST*

The paper by Balzarotti et al. (2008) shows another approach that utilizes the same concept of using static analysis to aid dynamic analysis. The authors present a method that works to address the condition where the sanitization of input in Web Applications is not done correctly. The proposed approach includes the static analysis of the Web Application, where the process marks all the variables that may move from sources to sensitive sinks. The approach marks all the non-sanitized data as tainted and sanitized as non-tainted. Furthermore, using only static analysis to find such data that is tainted will produce a large number of results that are false positives. The authors use dynamic analysis on the data marked as tainted to track the data in real-time in the Web Application. The approach poses an error as soon as the tainted data is about to be included in the sensitive pools. Inclusion of dynamic analysis therefore decreases the number of false positives and tracks the tainted data in real-time. Another technique demonstrated by Halfond and Orso (2005) shows an approach that combines static analysis and dynamic analysis to stop the SQL Injection attack in the run time in the Web Application. The paper demonstrates a tool Amnesia that uses the static analysis to build a model of valid SQL queries that are legit, and then uses the dynamic analysis to compare the dynamically created queries in the run time of the Web Application to the model prepared in the static phase, and checks if the dynamically created queries sustain the static model standard.

5.5. DAST using user session

DAST using user session is a technique that uses the data that are generated by the user when they interact with the Web Application. This technique focuses upon using this user generated data to perform dynamic analysis more effectively. It uses the user session data to generate test suites that are more effective than the test suites generated using the White Box technique, as only the static data are analyzed during White Box test suite generation, whereas in this DAST using user session, dynamic data generated by the user are used to generate test cases.

5.5.1. *Current implementation*

The paper by Elbaum et al. (2005) demonstrates a technique that utilizes DAST leveraging user session data. The paper basically uses user session data to generate test cases that can be used in dynamic testing of the Web Application. The paper demonstrates various approaches that could be used to generate and capture user data; the first approach demonstrates a model where each request made by a user is captured by the server in a log, and then name-value pairs are made that can be used to prepare test cases. Another approach that the paper demonstrates is where the collected user data are used directly, without any modifications. Another way that this paper demonstrates is to use cross user data to generate test cases. This technique uses data generated by various users and compiles them to generate test cases. The third approach includes using the exception request that is created by the user. This approach uses coupling of a normal user request with a request that can be considered as an exception request such as an anomaly of pressing back while submitting forms or navigating through a Web Application while making payments, and these requests are used to generate test cases. These test cases so generated are used to test the Web Application using dynamic testing, and these test cases are provided to the Web Application in running state and the anomaly in the behavior of the Web Application is marked to further test for the existence of a particular type of vulnerability. Another paper by Zhongsheng (2010) demonstrates DAST using the user session technique. This paper goes beyond this and collects the data and also sanitizes the data to decrease the data that are redundant and similar. The paper shows an approach where a large amount of user session data is collected and then those data are refined using logs on the Web Server and other session parameters. Furthermore, the approach divides the data into collective groups that signify one variety of data or user action. These collections are called test suites and each test suite contains almost the same type of session data parameters that are called test cases. Furthermore, the paper demonstrates a prioritizing algorithm to prioritize test suites to achieve effective results. These generated test suites are used effectively as if any test case within the test suite fails, then all other test cases in that suite will fail, thus decreasing the time spent on a test suite, and the variety of test suites generated can be categorized according to the functionality of Web Application they test. These generated test cases increase the efficiency of dynamic analysis and make it easier to test the Web Application against a certain type of functionality. Figure 5.4 shows the flow of the above-mentioned approach.

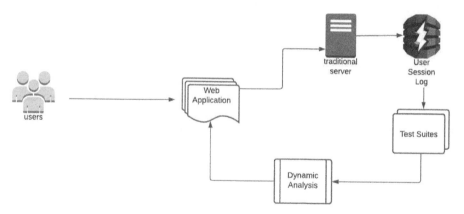

Figure 5.4. *The workings of DAST with user session*

Figure 5.4 shows the workings of how the users interact with the Web Application and how the traditional server records the session log of the user session. These stored user session logs are used to generate test suites which comprise various test cases, which are used by the DAST technique to perform a dynamic analysis on the Web Application.

The DAST with user session approach heavily depends upon the test cases that are generated using user session data, but these test cases cannot be generated directly, without refining or removing the data that are redundant or not relevant. One such approach is proposed by Sampath et al. (2008). The paper discusses various prioritization techniques to form test cases that can effectively detect faults in the Web Application. The paper also shows various prioritization techniques like the prioritization of test cases based on their length, prioritization based on the frequency of appearance of test cases, followed by prioritization based on the coverage given by parametric values in terms of interaction with the Web Application. All the above prioritization techniques help the dynamic testing in increasing the number of faults discovered in contrast to test cases that are randomly picked and used. The prioritization by length technique orders the base requests in test sets in both formats of arranging them from larger to shorter and shorter to larger. These large length test cases test more parts of the functionality of the Web Application. The prioritization by frequency technique first uses those request test cases that were invoked more to access a web page or web functionality rather than in comparison to those request test cases where the web pages were invoked least. So in the frequency technique, requests that accessed more pages are taken first. This model of generating test cases is very effective, but another hybrid model of generating test cases is shown in the paper by Maung (2014). The approach shown in this paper not only utilizes the user session data to generate cases but also uses the structural analysis of the working of the Web Application in the generation of test cases, combining both session data and structural analysis to generate test cases. The approach first accomplishes the structural analysis of the Web Application, to gather various dependency pages and to order the time of request to these pages, followed by a structural analysis; the approach generates test cases using a technique known as entropy gain theory by utilizing the gain in user sessions. Following this, the effectiveness of the test case generated is tested by monitoring the fault detection rate in the Web Application. Figure 5.5 shows the steps in the process of generating test suites.

Figure 5.5 shows the working of how the test cases are generated. Firstly, the user session log files are generated by the server and they are then processed to generate in bulk test cases. These bulk generated test cases are then optimized and prioritized with techniques mentioned in the above sections, and the optimized test cases are further used for testing of the Web Application.

Figure 5.5. *The process of generation of test cases*

5.6. DAST using Extended Tainted Mode Model

The Tainted Mode Model is a technique where a model of policies is prepared and testing of Web Application is done under those policies; under the model many assumptions are made, such as all data coming from an HTTP request are considered tainted and cannot be trusted, all data native to the web app is considered to be trustworthy or non-tainted, followed by that no tainted data will be used in the construction of the HTTP response. All these rules or policies define the Tainted Mode Model and any violation of these rules or policies detected in dynamic analysis of the Web Application is considered to be a violation of the model or presence of a potential vulnerability.

5.6.1. *Current implementation*

The Tainted Mode Model is a famous approach that is used while performing static and dynamic testing. One such approach is demonstrated by Petukhov and Kozlov (2008b). In their paper they demonstrate an approach that shows an Extended Tainted Mode Model, which overcomes a few weaknesses in the usual Tainted Mode Model. The weaknesses spotted in the usual Tainted Mode Model are as shown. Firstly, the usual Tainted Mode Model removes the tainted flag from data after one sanitization of the data is done for a particular type of operation, such as a dataset as non-tainted for HTTP response creation cannot be considered non-tainted for the creation of a particular SQL query as well, so this weakness of removing the tainted flag from data after one sanitization causes a problem. Secondly, the Tainted Mode Model is unable to address the situation where the tainted data are being passed through branching statements, where branching statements handle the future scope of execution. Thirdly, the Tainted Mode Model has no mechanism to deal with the situation where the sanitization mechanism is corrupted or not working properly. Fourthly, the Tainted Mode Model assumes that any data saved locally is trusted, which could mean that no external data could be saved at the local storage. So the paper proposes an Extended Tainted Mode Model which addresses all the above-mentioned issues. The Extended Tainted Mode Model addresses the problem of one-time sanitization by providing an extra set of classes for each type of sanitization behavior and then mapping the input to each type of sanitization class before they are used in a critical operation in the Web Application. The approach in the paper uses the extended tainted model with dynamic analysis and penetration testing combined. The Extended Tainted Mode Model helps the dynamic analysis of the Web Application to easily identify the presence of the vulnerability in the Web Application or the presence of any type of anomaly. This capability of dynamic analysis and Extended Tainted Mode Model is combined with penetration testing to come up with an effective way to implement the testing of Web Applications. Another paper by Pandikumar and Eshetu (2016) shows another approach that uses an Extended Tainted Mode Model with dynamic analysis to aid penetration testing. This approach uses extended tainted analysis to detect inter-modular vulnerabilities that arise mainly due to no sanitized input. Another paper by Sreenivasa Rao and Kumar (2012) talks about the same Extended Tainted Model approach to detect the vulnerabilities related to input sanitization. The Extended Tainted Mode Model in this approach is used to classify the policies which if not followed indicates the presence of an anomaly or vulnerability. The paper uses the Extended Tainted Mode Model to aid dynamic analysis of the Web Application to effectively spot vulnerabilities of the type which include bad input. Figure 5.6 shows how the Extended Tainted Mode Model with dynamic analysis aids penetration testing of a Web Application.

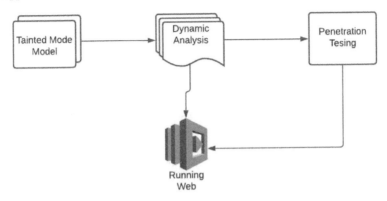

Figure 5.6. *Workings of the Tainted Model*

Figure 5.6 shows the process of the Tainted Mode Model used with dynamic analysis and penetration testing. It demonstrates that the first Tainted Mode Model is prepared and then the dynamic analysis of the Web Application is conducted according to the Tainted Mode Model. The data collected from dynamic analysis are used to enhance the accuracy of penetration testing of the Web Application to spot vulnerabilities with more accuracy. The vulnerabilities that are targeted through the Tainted Mode Model concern a class of vulnerabilities that arises due to non-proper sanitization of the input.

5.7. Current issues and research directions

As DAST testing evolves with the evolution of the Web Application in terms of size and technology, DAST testing relies heavily on open-source scripts or test cases that come from the open-source community, with a variety of scripts to perform testing. There are also scripts that are designed maliciously to disrupt the testing, so one major challenge while doing Dynamic Application testing is for the tester to choose automated tools and script wisely. Second, as the technology stack increases, the dynamic testing coverage over the Web Application is decreasing, and the complexity of dynamic testing is increasing as the testing of each different stack is done differently. Third, as the technology stack increases, the generation of test cases for each stack also changes, and so the manual procedure of generating test cases for each technology stack is not productive. Fourth, dynamic testing alone yields fewer false positives but covers only a small area of the Web Application as discussed by You et al. (2018b).

Research directions in the future must first focus upon increasing the ability of dynamic testing to increase its coverage more with fewer false positives. Secondly, the inclusion of machine learning in the generation of test cases for each technology stack would be a great area to generate test cases that are effective and productive in terms of the testing of Web Applications and finding vulnerabilities. Thirdly, the use of dynamic testing with another testing stack like White Box testing and Model Testing, to decrease the overall invested time of testing, along with DAST would be more efficient as explained by Astillo et al. (2021).

5.8. Conclusion

Dynamic Web Application testing is an area of high interest as the demand for Web Applications increases every day. But with this demand also comes the responsibility of security of the Web Applications and the users who use them, so the area of Web Application testing holds an important vitality as it is so wide and heavily used. The main challenges that Dynamic Web Application testing faces are its inability to cover a large part of the Web Application and the large duration of time it takes to do it. The challenge of low coverage and more time to complete it in testing are such issues that if they are not addressed then the number of vulnerabilities that occur in a Web Application will increase and the rate to detect them will decrease, which will lead to attackers attacking the Web Application and compromising it.

In this chapter, we have focused on the insights to various methodologies and techniques that have been devised by researchers to increase the power of dynamic testing by incorporating it with other methodologies like taint analysis, static analysis and the use of user session data to increase the quality of generation of test cases. These methodologies and techniques combined with dynamic analysis make it more powerful by addressing the problems like less coverage of Web Application by mixing static analysis with dynamic analysis to increase the coverage. A future direction of research would be to analyze more techniques that come into existence and address the problem of time consumption when dynamic testing is done on a large Web Application.

5.9. References

Alshahwan, N. and Harman, M. (2011). *Automated Web Application Testing Using Search Based Software Engineering*. CREST Centre, University College London, London.

Artzi, S., Kiezun, A., Dolby, J., Tip, F., Dig, D., Paradkar, A., Ernst, M.D. (2010). Finding bugs in web applications using dynamic test generation and explicit-state model checking. *IEEE Transactions on Software Engineering*, 36(4), 474–494.

Astillo, P.V., Choudhary, G., Duguma, D.G., Kim, J., You, I. (2021). TrMAps: Trust management in specification-based misbehavior detection system for imd-enabled artificial pancreas system. *IEEE Journal of Biomedical and Health Informatics*, 25(10), 3763–3775.

Balzarotti, D., Cova, M., Felmetsger, V., Jovanovic, N., Kirda, E., Kruegel, C., Vigna, G. (2008). Saner: Composing static and dynamic analysis to validate sanitization in web applications. *IEEE Symposium on Security and Privacy (sp 2008)*, Oakland.

Benedikt, M., Freire, J., Godefroid, P. (2002). Veriweb: Automatically testing dynamic web sites. *Proceedings of 11th International World Wide Web Conference (WWW–2002)*. Citeseer [Online]. Avaialble at: https://www.researchgate.net/publication/2909253_VeriWeb_Automatically_Testing_Dynamic_Web_Sites.

Curphey, M. and Arawo, R. (2006). Web application security assessment tools. *IEEE Security & Privacy*, 4(4), 32–41.

Doğan, S., Betin-Can, A., Garousi, V. (2014). Web application testing: A systematic literature review. *Journal of Systems and Software*, 91, 174–201 [Online]. Available at: https://www.sciencedirect.com/science/article/pii/S0164121214000223.

Elbaum, S., Rothermel, G., Karre, S., Fisher II, M. (2005). Leveraging user-session data to support web application testing. *IEEE Transactions on Software Engineering*, 31(3), 187–202.

Halfond, WG. and Orso, A. (2005). AMNESIA: Analysis and monitoring for neutralizing SQL-injection attacks. *Proceedings of the 20th IEEE/ACM International Conference on Automated Software Engineering* [Online]. Available at: https://doi.org/10.1145/1101908.1101935.

Huang, Y.-W., Huang, S.-K., Lin, T.-P., Tsai, C.-H. (2003). Web application security assessment by fault injection and behavior monitoring. *Proceedings of the 12th International Conference on World Wide Web* [Online]. Available at: https://doi.org/10.1145/ 775152.775174.

Imran, M., Eassa, F., Jambi, K. (2016). Dynamic analysis for security testing of web based applications using agent technology. *Proceedings of the 4th International Conference on Advances in Computing, Communication and Information Technology (CCIT) 2016*, Institute of Research Engineers and Doctors.

Lakshmi, D.R. and Mallika, S.S. (2017). A review on web application testing and its current research directions. *International Journal of Electrical and Computer Engineering (IJECE)*, 7(4), 2132–2141.

Maung, H.M. (2014). Test case reduction approach in user session based testing for web application. *12th International Conference on Computer Applications (ICCA 2014)* [Online]. Available at: https://onlineresource.ucsy.edu.mm/handle/123456789/18.

Pandikumar, T. and Eshetu, T. (2016). Detecting web application vulnerability using dynamic analysis with penetration testing. *International Research Journal of Engineering and Technology*, 3(10).

Petukhov, A. and Kozlov, D. (2008a). *Detecting Security Vulnerabilities in Web Applications Using Dynamic Analysis with Penetration Testing*. Computing Systems Lab, Department of Computer Science, Moscow State University, Moscow.

Petukhov, A. and Kozlov, D. (2008b). Detecting security vulnerabilities in web applications using dynamic analysis with penetration testing. *Application Security Conference* [Online]. Available at: https://owasp.org/www-pdf-archive/OWASP-AppSecEU08-Petukhov.pdf.

Sampath, S., Bryce, R.C., Viswanath, G., Kandimalla, V., Koru, A.G. (2008). Prioritizing user-session-based test cases for web applications testing. *2008 1st International Conference on Software Testing, Verification, and Validation* [Online]. Available at: https://www.computer.org/csdl/proceedings/icst/2008/12OmNxdVh2n.

Sharma, V., Choudhary, G., Ko, Y., You, I. (2018). Behavior and vulnerability assessment of drones-enabled Industrial Internet of Things (IIoT). *IEEE Access*, 6, 43368–43383.

Sönmez, F.Ö. and Kiliç, B.G. (2021). Holistic web application security visualization for multi-project and multi-phase dynamic application security test results. *IEEE Access*, 9, 25858–25884.

Sreenivasa Rao, B. and Kumar, N. (2012). Web application vulnerability detection using dynamic analysis with peneteration testing. *International Journal of Computer Science and Security (IJCSS)*, 6(2).

Vogt, P., Nentwich, F., Jovanovic, N., Kirda, E., Kruegel, C., Vigna, G. (2007). *Cross-site Scripting Prevention with Dynamic Data Tainting and Static Analysis*. Secure Systems Lab, Technical University Vienna, Vienna, and University of California, Santa Barbara.

You, I., Kwon, S., Choudhary, G., Sharma, V., Seo, J.T. (2018a). An enhanced LoRaWAN security protocol for privacy preservation in Iot with a case study on a smart factory-enabled parking system. *Sensors*, 18(6), 1888.

You, I., Yim, K., Sharma, V., Choudhary, G., Chen, I.-R., Cho, J.-H. (2018b). Misbehavior detection of embedded IoT devices in medical cyber physical systems. *Proceedings of the 2018 IEEE/ACM International Conference on Connected Health: Applications, Systems and Engineering Technologies*, Association for Computing Machinery, New York.

Zhongsheng, Q. (2010). Test case generation and optimization for user session-based web application testing. *Journal of Computers*, 5(11).

Zou, Y., Chen, Z., Zheng, Y., Zhang, X., Gao, Z. (2014). Virtual DOM coverage for effective testing of dynamic web applications. *Proceedings of the 2014 International Symposium on Software Testing and Analysis* [Online]. Available at: https://doi.org/10.1145/2610384.2610399.

SciFiOnto: Modeling, Visualization and Evaluation of Science Fiction Ontologies Based on Indian Contextualization with Automatic Knowledge Acquisition

There is a need for knowledge synthesis for science fiction as an independent domain, owing to its omnipotent nature of being socio-technical, scientific and exhibiting a perspective of humanities and culture within it. In this chapter, an ontology for science fiction has been modeled, considering the vocabulary of terms based on an extensive survey conducted by subjects who were either Generation Z or millennials. The ontology has been an extension to the existing science fiction ontology and has a regulatory mechanism to increase the number of concepts and individuals. Several classifications and terms have been added, with a specific focus on the Indian context. The proposed ontology model is quite rich in its population of terms and is the only ontology that unifies science fiction in the Indian context to the vocabularies of the existing science fiction ontology. Automatic Knowledge Base Generation is quite important and is a prerequisite for several information systems in the current era, where most of the applications are knowledge centered. The availability of an extensive amount of data and the non-availability of knowledge make reasoning and inferencing quite cumbersome for information systems. Knowledge representation and reasoning is essential as symbolic artificial intelligence and collective artificial intelligence require knowledge models to deduce inferences. A knowledge integration framework based on a Binomial Deep Neural Network has also been proposed to densely populate the entities in the existing science fiction ontology based on several heterogenous dynamic knowledge sources, based on SPARQL based querying and closed world semantics. The proposed Deep Neural Network is a customized layered neural network which has been formalized using Binomial Series. Apart from this, an inferential scheme that encompasses an Entity Graph for reasoning has been instilled into the approach. A reuse ratio of 91.43 with a domain regulatory Precision of 87.57% and a domain regulatory F-Measure of 88.6% has been achieved for the modeled seed ontology. A massive knowledge base for science fiction as an independent domain has been automatically generated using RDF (Resource Description Framework) mapping regulated by the proposed Binomial Deep

Chapter written by Gerard Deepak, Ayush A. Kumar and Sheeba J. Priyadarshini.

Neural Network, and a domain compliance F-Measure of 92.69% with an FNR of 0.06 and a reuse ratio of 93.21 has been achieved for the automatically synthesized knowledge base for science fiction as the domain.

6.1. Introduction

Ontologies are the most vital elements for knowledge modeling owing to their reusability and ability to connect with real-world domains. Ontologies serve as explicit and expressible knowledge description models that act as a cognitive bridge between human intellect and information systems. Ontologies are typically domain-centric and it is reasonable to model them based on the intervention of human cognition. Libraries use several traditional approaches for storing and monitoring literary pieces. Usually, they are based on a syntactic approach and there are several inconsistencies in the architecture. Despite having several attributes and properties, textbooks are not stored in accordance with the remarkable knowledge and information that they carry. Based on certain vague classifications like the author's name and the book's title, these huge amounts of literary masterpieces are being underutilized. Unification with respect to modern information systems can be done, perhaps with some effort for books pertaining to science and technology, but for books on fiction, this is not the case. There are a plethora of themes for science fiction (Sci-Fi), ranging from fantasies about the cosmos, to daily human life and nature. Hence, there is a need to structure this information to effectively utilize the knowledge and data on Sci-Fi. The present syntactic version prompts us to remember data and search for ourselves. But, if structured, the semantic version would exploit the computer to do all of the work for us, and the information would be organized for greater purpose. For example, if the domain knowledge on Sci-Fi is captured and clustered effectively for rigorous classification, several sophisticated processes and computations can be performed on the data to get valuable information and results from the unstructured form of raw facts stored in the Sci-Fi books. Hence, the Semantic Web can aid in this unification by using ontologies and semantic relationships to categorize and retrieve various Sci-Fi data.

The integration of literary data using ontologies can also satisfy several crucial requirements of library science such as the indexing and retrieval of works of importance. The ontological methods can then be applied, along with statistical and semantic approaches for the proper representation and storage of content in digital format. Conceptualized ontologies can aid in this purpose of preserving data and making library science prepared for the advent of the Semantic Web. There are a huge number of attributes which can be utilized for indexing and the recovery of philosophical data. For instance, in Sci-Fi, there are several ideas and fantasies that overlap with each other and, if integrated, can form another new theory that may be more detailed than the previous ones. One of the challenges in Sci-Fi ontology modeling is the complex relationships that the entities share with each other. These relationships depend on the interpretations and often have more than one meaning. All of these attributes must be stored, and it is difficult to do so in traditional approaches of manual indexing. Hence, equipped with a relationship extractor, literary works can be modeled as robust and dynamic ontologies which describe several viewpoints, regardless of the controversies attached to them.

For domains like science fiction, an ample amount of knowledge and literature is available in several digital forms over the Internet. Science fiction emerged into a concrete domain in the 1990s when computers and technology advancements became popular. Several conspiracy theories such as cyberpunk and computer theories and fiction (Bacon-Smith 2000) contributed to the gain in momentum in science fiction, allowing it to succeed in becoming an independent domain. To form a successful ontological model for Sci-Fi, Automatic Knowledge Acquisition (AKA) can be highly beneficial and time and energy efficient. Internet crawlers that search websites and traverse a plethora of related websites, mining information from all of the possible sources can result in the large-scale facilitation of automated ontology modeling. There is a need for such approaches because the current manual approach is not very suitable for vast domains like Sci-Fi. For scientific domains that do not depend on the perspectives of the reader and are universal in appeal, the Sci-Fi domain has its own challenges. The unification of the Sci-Fi domain takes a lot of time and effort because of its vast and inclusive nature. Almost everything that a human can dream of can be coupled with logical reasoning or fantasies and included in Sci-Fi. That is one of the prime reasons to refer as many books as possible for Knowledge Acquisition (KA) for Sci-Fi domains. If several viewpoints of several readers are present in the ontology, the ontology becomes complete and inclusive.

Automatic knowledge acquisition is the automated approach of knowledge inclusion in a target usually from predefined sources. This ensures minimal manual labor and a higher precision in the construction and modeling of ontologies. The website crawler works for automatic knowledge acquisition to facilitate information retrieval using ontologies. The basis of this problem is the classic issues in the handling and management of data, and the usage of ontologies to store the given data in forms of knowledge graphs with all the possible relations and properties of the classes. Also, there is no centralized storage and management system for the Sci-Fi domain, which makes this problem necessary to solve.

Using the modeled ontology, the user would be able to find a particular character of any Sci-Fi related subject, and along with that, well-defined information about the properties and relationships of the subject will be present. Hence, moving toward a central repository of the Sci-Fi domain, these collections of data usually range up to several million instances. The automatic acquisition of already present knowledge and the suitable induction of terms into an ontology are required to develop a unified source of Sci-Fi data. All of the data present are unstructured in forms of books and documents where relationships are not explicitly defined, and there is a lack of consistency due to speculation differences and biases.

Motivation: The motivation of this work lies in the absence of the widespread application of the Semantic Web and ontologies for the literary domain. Since their inception, ontologies are often used in medical, biological and even chemical domains. But seldom do people implement ontologies for literary information and sciences because of the vast level of complexity associated with them. As described, different literary stances require different graphs in the traditional approach, and they may often lead to completely different results. Hence, application of ontologies in literary sciences can lead to the unification of several philosophical thinkers and improve the already existing knowledge sources on Sci-Fi and related domains. The methodological practices which are associated with the modeling of scientific ontologies cannot be used for literary ontologies because of a difference in the fundamental nature of the sciences. Hence, an attempt has been made to form a hybrid ontological modeling system for Sci-Fi. For a wide domain like Sci-Fi, where there are different theories for the same concept, manual population of ontological terms is not efficient as there is no one unified source. Hence, to form dynamic and extensive domain ontologies for the Sci-Fi domain, the KA process must be automated for viable storage and retrieval of data. Using the SPARQL querying mechanism, extensive knowledge sources such as LOD Cloud, DBPedia and Wikidata are traversed, and ontological classes are retrieved. The induction is made using the Hyperlink-Induced Topic Search (HITS) algorithm, which only allows the relevant classes to be stored in the ontology, hence maintaining the quality of the data stored. A neural network is used for mapping, with a vision to make a unified ontology for the Sci-Fi domain.

Contribution: In this work, an attempt to generate and synthesize knowledge by aggregating entities has been made for Sci-Fi as a domain. Methontology has been used with several changes that make it suitable for modeling Sci-Fi ontologies. The entire process of modeling and visualizing a Sci-Fi ontology has been depicted with deep interest in this work, and entity graphs have been generated for Sci-Fi ontologies. Crowdsourced automatic knowledge acquisition for Sci-Fi has also been proposed for the existing manually modeled sparse domain-specific ontologies. This work aims to provide a robust framework for AKA for the population of sparse modeled ontologies with classes and related data in the form of relationships, properties, comments and other RDF entities. A Binomial Deep Neural Network model for mapping RDF and generating large and yet domain relevant knowledge bases has been proposed. SPARQL querying is used to search several repositories such as Wikidata, Linked Open Data (LOD) Cloud and DBPedia. The proposed Binomial Deep Neural Network has been utilized to facilitate the RDF-to-RDF entity mapping for automated population of the ontology. The approach uses the HITS algorithm for automated term induction into the ontology.

Organization: The remainder of this chapter is organized as follows. Section 6.2 contains the relevant literature survey. Section 6.3 describes ontology modeling, its phases of conceptualization and implementation, and also ontology evaluation. Section 6.4 depicts the proposed Automatic Knowledge Acquisition approach of populating ontology terms. The chapter is concluded in section 6.5.

6.2. Literature survey

6.2.1. *Formulation and modeling of ontologies for varied domains of importance*

Sheridan et al. (2019) have formulated an ontology for media annotation of literature. This Literary Theme Ontology (LTO) has been framed from several online sources, books and personal experiences. Eco (2009) used an ontology of semiotic characters, put forth a framework to consider fictional characters as semiotic characters and worked on modeling an ontology for these entities. For the domain of additive manufacturing in the historical domain, Shimizu et al. (2020) have formed an ontology using the best practices of several methods including Methontology. Available in OWL, this ontology consists of data regarding the archaic practices of the slave trade and accompanied with provenance modeling. Sanfilippo et al. (2019) have proposed a model to organize the data and have shown numerous examples for the application of computational ontological models for the scientific domain. They have defined several attributes representing the processes, objects, material types and descriptions of several complicated data for manufacturing. For the purpose of analyzing the videos recorded by Unmanned Aerial Vehicles (UAVs), Rai et al. (2021) have presented varied conceptual models for knowledge representation and management pertaining to a specific domain. Hitzler et al. (2018) have represented an ontology for cooking recipes using strategic modular ontology modeling, by making use of design patterns. Nandhakishore et al. (2022) have formulated a model for the conceptualization, modeling and evaluation of ontologies for Kinematics as a strategic domain. An explicit scientific domain knowledge modeling has been carried out by them for reasoning and representing scientific knowledge.

6.2.2. *Auxiliary automatic and semi-automatic models in ontology synthesis*

Cavaliere et al. (2019) have proposed an ontological model. A deeper interpretation is given by this model. It describes several objects and recognizes the data based on semantic querying. Aziz et al. (2019) have formed an ontology for hazard analysis by graphical representation. Using Protégé and Bayesian probabilistic networks, this ontology has been formed from the data acquired from the chemical safety database. There are several challenged in RDF querying due to the recent developments of web information. Conventional social information base frameworks effectively adjust and question circulated information. Banane et al. (2019) have proposed SPARQL2Hive, which utilizes the inquiry language of Hive, situated above Hadoop MapReduce, as a moderate layer alongside SPARQL and MapReduce, for effective mapping in place of direct mapping for RDF data. Adetunji et al. (2020) have formulated an ontological model-based knowledge acquisition system for analyzing software anomalies. The Protégé tool is used to build a prototype ontology for software-based usage. Kestel et al. (2019) have designed a system for the simulation of knowledge acquired by data mining and other AKA techniques. Systems like this can be highly useful for problems in numerical simulation domains like the Finite Element Analysis. Hence, using these techniques, even beginners in simulation can visualize the data needed for the domain, making the work even more human-friendly. Chen et al. (2019) have proposed a method to represent the abstract data of the ontologies based on a BERT model. To accomplish the task of maintaining and reviewing academic literature automatically, they have formed a methodology to create knowledge graphs and represented the relationships and properties of the system using ontologies.

6.2.3. *Ontology-driven systems and applications*

Laaz et al. (2019) have proposed a system of automatic web pages generation from ontologies. To develop the web applications, which are supported by semantic technologies, they have designed OntoIFML, which automates the generation of ontologies based on the web pages. Chen et al. (2020) have modeled an ontology for the IoT domain with semantic relationships. By achieving automated classification and behavior analysis of the IoT systems, they have proposed a framework for real-time ontology modeling, which works for dynamic continuous data and not only for static ontologies. Subramaniyaswamy et al. (2019) have proposed an ontology-based model for personalized food recommendations for an IoT domain-specific healthcare system. Such systems ensure the utility of domain-specific knowledge authored and make use of them to yield personalized recommendations. Cantador et al. (2008) have proposed a model that is multilayered and yields recommendations using domain-specific ontologies. The model uses the terms of semantic concepts and user preferences and item spaces which are subject to clustering to yield multiple semantic layers to facilitate recommendations. Shahzad et al. (2021) have proposed a framework for the integration of services for smart health using ontologies, where an ontology-driven classification has been realized.

6.2.4. *Automatic Knowledge Acquisition systems*

Coletti et al. (2019) have proposed a semantic modeling technique for cascading risks. To create the semantic model, they have made use of the semantic and computational techniques, which run with an application called the CREAtivity machine. Wang et al. (2019) have built a framework for the automated development of coal mine accident knowledge in the form of an ontological model. The classes are automatically extracted using BP neural networks, and the Protégé tool is used to add the attributes to the model. This ontology can be used to save human effort and improve precision in the storage and retrieval of sensitive data like those of coal mine accidents. Colloc et al. (2020) have described an object-oriented strategy for modeling expert systems, which incorporates the detection of similarities for provisioning reasoning and similarity detection. The reasoning mechanisms are a composition of induction, deduction and simulation models for automatic knowledge acquisition. Liu et al. (2019) have proposed a strategic scheme for automatic knowledge acquisition for ordered information systems using the inclusion degree paradigm and concept lattice. Leng et al. (2019) have proposed automatic knowledge acquisition for mechanical, electrical and plumbing systems using Natural Language Processing (NLP) and AI techniques using the Bi-LSTM-CRF model and knowledge graphs. The approach focuses on entity extraction and population. Grasso et al. (2021) have proposed a paradigm for KA based on multilingual word alignment integrating knowledge that is not biased and is disambiguated text.

6.2.5. *Science fiction as an independent domain of existence*

Science fiction is a designated genre of speculative fiction that instills imaginative concepts that are typically from the future. It is an imaginative exploration of science and technology using the personification of surreal characters or things. It is termed as the "literature of ideas" and is subjected to enlisting the consequences of socio-scientific innovations and advancement in technologies (Thorn et al. 2002; Gilks et al. 2003). Science fiction is composed of time travel, space exploration, mythology, alien universe and life on extraterrestrial existence. It can always be a speculative intersection of science, humanities, horror, super heroism, ancient mythology (Luchurst 2005) and fiction. Nicholes (2018) has developed Genre Knowledge and STEM interest using a prototype for Science Fiction. Banerjee (2020) has pointed out several facets of science fiction for Indian contextualization and has composed several Indian science fiction in various genres. Owing to the diversity of several cultures, geographical boundaries, off space openness and technology driven theories in science fiction, which emerge as socio-technical with a convergence of scientific imaginative theories, making science fiction an independent domain, there is a need to model ontologies and generate knowledge for science fiction as a strategic domain of choice.

Knowledge graphs have impacted present-day knowledge organization (Gaurav et al. 2021), wherein ontological concepts for a specific designated domain laid a basis for the same (Pushpa et al. 2015). The modeling and evaluation of ontologies requires human comprehension and verification. In Kumar et al. (2020) and Deepak et al. (2019), ontological models are depicted for specialized scientific domains, which have been comprehended based on the human-in-the-middle model. It is clear from the literature that Automatic and Semi-Automatic Knowledge Modeling Frameworks are of utmost importance, and it is almost impossible to automatically generate knowledge for a scientific and a socio-scientific domain without human interference or cognition. As a result, manual modeling of ontologies is the basis for automatic knowledge synthesis. Science fiction is more of a socio-technical, scientific, multi-cultural domain. As a result, manual modeling of ontologies and thereby Automatic Knowledge Graph Generation are a mandate for the conception of knowledge which is not only of relevance to the domain, but also widely acceptable by the science fiction community at large to facilitate use and inferencing in real-world information and intelligent systems.

6.3. Modeling and evaluation of the ontology

6.3.1. *Ontology modeling*

To model the ontology on Sci-Fi characters, this work uses a modified approach of the Methontology (Corcho et al. 2005) framework. These applied ontologies preserve the data and aid in the efficient search and indexing of knowledge. Moreover, for domains like Sci-Fi, it is a requirement to develop a descriptive ontology because of the sheer amount of valuable information they can carry. The Methontology approach is basically an approach of descriptive modeling of ontologies by planning several important parts of the process and their prospective impacts on the modeled work in advance.

6.3.1.1. *Planning*

The first level of the Methontology approach is to plan the activities present in the development phase. The developed plan must be executed as per the discussions and all of the key steps are perfectly performed. The scope of the ontology is Sci-Fi works and their related metadata. This ontology is being built for the efficient storage and retrieval of Sci-Fi data, along with all of the relationships and attributes which the data carry. All of the plausible fantasies must be stored because of immense future uses of ontologies related to the domain. The domain is fixed to be science fiction and related genres of literature. The super-domain can be formalized as all the literary works as in future, a need may arise to bring the entire literature into one single ontology for retrieval and knowledge visualization of the data.

6.3.1.2. Definition and scope

The prospective users of the ontology are research scholars, literary critics or even casual readers who want to grasp the knowledge of science fiction on a greater level. Ontologies are developed to make the computer understand the knowledge and not vice versa, which is done in the syntactic web. In the conventional systems, Cascading Style Sheets (CSS) are used to make the content of the web understandable to human users. But, in the Semantic Web, more emphasis is given to the understanding of the domain knowledge by the computer, so that the complex decisions can be performed by the computer using numerical intensive computations to aid human users (Breitman et al. 2007).

6.3.1.3. Knowledge acquisition

For KA of the ontology, several different approaches can be used to make the ontology as inclusive as possible. For specialized domains such as engineering or sciences, direct KA from scientific literature can be made as the theories are largely absolute and universal. But, for Sci-Fi and related approaches, theories are based on the interpretation from person to person and for an inclusive ontology, each of their plausible interpretations can be included in the ontology. This work also talks about the use of Crowdsourced Knowledge Acquisition (CSKA) for developing a database of concepts and their related entities. For Sci-Fi ontologies, the process can be automated by the Altruistic Crowdsourcing (ACS) (Sabou et al. 2013) technique, where a large number of volunteers take part in the process of KA. For example, several questionnaires can be circulated for the purpose of KA. This reduces the motivation for malpractices and cheating because the incentive provided is small. Malpractices have a chance in processes where there is a high incentive to cheat because of the importance of individual opinions. Here, in ACS, individual opinions are added to the ontology, and since the ontology is based on data from an extremely large crowd, there is not much motivation to cheat. For an efficient modeling of the ontology, crowd diversity must be taken care of, and efforts must be made for the inclusion of all of the opinions, regardless of the controversies present.

6.3.1.4. Data elicitation

This process can be automated by Internet forms and surveys leading to efficient data acquisition and indexing. Focusing on the performance of the ACS system, protocol analysis is crucial because of the presence of several non-observable facts prevalent in the domain. Sci-Fi is one such domain where there is easy access to information sources, but the interpretation of these points from several viewpoints takes a large amount of effort. So, extra-domain visualization can also be required at times, leading to anthropological studies which yield exceptional results but are less systematized.

6.3.1.5. *Domain analysis*

The ontological domain for this work is Sci-Fi and related areas. Several domains under Sci-Fi, such as space fantasies, chemical and biological speculations and mutant being fiction, can be included under one domain of life containing fiction. But there are other domains where the attributes relate much to physics and can be worked out mathematically. Utopia and dystopian fiction are domains which talk about the prospective future worlds with varied scientific development than the current speculated one. Alternate history, anthropological fiction, dying earth and apocalyptic fantasies are the domains which are more closely related to humanities and social sciences, than other genres which are mostly science related. All of these domains can be closely knit together to analyze the metadata of these genres and develop intra-Sci-Fi relationships.

6.3.1.6. *Ontological relationships*

Relations among scientific entities are largely defined and can be extracted using taxonomic and non-taxonomic approaches. Several hypernym-hyponym based axioms can be defined for specialized domains like chemistry and biology. For Sci-Fi, there can be more than one relationship between the living characters and other entities, which can be tedious to model. Hence, an ACS-based approach can be vastly useful in understanding these complex relationships. An entity in the Sci-Fi ontology can be defined by several attributes like continuants, which can later be dependent or independent. Occurrents can be defined as a set of continuants. For example, a class hierarchy for any ontological entity is defined in Table 6.1.

The generic class hierarchy to automatically model Sci-Fi ontology comprises the SciFiOntologicalEntity, which describes any specific entity that belongs to science fiction as a broad area domain. The Ontological Entity comprises the Metadata, *Occurrents* and Continuants for structuring the composition of the Ontological Entity. The Metadata comprises the genre, subgenre, occurrence and the domain which the entity belongs to. The reason why the domain needs to be specified every time as a Metadata instance is to assimilate intelligence to the information system irrespective of where it is accessed. This is the reason why the domain of the entity is a mandate at every entity metadata description. The Occurrents are composed of Non-Fictional Occurrents, which describe the timeline of the entity, the zone and the country of the entity to ensure the geographical positioning of a science fiction character and if it occurs in the global positioning of it with a geographical stand. The timeline assures the positioning of the character in the present or in the past, or even in the future. The Fictional Occurrents, which are another composition of the Occurrents, compose entity afterlife, time travel and space travel. This clearly designates the conception and positioning of the character based on a fictional standpoint. The Continuants are composed of Fictional Continuants like name, age and location. However, the non-fictional continuants are absent as the Fictional Continuants alone are sufficient, as once a character is positioned in the Science Fiction Backdrop, it automatically becomes fictional, even if it is capable of possessing non-fictional properties.

```
SciFiOntologicalEntity:

        MetaData

                    entity.genre

                    entity.subgenre

                    entity.occurrence

                    entity.domain

        Occurrents

                    Non-fictional Occurrents:

                                entity.timeline

                                entity.zone

                                entity.country

                    Fictional Occurrents:

                                entity.afterlife

                                entity.timetravel

                                entity.spacetravel

        Continuants

                    Fictional Continutants

                                entity.name

                                entity.age

                                entity.location
```

Table 6.1. *Class hierarchy*

For example, in Figure 6.1, an entity graph for the Indian epic fantasy novel, Chandrakanta, is shown. The base class is Princess Chandrakanta, who is the central character of the novel. Several ontological relationships centric to the character are shown in the entity graph. Chandrakanta "loves" Prince Virendra Singh is the implication by the relation attribute "loves". Similar relationships are shown by several attributes such as "author", "publishedYear" and "kingdom". If a class contains several subclasses, the relationship "contains" is used. For example, Tilism contains several fields such as "Magic", "Martial Arts" and "Fine Arts". Hence, the keyword "contains" is used. Similar ontologies for different novels can be modeled to preserve the knowledge forever and perform intensive numerical computations easily.

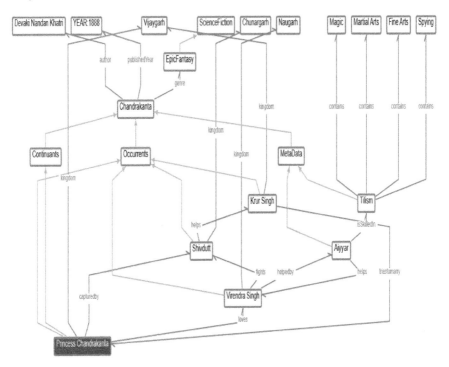

Figure 6.1. *Entity graph for a sample class. For a color version of this figure, see www.iste.co.uk/mehta/tools.zip*

6.3.2. *Ontology visualization*

The modeled ontology is visualized using WebVOWL 1.1.7. The visualization results provide a comprehensive view of the ontology, along with all of the relations and subclasses in a graphical format. Automatic ontology visualization is performed to save human time and effort to reduce computation time. The OWL format of the ontology is uploaded to the WebVOWL server, and a graphical view of the classes, along with the related subclasses and relationship annotations are provided. Figure 6.2 shows the ontology visualization results for a small part of the SciFiOnto.

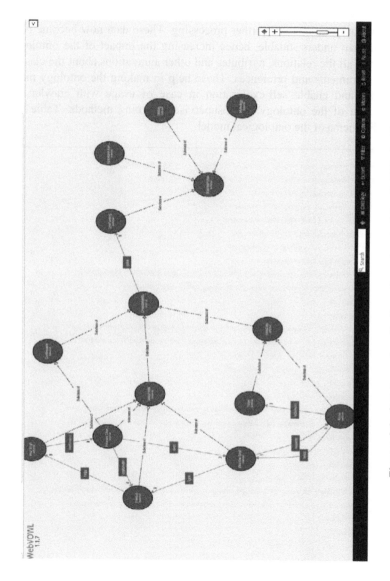

Figure 6.2. *Ontology visualization of a snippet of the SciFiOnto. For a color version of this figure, see www.iste.co.uk/mehta/tools.zip*

6.3.2.1. *RDF schema of the ontology*

Table 6.2 shows the class RDF schema of the ontology. RDF stands for Resource Description Framework and is the most popular method of storing and developing ontologies. XML to RDF transition of the ontology makes it more machine readable and suitable for computations and further processing. These data now become both machine and human understandable, hence increasing the impact of the ontology. RDF can describe all the relations, attributes and other annotations about the classes such as labels, comments and references. These help in making the ontology more machine-friendly and enable self-exploration in case of usage with crawlers to increase the scope of the ontology by unsupervised learning methods. Table 6.2 shows the RDF schema of the ontological model.

```xml
<?xml version="1.0"?>
<rdf:RDF xmlns="urn:webprotege:ontology:6ce3293a-0c56-48de-9a03-875451936ee7#"
    xml:base="urn:webprotege:ontology:6ce3293a-0c56-48de-9a03-875451936ee7"
    xmlns:owl="http://www.w3.org/2002/07/owl#"
    xmlns:rdf="http://www.w3.org/1999/02/22-rdf-syntax-ns#"
    xmlns:xml="http://www.w3.org/XML/1998/namespace"
    xmlns:xsd="http://www.w3.org/2001/XMLSchema#"
    xmlns:rdfs="http://www.w3.org/2000/01/rdf-schema#"
    xmlns:webprotege="http://webprotege.stanford.edu/">
    <owl:Ontology rdf:about="urn:webprotege:ontology:6ce3293a-0c56-48de-9a03-875451936ee7"/>
    <owl:Class rdf:about="http://webprotege.stanford.edu/R8o9hqlgrc44xqDefD4RK6Q">
        <rdfs:subClassOf>
            <owl:Restriction>
                <owl:onProperty rdf:resource="http://webprotege.stanford.edu/R2P4H50F7rRmo3liOORdye"/>
                <owl:someValuesFrom rdf:resource="http://webprotege.stanford.edu/R8kjeNeQloanfAr8QV4S1Z2"/>
            </owl:Restriction>
        </rdfs:subClassOf>
        <rdfs:subClassOf>
            <owl:Restriction>
                <owl:onProperty rdf:resource="http://webprotege.stanford.edu/R7eYS7k5ipf69PnVZk46lJB"/>
                <owl:hasValue rdf:resource="http://webprotege.stanford.edu/R9i6Yrl9wD2k6aQqleM5DtF"/>
            </owl:Restriction>
        </rdfs:subClassOf>
        <rdfs:subClassOf>
            <owl:Restriction>
                <owl:onProperty rdf:resource="http://webprotege.stanford.edu/R7l2qWwTmdKNt90VmCbc3cs"/>
                <owl:hasValue rdf:resource="http://webprotege.stanford.edu/RBV316L1AUszzpa1qpKzSj6"/>
            </owl:Restriction>
        </rdfs:subClassOf>
        <rdfs:label>Chandrakanta</rdfs:label>
    </owl:Class>
</rdf:RDF>
```

Table 6.2. *RDF schema of the ontology*

6.3.3. *Ontology evaluation*

After the modeling and visualization of any ontology, it must be evaluated by some definite approach so that the chances of improvement increase, and apt modifications are made to make the ontology even more robust and useful. A hybrid method of ontology evaluation is used in this work, which evaluates several aspects of ontology modeling and deployment.

6.3.3.1. *Quantitative evaluation*

In quantitative evaluation, the count of classes and other quantitative data about the classes are evaluated to find out the reuse ratio of the ontology to quantify the ontology's impact. The count of classes, subclasses, leaf classes, class attributes, properties and relationships per class are evaluated in this part of ontology evaluation. If the ontology has its base structure from an already existing ontology, then adequate reference is included, and the reference ratio is calculated. Table 6.3 shows the quantitative evaluation report of the Modeled Sci-Fi Ontology based on human cognition.

Number of classes	85
Number of subclasses	36
Number of leaf classes	10
Number of attributes	31
Number of properties	20
Number of relations	25
Depth of inheritance	4
Reuse ratio	91.43
Reference ratio	0

Table 6.3. *Quantitative data of the modeled Sci-Fi ontology*

The initially conceived ontology has 85 classes with 36 subclasses and 10 leaf classes. The associated number of attributes was 31 and the number of properties in the ontology was 20. The ontology had 25 relations with a depth of inheritance of 4. The proposed Sci-Fi ontology conceived based on human cognition exhibited a reuse ratio of 91.43, which indicated its reusability. The proposed Sci-Fi ontology was associated with a reference ratio of 0, which indicates that this is the first formal independent ontology that is designated to a domain like Sci-Fi.

6.3.3.2. *Qualitative evaluation*

The qualitative evaluation of an ontology is performed by crowd knowledge-based evaluation by recording and analyzing the reviews of a panel of experts who are to use the ontology in future. The qualitative metrics which are to be evaluated are Accuracy of the class hierarchy of the ontology, Clarity on the domain and arrangement of the classes, Coherence among the relationships defined and implemented, Consistency in using the same attributes and relationships for similar classes and objects, Interpretability of the final ontology, Methodology and its compatibility with the domain and knowledge hierarchy, Relevance of the classes and relations with the domain and ontology, and Richness of the ontology in terms of classes and their individual impact on the ontology. The qualitative evaluation by a panel of 100 experts for Sci-Fi based ontologies is shown in Table 6.4 and its graphical visualization is shown in Figure 6.3. The domain experts chosen for the Sci-Fi domain were either candidates who were aware of Sci-Fi or who are regular readers of Sci-Fi, searched using a local library circulating Sci-Fi books. Subjects from an online community of Sci-Fi interests were also picked up randomly from Quora groups on the basis of their availability. Also, Masters and final year Bachelor students in English Literature who had a viable knowledge of Sci-Fi as an independent domain were chosen as subjects for knowledge modeling.

Metric	Very high	High	Medium	Low
Accuracy	61	34	5	0
Clarity	59	33	8	0
Coherence	56	37	7	0
Consistency	67	28	5	0
Interpretability	62	29	9	0
Methodology	60	33	7	0
Richness	65	29	6	0
Relevance	63	27	10	0

Table 6.4. *Qualitative evaluation*

From Figure 6.3, it is notable that the qualitative evaluation of the ontologies that are manually modeled and conceived based on the human cognition has a majority of very high voting for each of the parameters, namely, Accuracy, Clarity, Coherence, Interoperability, Methodology, Richness and Relevance. However, the second majority of voting for the terms conceived into the ontological domain goes to high, which is followed by medium for each of the parameters for which the Sci-Fi ontology was modeled. There were no votes received for low, which was NULL. This clearly indicates that the manually modeled seed ontology for science fiction as a domain is widely accepted against several evaluation parameters by a community of experts, who were involved in modeling the initial seed ontology for a socio-technical domain like science fiction.

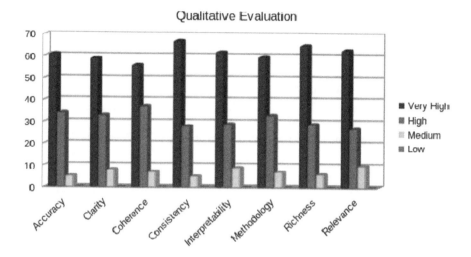

Figure 6.3. *Qualitative evaluation datasheet. For a color version of this figure, see www.iste.co.uk/mehta/tools.zip*

6.3.3.3. *Crowd knowledge-based evaluation*

The principal ontology classes and structures are shared with 240 users who are experts in the field of ontologies and the domain that is Sci-Fi. The ontology vocabulary is hence validated based on the conceived ontologies and ontology vocabulary formed by the inputs given by these experts, and a similarity index-based mapping is done between the developed ontology vocabularies and the original classes and relations defined in the modeled ontology. The overall deviance is calculated, and the Precision, Recall, Accuracy and F-Measure are calculated. Precision shown in equation [6.1] represents the ratio of the count of instances correctly labeled versus the count of instances labeled. Recall described in equation [6.2] is known as the ratio between the number of instances appropriately labeled and the number of correct labels. Accuracy depicted in equation [6.3] and F-Measure shown in equation [6.4] signify the arithmetic and harmonic mean of the precision and recall, respectively. Also, the False Negative Rate (FNR) is used as a comparison metric to evaluate the qualities of the ontologies conceived. Table 6.5 shows the results of the hybrid evaluation of the ontology.

$$Precision = \frac{\text{No. of ontological entities originally conceived and relevant}}{\text{Total no. of ontological entities in the modeled ontology}} \qquad [6.1]$$

$$Recall = \frac{\text{No. of ontological entities originally conceived and relevant}}{\text{Total no. of ontological entities in the experts vocabulary}} \qquad [6.2]$$

$$Accuracy = \frac{Precision + Recall}{2} \qquad [6.3]$$

$$F - Measure = \frac{2*Precision*Recall}{Precision+Recall} \qquad [6.4]$$

$$FNR = 1 - \text{Specificity} \qquad [6.5]$$

Number of instances selected	Precision (%)	Recall (%)	Accuracy (%)	F-Measure (%)	FNR
20	86.66	88.73	87.7	87.68	0.12
40	86.92	89.23	88.08	88.06	0.11
60	87.51	89.99	88.75	88.73	0.11
80	87.9	90.23	89.07	89.05	0.10
100	88.88	90.69	89.79	89.78	0.10
Average	87.57	89.77	88.67	88.66	0.11

Table 6.5. *Hybrid evaluation of the manually conceived Sci-Fi domain ontology based on ground truth collected using experts' contribution*

It is notable from Table 6.5 that the percentages of Precision, Recall, Accuracy, F-Measure and FNR are depicted with the number of instances validated. Instead of validating all of the instances at once, since there are a good number of instances (composition of classes, subclasses, leaf classes and individuals), the performance is evaluated by selecting a specific number of instances incrementally and validating based on the expert opinion of whether a particular entity belongs to a prospective domain or not. An average Precision of 87.57%, an Overall Recall of 89.77%, an

Overall Accuracy of 88.67% with an average F-Measure of 88.66% and an FDR of 0.11 are furnished for the initially modeled crowdsourced ontology for the Sci-Fi domain.

6.4. Automatic Knowledge Acquisition model

6.4.1. *System architecture*

The system, shown in Figure 6.4, is designed to take inputs from a sparsely populated ontology and analyze the individual entity graphs of the ontology to search for related information using SPARQL querying in websites such as Wikipedia and DBPedia. The derived information is then categorized into the standard <Subject, Predicate, Object> format as per the RDF standards, using a neural network. Then, the terms are inducted into the ontology using a suitable ranking and induction algorithm. The HITS algorithm (Kleinberg 1999) is used for automated ontology population. For the initial phases, an already constructed ontology is used to provide the system with a backbone ontology to look up terms in the querying database. Separate entity graphs for the classes linked with each other are generated and they are then queried using SPARQL. The main reasoning behind this step is to make the entire process automatic, using the large amount of data available on the Internet, and at the same time, maintaining the precision and accuracy of the modeled ontological entity. So, the knowledge present in large sources such as Wikidata, DBpedia and LOD Cloud are integrated into a larger knowledge base, and it is then compared with the RDF entities of the skeleton ontological input.

In RDF, the data are present in the form of a Triadic Structure, which is formalized as a triplet consisting of the <S,P,O> format where S is the subject, P is the predicate and O is the object. Quite often, S denotes the name of the class, or the entity, and P stands for its hyperlink or the source of the information. O is the data, and it can be in a form of a dictionary containing all of the properties and relationships of the entity with the label: value type structure. The extracted terms are queried using a neural network, as neural networks are very efficient in extracting the taxonomic and non-taxonomic relationships between the classes. Hence, they are mapped to a certain RDF class and relation parameter during extraction. This leads to the mapping of new data to already existing relationship parameters in the ontology, which makes the ontology populated. The induction of these terms is carried on using the HITS algorithm. The terms are then included into the ontology based on their ranking and need in the ontology to make the model as precise as possible.

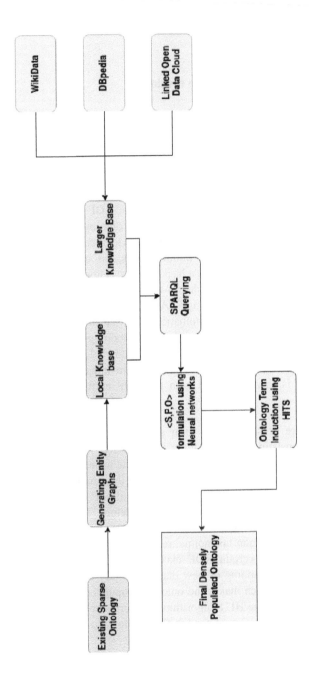

Figure 6.4. *System architecture of RDF-driven automatic ontology generator to synthesize knowledge. For a color version of this figure, see www.iste.co.uk/mehta/tools.zip*

6.4.2. *Acquisition algorithm*

Figure 6.5 shows the entity graph of a sample class called "Virendra Singh", who is a character of the fictional Indian novel "Chandrakanta". This class has several relationships with other classes: he "fights" Shivdutt, is helped by "Aiyyar" and so on. The entity graphs consist of several properties and relationships pertaining to the class of instance. The relation attribute "loves" shows love interest among two characters and is hence a property that exists mutually between two classes. Attributes such as "author" and "publishedYear" show the characteristics of the novel to which the class taken into consideration belongs to. In the case of a class being a holonym of several classes, the "contains" attribute is used. For example, Tilism in the above example contains several fields such as "Magic", "Martial Arts" and "Fine Arts". Hence, the keyword "contains" is used. Similar ontologies for different novels can be modeled to preserve the knowledge forever and perform intensive numerical computations easily. So, for entity graphs like this, the information can be extracted and more data about the class can be extracted by web querying. SPARQL is used for the querying operation. The acquired data are then sent through a neural network to enable the mapping from RDF to RDF.

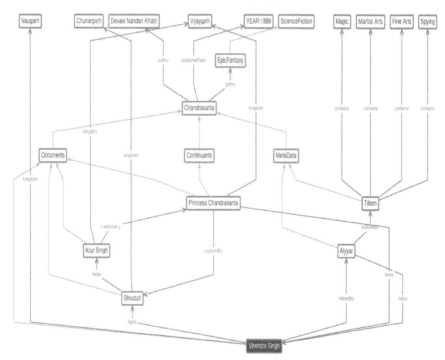

Figure 6.5. *Entity graph for one of the classes. For a color version of this figure, see www.iste.co.uk/mehta/tools.zip*

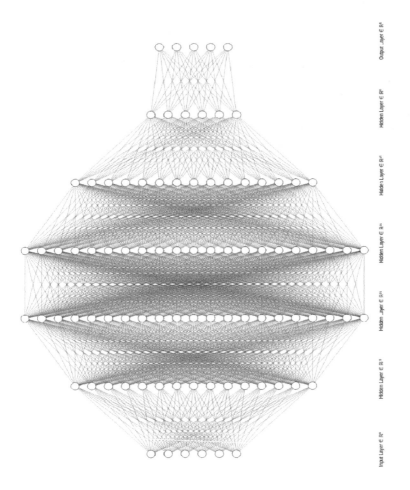

Figure 6.6. *Proposed Binomial Neural Network Architecture*

For this system, a neural network which has the number of nodes based on the binomial number series based on the number of objects in the class is used. For example, a class with six objects has six input nodes followed by 15, 21, 21, 15, 6, and finally five output nodes. This helps build the neural network based on the number of objects in the classes. The Binomial Deep Neural Network architecture, depicted in Figure 6.6, is based on the number of classes or properties which are present in the ontology, and the number of entities the objects can belong to. So, a class with six objects needs to find the correct label for an RDF entity queried over the database. The neural network algorithm is shown in Table 6.6.

Input: Class from the ontology

Output: Corresponding property and RDF mapping Algorithm

Start

      for each class in the skeleton ontology:

          generate entity graph

          extract the classes and relations

          use SPARQL to query the relations in the listed sources

          extracted_entities = list (acquired_classes from SPARQL)

          for each new_class in extracted_entities:

              RDF_mapping = BinNeuralNetwork(new_class)

              make a list of prospective classes and RDF mappings

          end for

          n_terms = number of required terms in the ontology

          Induct n_terms terms into the ontology using HITS algorithm

          output the populated ontology

      end for

End

Table 6.6. *Algorithm for RDF mapping using the Binomial Deep Neural Network*

The neural network works for the RDF-to-RDF mapping between the classes which are obtained from the SPARQL querying with the classes on the skeleton ontology, which is used to get the relevant classes from the knowledge stores which have prospective classes for the ontology. The process workflow starts from selecting each class from the skeleton ontology. The entity graph of the class is generated and the relationships with other classes are extracted for further querying over the database. From SPARQL querying, the list of extracted classes is mapped from RDF to RDF using the Binomial Neural Network. Hence, a map of the prospective RDF mappings and classes is made. Based on the requirement of the user, the number of the required terms is defined, and the required number of terms is inducted into the ontology. Hence, the populated ontology is shown as the output of the system.

Expert judgment and similarity metrics are used to compute the Precision, Recall, Accuracy, F-Measure and the FNR of the proposed model. The SPARQL querying algorithm is executed along with pellet reasoning for data acquisition. Cosine similarity indices of the new classes are calculated with the old classes, and expert judgments are used to demonstrate the similarity between the classes. These metrics are used to classify the classes as matching or not matching with the original classes and the metrics are calculated. The principal ontology classes and structures are shared with 110 users who are experts in the field of Sci-Fi. The expanded ontology vocabulary and relationships are studied by these experts and are classified as relevant or not. The overall deviance is calculated, and the Precision, Recall, Accuracy, F-Measure and FNR are computed.

Number of Instances Selected	Precision (%)	Recall (%)	Accuracy (%)	F-Measure (%)	FNR
20	90.13	91.72	90.93	90.92	0.08
40	90.56	92.5	91.53	91.52	0.08
60	91.23	93.69	92.46	92.44	0.06
80	92.8	94.56	93.68	93.67	0.05
100	94.28	95.53	94.91	94.9	0.04
Average	**91.8**	**93.6**	**92.7**	**92.69**	**0.06**

Table 6.7. *Evaluation results for Automatic Knowledge Base Generation*

Table 6.7 shows the results of the hybrid evaluation technique on the proposed SciFiOnto model on the basis of the number of selected instances from the original human conceived seed ontology model, which is further liasoned with the auxiliary knowledge stores. From Table 6.7, it is inferable that even as the number of instance increases, the percentages of Precision, Recall, Accuracy and F-Measure increase and the FNR value decreases. The reason for this increasing gradient in percentages of Precision, Recall, Accuracy and F-Measure and the decreasing gradient of FNR is mainly due to the reason that, as the number of instances increases, a greater number of principal concepts increases, and thereby a higher number of auxiliary knowledge and vertical knowledge dentistry within a specific instance, which is visualized as a class or concept. This enhances the robustness of the model to accommodate the knowledge within the framework, thereby ensuring the performance metrics relevant to the seed ontology as it is accommodated within the core seed concepts which are used. It is indicative that the proposed SciFiOnto furnishes an average Precision of 91.8%, an average Recall of 93.60%, an average Accuracy of 92.70%, an average F-Measure of 92.69% with a very low average FNR of 0.06 for Automatic Knowledge Base Generation based on the conceived seed ontologies based on human conceptual understanding. The encompassment of the proposed Binomial Neural Network upon a user conceived domain ontological model ensures learning of data from the entities and instances on the basis of human conceptual interpretation for a specialized literary domain like science fiction with socio-technical awareness.

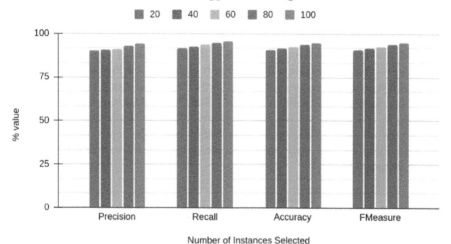

Figure 6.7. *Hybrid evaluation results chart. For a color version of this figure, see www.iste.co.uk/mehta/tools.zip*

Using a Binomial Neural Network, several concepts and their classes are matched with the literals and hence the required KA for the ontology is carried on. The modeling results are depicted in Figure 6.7. It is inferable from Figure 6.7 that as the number of instances to the Binomial Neural Network increases, the auxiliary knowledge also increases, and is passed into the framework. This ensures that the number of concepts also increases, which demands lateral cognitive knowledge. As a result, the Precision, Recall, Accuracy and F-Measure also increase as the number of instances increases, owing to the density of knowledge which gets fed into the framework, which acts as an interface for designating associated entities and instances to leverage with the existing underlying seed ontology from the data on the World Wide Web. This helps in Knowledge Assimilation with the already existing knowledge that has been verified by the experts to imbibe human cognition.

Table 6.8 shows the quantitative aspects of the populated ontology based on the system. From the skeleton ontology, the number of classes becomes 417 and the number of subclasses increases to 2,143. Similarly, the ontology becomes in-depth, with the inheritance depth increasing to 18, and by the addition of 2,471 individuals and 563 new attributes to relate the classes. Real-world data are amalgamated in the ontology by crowdsourced KA techniques and intelligent semantic techniques. When using web scraping tools, the entire domain knowledge is categorized, and appropriate labeling is implemented using neural networks. These are used for operations like finding the POS (Part of Speech) of the word, and the category in which it will fit. Then, the attributes and the labels are embedded in the classes and a dynamic ontology is formed. There is a clear increase in the number of classes, subclasses, individuals, attributes, number of relations, depth of inheritance and reuse ratio owing to the automatic knowledge aggregation. However, the aggregated knowledge is relevant in terms of Precision, Recall, Accuracy and F-Measure. The main reason is due to the quality of the initially conceptualized seed ontology, which was conceived using domain experts and further enhanced using LOD Cloud. It is evident that there is an increase in Precision, Recall, Accuracy and F-Measure, and a decrease in the FNR value. This indicates that the proposed SciFiOnto is significantly efficient in Automatic Knowledge Base Generation using an expert contributed and verified seed domain ontology for a socio-technical domain like science fiction.

Number of classes	417
Number of subclasses	2,143
Number of individuals	2,471
Number of attributes	563
Number of relations	86
Depth of inheritance	18
Reuse ratio	93.21
Reference ratio	0

Table 6.8. *Quantitative aspects of the obtained automatically generated ontology*

6.5. Conclusion

An ontology pertaining to the Sci-Fi domain was modeled using human cognition. A hybrid crowdsourced method has been proposed for data acquisition. Several classifications have been made for the Sci-Fi data based on the properties of the objects in various Sci-Fi novels, fantasies and different genres of the domain. With special focus on the Indian context, the example of the Sci-Fi novel "Chandrakanta" is depicted in this chapter to show the relationships with the entity graphs and RDF schema. The ontology is evaluated using the semiotics approach of ontology evaluation and a reuse ratio of 91.43% is obtained with an accuracy of 88.67%, which is computed by estimating domain relevance using experts' opinion. Also, an Automatic Knowledge Acquisition model for the Sci-Fi domain is used to populate the existing skeleton ontology, which is sparse. A data and information integration model is developed, which works on RDF-to-RDF mapping between the newly acquired classes and the baseline ontology using a Binomial Deep Neural Network that has been put forth. Based on several sources having highly dispersed data on Sci-Fi and related genres, these terms and classes are acquired and integrated with the ontology using HITS algorithm. Finally, the proposed approach is evaluated using crowd intelligence for semantic fitness, which yields the confusion matrix of the acquired classes being classified accurately or not based on the cosine similarity index and classification by domain experts. An average accuracy of 92.7% with an FNR of 0.06 has been obtained for the automatically synthesized knowledge, which shows the potential widespread application of the system, even in other domains.

6.6. References

Adetunji, T., Vincent, O.R., Ugwunna, C.O., Odeniyi, L.A., Folorunso, O. (2020). An ontology-based knowledge acquisition model for software anomalies systems. *International Conference in Mathematics, Computer Engineering and Computer Science (ICMCECS)*, Ayobo, 18–21 March.

Aziz, A., Ahmed, S., Khan, F.I. (2019). An ontology-based methodology for hazard identification and causation analysis. *Process Safety and Environmental Protection*, 123, 87–98.

Bacon-Smith, C. (2000). *Science Fiction Culture*. University of Pennsylvania Press, Philadelphia, Pennsylvania.

Banane, M., Erraissi, A., Belangour, A. (2019). SPARQL2Hive: An approach to processing SPARQL queries on Hive based on meta-models. *8th International Conference on Modeling Simulation and Applied Optimization (ICMSAO)*, Manama, 15–17 April.

Banerjee, S. (2020). *Indian Science Fiction: Patterns, History and Hybridity*. University of Wales Press, Cardiff.

Breitman, K., Casanova, M.A., Truszkowski, W. (2007). *Semantic Web: Concepts, Technologies and Applications*. Springer Science & Business Media, London.

Cantador, I., Bellogín, A., Castells, P. (2008). A multilayer ontology-based hybrid recommendation model. *AI Communications*, 21(2/3), 203–210.

Cavaliere, D., Loia, V., Senatore, S. (2019). Towards an ontology design pattern for UAV video content analysis. *IEEE Access*, 7, 105342–105353.

Chen, H. and Luo, X. (2019). An automatic literature knowledge graph and reasoning network modeling framework based on ontology and natural language processing. *Advanced Engineering Informatics*, 42, 100959.

Chen, G., Jiang, T., Wang, M., Tang, X., Ji, W. (2020). Modeling and reasoning of IoT architecture in semantic ontology dimension. *Computer Communications*, 153, 580–594.

Coletti, A., De Nicola, A., Vicoli, G., Villani, M.L. (2019). Semantic modeling of cascading risks in interoperable socio-technical systems. *Enterprise Interoperability VIII*. Springer, Cham.

Colloc, J. and Boulanger, D. (2020). Automatic knowledge acquisition for object-oriented expert systems. arXiv preprint arXiv:2005.08517.

Corcho, O., Fernández-López, M., Gómez-Pérez, A., López-Cima, A. (2005). Building legal ontologies with methontology and WebODE. *Law and the Semantic Web*. Springer, Berlin, Heidelberg.

Deepak, G., Kumar, A.A., Santhanavijayan, A., Prakash, N. (2019). Design and evaluation of conceptual ontologies for electrochemistry as a domain. *IEEE International WIE Conference on Electrical and Computer Engineering (WIECON-ECE)*, Bangalore.

Eco, U. (2009). On the ontology of fictional characters: A semiotic approach. *Sign Systems Studies*, 37(1/2), 82–98.

Gaurav, D., Rodriguez, F.O., Tiwari, S., Jabbar, M.A. (2021). Review of machine learning approach for drug development process. *Deep Learning in Biomedical and Health Informatics*. CRC Press, Boca Raton, Florida.

Gilks, M., Fleming, P., Allen, M. (2003). *Science Fiction: The Literature of Ideas*. WritingWorld.com. Archived from the original on 15 May 2015 [Accessed 22 December 2006].

Grasso, F. and Di Caro, L. (2021). A methodology for large-scale, disambiguated and unbiased lexical knowledge acquisition based on multilingual word alignment. CEUR Workshop Proceedings, 3033(18).

Gupta, S., Tiwari, S., Ortiz-Rodriguez, F., Panchal, R.K. (2021). KG4ASTRA: Question answering over Indian Missiles Knowledge Graph. *Soft Computing*, 25, 13841–13855.

Hitzler, P. and Krisnadhi, A. (2018). A tutorial on modular ontology modeling with ontology design patterns: The cooking recipes ontology. arXiv preprint arXiv:1808.08433.

Kestel, P., Kügler, P., Zirngibl, C., Schleich, B., Wartzack, S. (2019). Ontology-based approach for the provision of simulation knowledge acquired by Data and Text Mining processes. *Advanced Engineering Informatics*, 39, 292–305.

Kleinberg, J. (1999). Authoritative sources in a hyperlinked environment. *J. of the ACM*, 46(5), 604–632.

Kumar, A., Deepak, G., Santhanavijayan, A. (2020). HeTOnto: A novel approach for conceptualization, modeling, visualization, and formalization of domain centric ontologies for heat transfer. *IEEE International Conference on Electronics, Computing and Communication Technologies (CONECCT)*, Bangalore.

Laaz, N. and Mbarki, S. (2019). OntoIFML: Automatic generation of annotated web pages from IFML and ontologies using the MDA Approach: A case study of an EMR management application. *Proceedings of the 7th International Conference on Model-Driven Engineering and Software Development (MODELSWARD 2019)*, SCITEPRESS – Science and Technology Publications, 353–361.

Leng, S., Hu, Z.Z., Luo, Z., Zhang, J.P., Lin, J.R. (2019). Automatic MEP knowledge acquisition based on documents and natural language processing. *Proceedings of the 36th International Conference of CIB W*, 78, 800–809.

Liu, Y., Kang, X., Miao, D., Li, D. (2019). A knowledge acquisition method based on concept lattice and inclusion degree for ordered information systems. *Int. J. Mach. Learn. & Cyber.*, 10, 3245–3261.

Luckhurst, R. (2005). *Science Fiction*. Polity Press, Wiley Publishing House, Hoboken, New Jersey.

Nandhakishore, C.S., Deepak, G., Santhanavijayan, A. (2022). Conceptualization, visualization, and modeling of ontologies for elementary kinematics. *Advanced Computing and Intelligent Technologies*. Springer, Singapore.

Nicholes, J. (2018). Developing STEM interest and genre knowledge through science fiction prototyping. *The STEAM Journal*, 3(2), 14.

Pushpa, C.N., Deepak, G., Thriveni, J., Venugopal, K.R. (2015). OntoCollab: Strategic review oriented collaborative knowledge modeling using ontologies. *7th International Conference on Advanced Computing (ICoAC)*. Madras Institute of Technology, Chennai.

Rai, C., Sivastava, A., Tiwari, S., Abhishek, K. (2021). Towards a conceptual modelling of ontologies. *Emerging Technologies in Data Mining and Information Security: Proceedings of IEMIS 2020*, 1(1), 39.

Sabou, M., Scharl, A., Föls, M. (2013). Crowdsourced knowledge acquisition: Towards hybrid-genre workflows. *International Journal on Semantic Web and Information Systems (IJSWIS)*, 9(3), 14–41.

Sanfilippo, E.M., Belkadi, F., Bernard, A. (2019). Ontology-based knowledge representation for additive manufacturing. *Computers in Industry*, 109, 182–194.

Shahzad, S.K., Ahmed, D., Naqvi, M.R., Mushtaq, M.T., Iqbal, M.W., Munir, F. (2021). Ontology driven smart health service integration. *Computer Methods and Programs in Biomedicine*, 207, 106146.

Sheridan, P., Onsjö, M., Hastings, J. (2019). The literary theme ontology for media annotation and information retrieval. arXiv preprint arXiv:1905.00522.

Shimizu, C., Hitzler, P., Hirt, Q., Rehberger, D., Estrecha, S.G., Foley, C., Carty, R. (2020). The enslaved ontology: Peoples of the historic slave trade. *Journal of Web Semantics*, 100567.

Subramaniyaswamy, V., Manogaran, G., Logesh, R., Vijayakumar, V., Chilamkurti, N., Malathi, D., Senthilselvan, N. (2019). An ontology-driven personalized food recommendation in IoT-based healthcare system. *The Journal of Supercomputing*, 75(6), 3184–3216.

Thorn, A. (2002). Aurora Award. Acceptance speech, Calgary.

Wang, X., Gui, D., Li, H., Gui, H. (2019). Automatic construction of coal mine accident ontology. *International Conference on Applications and Techniques in Cyber Security and Intelligence*. Springer, Cham.

Semantic Web-Enabled IoT Integration for a Smart City

On top of the Internet, the web illustrates how a set of relatively simple and open standards can be used to build very flexible systems while preserving efficiency and scalability. The cross-integration and developments of composite applications on the web, alongside its ubiquitous availability across a broad range of devices (e.g. desktops, laptops, mobile phones, set-top boxes and gaming devices), make the web an outstanding candidate for a universal integration platform. Websites no longer only offer pages; now Application Programming Interfaces (API) can be used by other web resources to create new, ad hoc and composite applications that run in the computing cloud and able to be accessed with desktops or mobile computers. In this chapter, we use the web and its emerging technologies as the basis of a smart things application integration platform. We propose a Web of Things (WoT) application architecture offering four layers that simplify the development of applications involving smart things. In this chapter, a WoT application has been applied by taking the dataset of famous cities like New York.

7.1. Introduction: Semantic Web and sensors

The integration of gigantic datasets brings a rise in knowledge discoveries and ontologies organize the domain knowledge as important concepts, relations, axioms and instances. In forest panting domains, ontologies organize the forest planting information for encoding tree or planting space, geographical locations, park and sanctuary details. A hierarchical relationship of concepts in ontology plays an important role in data integration, knowledge representation and decision support systems. Internet of Things (IoT) technologies offer to exchange the data between entities through sensing devices in order to find and detect the empty space or location using IoT-based forest planting systems. The data can be a smart city like New York,

Chapter written by Ronak PANCHAL and Fernando ORTIZ-RODRIGUEZ.

New York's sensing data, the user's information, or device and other domain-specific data. A specific data structure is required to generate the desired information in the IoT-based planting system to interact with the connected devices. Semantic models are based on ontologies that are significant for the modeling of concepts and the relationship between the concepts. These models include forest planting terminologies and relationships of terms for the representation of free space information with radio-frequency identification (RFID) devices. Semantic Web technologies are recognized as promising tools for interacting with several smart devices as they are excellent when it comes to exchanging their services and sharing data precisely.

7.2. Motivation and challenge

This chapter addresses the main contributions in the assessment of the Forest Planting Ontology (FPO) using IoT in smart cities like New York, so inconsistencies and modeling errors can be removed from the ontology. They are:

1) Proposed methodology and approaches to evaluate the ontology quality.

2) Modeled test cases for the assessment of FPO.

3) Evaluation of all test cases on several tools (Protégé and Jena Fuseki).

4) Geolocation Sensor, Real-Time Location Tracking and detection of empty park, sanctuary for planting.

7.3. Literature review

According to Sanju Tiwari and Ajith Abraham:

> In health-care systems, Internet of Technology (IoT) technologies provide data exchange among various entities and ontologies offer a formal description to present the knowledge of health-care domains. As of the best knowledge, no other study has been presented earlier to conduct the integrated assessment on different tools. All test cases are successfully analyzed on these tools and results are drawn and compared with other ontologies. (Tiwari and Abraham 2020)

Pandey said:

> The paper deals with challenges to integrate the data coming from heterogeneous sensor networks coming from various geographical locations. A Sensor Web Registry is proposed to achieve this task. The outcome of this effort is further realized by using Semantic Web Technologies like Ontologies, OWL, SPARQL and Python. The paper

used all this practically using a Micaz Sensor Boards with Zigbee protocol in a lab setup. (Pandey and Panchal 2019)

Paola and María study smart city ontology and create the documentation, so:

the review reveals some gaps in the ontologies available for this field. First, there are smart city ontologies that are not available, a fact that completely hinders their reuse. Second, each ontology provides its custom model adapted to its specific needs, which makes it difficult to increase the interoperability among models, beyond common points, such as the modeling of time and units of measurement, where standards and well-known ontologies are usually reused. Third, some ontologies do not provide a clear documentation or the ontology requirements specification from which they are built. (Espinoza-Arias et al. 2018)

Antonio De Nicola said:

Ontologies have become viable and effective tools to practitioners for developing applications requiring data and process interoperability, big data management, and automated reasoning on knowledge. We investigate how and to what extent ontologies have been used to support smart city services and we provide a comprehensive reference on what problems have been addressed and what has been achieved so far with ontology-based applications. (De Nicola and Villani 2021)

Anastasija et al. (2022) focuses on the current visualization techniques to understand and process healthcare data by concentrating on biomedical subdomain.

Ontologies are represented as a semantic model with IoT by Mishra and Jain (2020) (Tiwari et al. 2022). Semantic approaches appear with heterogeneous sensor data from IoT devices. The data thus captured should be represented in the form of ontologies for information extraction, knowledge sharing, information integration and more.

7.4. Implementation of forest planting using SPARQL queries

7.4.1. *Architecture sketch with conceptual diagram*

Researchers have designed conceptual diagrams from the Record dataset for forestry planting spaces for NYC parks.

There are five major classes which are formulated from this dataset. The different classes are: Park, Sanctuary, Borough, Planting Site and Planning Status (Empty and Populated).

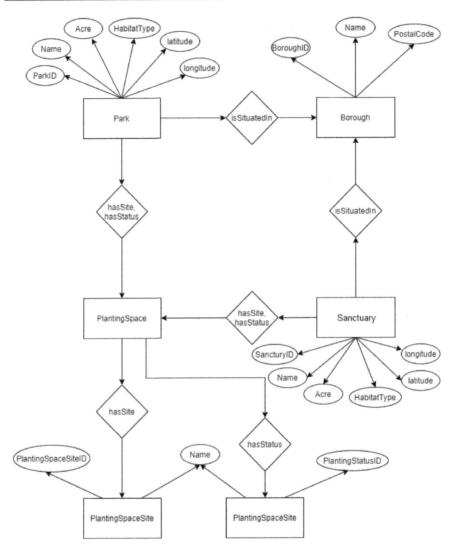

Figure 7.1. *Conceptual diagram of forest planting space*

7.4.2. *Implementation ontology from the dataset*

The ontology has been designed and includes Object Properties, Data Properties and instances in the PlantingSpace ontology of a given dataset.

1) Active ontology URI is given in Figure 7.2.

Figure 7.2. *Active ontology URI. For a color version of this figure, see www.iste.co.uk/mehta/tools.zip*

2) There are classes of PlantingSpace ontology, as shown in Figure 7.3.

Figure 7.3. *Classes of PlantingSpace ontology. For a color version of this figure, see www.iste.co.uk/mehta/tools.zip*

3) Object properties are given in Figure 7.4.

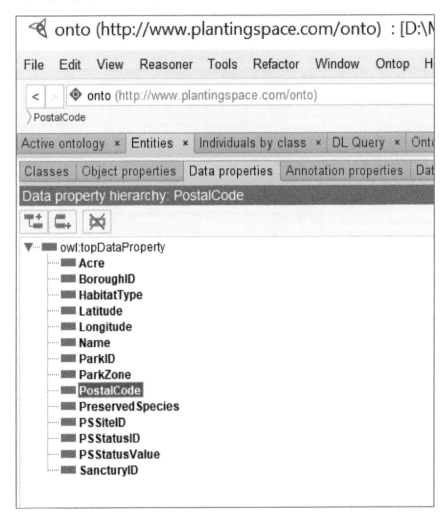

Figure 7.4. *Object properties. For a color version of this figure, see www.iste.co.uk/mehta/tools.zip*

4) Data properties are given in Figure 7.5.

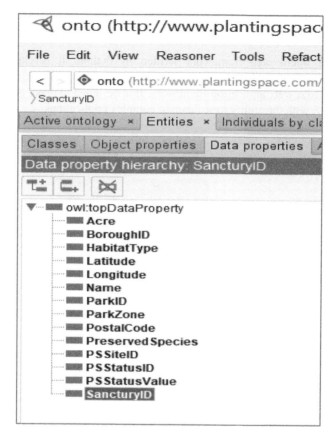

Figure 7.5. *Data properties. For a color version of this figure, see www.iste.co.uk/mehta/tools.zip*

7.4.3. *Technologies and tools*

The Protégé tools were used to design an ontology and upload the ontology dataset on the Apache Jena Fuseki server. It was used with the Jena SPARQL endpoint inside the Python flask-based web application for displaying data.

– *Protégé*: a free, open-source ontology editor and a knowledge management system.

– *Apache Jena Fuseki server*: a SPARQL server. It can run as an operating system service, a Java web application (WAR file) and a standalone server.

– *Python*: a programming language. It can be used on a server to create web applications. It is a multi-paradigm programming language. Object-oriented programming and structured programming are fully supported, as are many of its features.

– *Flask*: a micro web framework written in Python. It is classified as a microframework because it does not require particular tools or libraries. Flask is a lightweight WSGI web application framework. It is designed to make getting started quick and easy, with the ability to scale up to complex applications.

Once the ontology dataset is ready, follow the given steps shown in Figure 7.6.

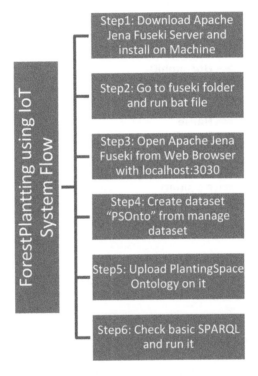

Figure 7.6. *Forest planting using IoT system flow*

Above is an image of the Apache Jena Fuseki with the SPARQL query of PlantingSpace ontology.

Results are integrated with the SPARQL query, and executed in the proposed web application in Python Flask.

Figure 7.7. *Apache Jena Fuseki with SPARQL query. For a color version of this figure, see www.iste.co.uk/mehta/tools.zip*

```
from flask import Flask, render_template
import requests

app = Flask(__name__)

prefixquery = """PREFIX rdf: <http://www.w3.org/1999/02/22-rdf-syntax-ns#>
        PREFIX owl: <http://www.w3.org/2002/07/owl#>
        PREFIX rdfs: <http://www.w3.org/2000/01/rdf-schema#>
        PREFIX xsd: <http://www.w3.org/2001/XMLSchema#>
        PREFIX test: <http://www.plantingspace.com/onto#> """

@app.route('/')
def Index():
  url = 'http://localhost:3030/PSOnto/sparql'
  query = prefixquery + """
      SELECT (MAX(?park_id)+1 AS ?pid) WHERE { ?x a test:Park . ?x
test:ParkID ?park_id . }
      """
  r = requests.get(url, params={'format': 'json', 'query': query})
  results = r.json()
  query1 = prefixquery + """
```

```
    SELECT (MAX(?sanctury_id)+1 AS ?sid) WHERE { ?x a test:Sanctury . ?x
test:SancturyID ?sanctury_id . }
                    """
    r1 = requests.get(url, params={'format': 'json', 'query': query1})
    results1 = r1.json()

    query2 = prefixquery + """
    SELECT (MAX(?borough_id)+1 AS ?bid) WHERE { ?x a test:Borough . ?x
test:BoroughID ?borough_id . }
                    """
    r2 = requests.get(url, params={'format': 'json', 'query': query2})
    results2 = r2.json()

    return render_template("index.html", data=results, data1=results1, data2=results2 )

@app.route('/park')
def Park():
    title="Park"
    url = 'http://localhost:3030/PSOnto/sparql'
    query = prefixquery + """ SELECT ?x ?parkname  ?acre ?htype ?bname ?status
?lati ?logi
                        WHERE
                        {
                        ?x a test:Park .
                        ?x test:Name ?parkname .
                         ?x test:Acre ?acre .
                        ?x test:HabitatType ?htype .
                        ?x test:Latitude ?lati .
                         ?x test:Longitude ?logi .
                        ?x test:isSituatedIn ?y .
                        ?y test:Name ?bname .
                        ?x test:hasStatus ?z .
                         ?z test:PSStatusValue  ?status .
                        FILTER regex(?htype, "forest", "i")
                        FILTER regex(?status, "popu", "i")
                        FILTER regex(?bname, "queen", "i")
                        FILTER regex(?parkname, "", "i")
                        }

            """
    r = requests.get(url, params={'format': 'json', 'query': query})
    results = r.json()
    #print(results)
    return render_template("park.html", data=results)

@app.route('/sanctury')
def Sanctury():
    title="Park"
    url = 'http://localhost:3030/PSOnto/sparql'
```

```
      query = prefixquery + """ SELECT ?x ?sancturyname ?boroghname ?acre ?htype
?status ?pcode WHERE
          {
          ?x a test:Sanctury .
          ?x test:Name ?sancturyname .
          ?x test:Acre ?acre .
          ?x test:HabitatType ?htype .
          ?x test:isSituatedIn ?y .
          ?y test:Name ?boroghname .
          ?y test:PostalCode ?pcode .
          ?x test:hasStatus ?z .
          ?z test:PSStatusValue ?status .
          ?y test:PostalCode ?pcode .
          ?x test:hasStatus ?z .
          ?z test:PSStatusValue ?status .
          FILTER regex(?status, "empty", "i")
          FILTER regex(?sancturyname, "preserve", "i")
          FILTER regex(?htype,"fresh","i")
          }
          order by ?x
          """
  r = requests.get(url, params={'format': 'json', 'query': query})
  results = r.json()
  return render_template("sanctury.html", data=results)


@app.route('/noofsanctury')
def NoofSanctury():
  title="NoofSanctury"
  url = 'http://localhost:3030/PSOnto/sparql'
  query = prefixquery + """ SELECT  ?species (count(?sancturyname) as
?numberofsanctury)  WHERE
              {
              ?x a test:Sanctury .
              ?x test:Name ?sancturyname .
              ?x test:Acre ?acre .
              ?x test:HabitatType ?htype .
              ?x test:PreservedSpecies ?species .
              }
              GROUP BY ?species
              HAVING(regex(?species, "herons", "i") )
              """
  r = requests.get(url, params={'format': 'json', 'query': query})
  results = r.json()
  return render_template("noofsanctury_specieswise.html", data=results)


if __name__=="__main__":
  app.run(debug=True)
```

For a color version of this code, see www.iste.co.uk/mehta/tools.zip

Now researchers have created a dashboard for the PlantingSpace ontology system which is given below:

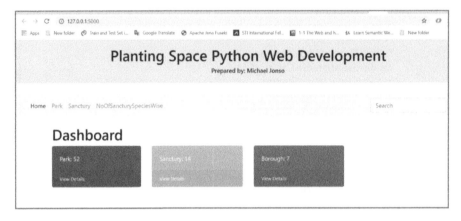

Figure 7.8. *Dashboard. For a color version of this figure, see www.iste.co.uk/mehta/tools.zip*

SPARQL result of PARK-related information is given in Figure 7.9.

Figure 7.9. *SPARQL result of PARK. For a color version of this figure, see www.iste.co.uk/mehta/tools.zip*

The following are sample queries which can be executed by using the proposed system. There are few questions that can be raised as a SPARQL query on

PlantingSpace ontology against an RDF graph. Those queries in question will follow. I have created some queries from PlantingSpace ontology.

1) Display park name, borough, its acre and habitat type based on status, park name and borough.

```
PREFIX rdf: <http://www.w3.org/1999/02/22-rdf-syntax-ns#>
PREFIX owl: <http://www.w3.org/2002/07/owl#>
PREFIX rdfs: <http://www.w3.org/2000/01/rdf-schema#>
PREFIX xsd: <http://www.w3.org/2001/XMLSchema#>
PREFIX test: <http://www.plantingspace.com/onto#>
SELECT ?x ?parkname ?acre ?htype ?bname ?status
WHERE
{
?x a test:Park .
?x test:Name ?parkname .
?x test:Acre ?acre .
?x test:HabitatType ?htype .
?x test:Latitude ?lati .
?x test:Longitude ?logi .
?x test:isSituatedIn ?y .
?y test:Name ?bname .
?x test:hasStatus ?z .
?z test:PSStatusValue ?status .
FILTER regex(?htype, "forest", "i")
FILTER regex(?status, "empty", "i")
FILTER regex(?bname, "queens", "i")
FILTER regex(?parkname, "cove", "i")
}
```

2) Count sanctuaries based on its species, of which there are more than two.

```
PREFIX rdf: <http://www.w3.org/1999/02/22-rdf-syntax-ns#>
PREFIX owl: <http://www.w3.org/2002/07/owl#>
PREFIX rdfs: <http://www.w3.org/2000/01/rdf-schema#>
PREFIX xsd: <http://www.w3.org/2001/XMLSchema#>
PREFIX test: <http://www.plantingspace.com/onto#>
SELECT ?species (count(?sancturyname) as ?cn) WHERE
{
?x a test:Sanctury .
?x test:Name ?sancturyname .
```

```
?x test:Acre ?acre .
?x test:HabitatType ?htype .
?x test:PreservedSpecies ?species .
}
GROUP BY ?species
HAVING(COUNT(?sancturyname) > 1)
```

3) Display "Herons" with species-wise sanctuary details.

```
PREFIX rdf: <http://www.w3.org/1999/02/22-rdf-syntax-ns#>
PREFIX owl: <http://www.w3.org/2002/07/owl#>
PREFIX rdfs: <http://www.w3.org/2000/01/rdf-schema#>
PREFIX xsd: <http://www.w3.org/2001/XMLSchema#>
PREFIX test: <http://www.plantingspace.com/onto#>
SELECT ?species (count(?sancturyname) as ?numberofsanctury) WHERE
{
?x a test:Sanctury .
?x test:Name ?sancturyname .
?x test:Acre ?acre .
?x test:HabitatType ?htype .
?x test:PreservedSpecies ?species .
}
GROUP BY ?species
HAVING(regex(?species, "herons", "i") )
```

7.5. Conclusion

After a quality assessment of FPO, it was successfully published on Linked Data for global community use. As a future scope, the ontology will be included in IoT-based devices for related vocabularies to make it public and easily accessed by Linked Open Data Cloud.

7.6. References

De Nicola, A. and Villani, M. (2021). Smart city ontologies and their applications: A systematic literature review. *Sustainability (Switzerland)*, 13(10), 5578.

Espinoza-Arias, P., Poveda-Villalón, M., García-Castro, R., Corcho, O. (2018). Ontological representation of smart city data: From devices to cities. *Applied Sciences (Switzerland)*, 9(1), 32.

Mishra, S. and Jain, S. (2020). Ontologies as a semantic model in IoT. *International Journal of Computers and Applications*, 42(3), 233–243.

Nikiforova, A., Tiwari, S., Rovite, V., Klovins, J., Kante, N. (2022). Evaluation and visualization of healthcare semantic models. *Evaluation*, 323, 91773–91775.

Pandey, K. and Panchal, R. (2019). Data capturing and retrieval from wireless sensor networks using Semantic Web [Online]. Available at: https://papers.ssrn.com/sol3/papers.cfm?abstract_id=3555014 [Accessed 10 February 2020].

Tiwari, S. and Abraham, A. (2020). Semantic assessment of smart healthcare ontology. *International Journal of Web Information Systems*, 16(4), 475–491 [Online]. Available at: https://doi.org/10.1108/IJWIS-05-2020-0027.

Tiwari, S., Ortiz-Rodriguez, F., Jabbar, M.A. (eds) (2022). Semantic modelling for healthcare applications: An introduction. In *Semantic Models in IoT and eHealth Applications*. Elsevier, Cambridge [Online]. Available at: https://www.elsevier.com/books/semantic-models-in-iot-and-ehealth-applications/tiwari/978-0-323-91773-5.

Heart Rate Monitoring Using IoT and AI

Health plays a crucial role in the lives of humans, irrespective of the remaining things on this Earth. To lead a good life with normal health, all health-related parameters must work properly and accurately. Regular heartbeat is one among them. One in four deaths and more than 10 million cases per year in India are due to heart disease and stroke. The percentage may increase when considering the rest of the world. An irregular heartbeat, also called arrhythmia, may not be recognized by a person who experiences it. It may not have real symptoms and may occur when the electrical signals or impulses do not function properly inside the cardiac system. But people can lead a normal life if it is identified and diagnosed properly. The idea is to design a small chip-like device that can be carriable and connected to the cloud using the Internet of Things (IoT). The sensors include a heartbeat sensor and temperature sensor that will collect and send heart signals and temperature continuously to the cloud. These signals will be scrutinized by an AI (Artificial Intelligence) model. This model will be trained to detect the different kinds of heartbeats as per the situation the person lives in. The model learns the patterns of heartbeat signals and tries to recognize the patterns. The learned model tries to predict irregular heartbeats in future recordings. This system is also capable of sending a message to the person if there is an irregular (unhealthy) heartbeat identified. It may encourage the person to visit a doctor if they find that it is a regular problem. The Semantic Web has its significance in exchanging and making use of collected information among systems. In this way, this work will help people to recognize and identify heartbeat-related problems at acute stages.

Chapter written by Kalpana Murugan, Cherukuri Nikhil Kumar, Donthu Sai Subash and Sangam Deva Kishore Reddy.

8.1. Introduction

The first code for 1,200 m distance communication was invented in 1833. Since then, many great mathematicians and scientists have made statements on wireless communications and equipped machines with the best senses to act intelligently. In 1966, German computer science pioneer Karl Steinbuch said: "In a few decades, computers will be interwoven into almost every industrial product". Twenty-four years after his statement, in 1990, the first IoT device named the "toaster" was considered and could be turned on and off over the Internet. In 1999, Kevin Ashton coined the phrase "Internet of Things (IoT)". It was a great year for the IoT era. IoT makes devices smart by connecting to the Internet and providing them with felicitous sense organs (sensors, actuators, more). The connections among them enable the exchange of data and the ability to act intelligently according to the situations.

According to the standards established by the World Wide Web Consortium (W3C), an extended version of the World Wide Web (WWW) is considered to be the Semantic Web. The aim is to make data on the Internet machine-readable and use the information on the Internet for several purposes, such as reusing and sharing. The web ontology language and Resource Description Framework (RDF) are the technologies utilized to authorize the encoding of semantic data. Formally, the aforementioned technologies utilized for encoding the semantic data are used to represent metadata. Tim Berners-Lee coined this term. The SWoT (Semantic Web of Things) is a field that has recently emerged, developed through the integration of two paradigms, the Semantics Web and the IoT. IoT interoperability is still in its infancy and poses challenges to its efficient development and use.

Health plays a crucial role in lives of humans, irrespective of the remaining things on this Earth. To lead a good life with normal health, all health-related parameters must function properly and accurately. Regular heartbeat is one among them. An irregular heartbeat, also called arrhythmia, may not be recognized by a person who experiences it. It may not have real symptoms experienced by humans and may occur when the electrical signals or impulses do not function properly inside the cardiac system. But people can lead a normal life if it is identified and diagnosed properly. Cardiovascular disease (CVD) is the main cause of death in the world, taking approximately 17.9 million people every year. CVDs are a set of vascular and heart diseases, including cerebrovascular disease, rheumatic cardiac disease, coronary cardiac disease etc. Cardiac strokes and attacks account for more than 85% of deaths from cardiovascular disease, and a third of deaths occur in people under the age of 70. After its onset, symptoms may be experienced by the patients. There are four types of arrhythmias: slow heartbeats, also called bradycardia, fast heartbeats, also called tachycardia, irregular heartbeats, also called fibrillation and early heartbeats or premature contraction. In addition, there are various kinds of arrhythmias, for instance atrial fibrillation and flutter, and long QT syndrome. Among these arrhythmias, most of them do not give rise to problems and are not serious; however, a few of them improve the risk of cardiac arrest or stroke.

The electrocardiogram (EKG) is the most widely used test for diagnosing irregular heartbeats because it presents information from each cardiac cycle through a series of wave groups in the PR and QT intervals. The P wave is the first group of waves in the series, followed by the QRS complex, and T wave with PR in the first segment and ST in the second segment. When the heart is excited by the sinus node and advances to the atrium, a P wave is generated due to atria depolarization and reflects the depolarization process of atria. The first and second halves represent the right atrium and left atrium. There are three groups of waves associated with a normal QRS complex: the first downward wave is known as the Q wave, the high peak after the downward wave is known as the R wave and the S wave is produced downward after the R wave. These three waves represent the electrical activation of the ventricles, and they are often referred to as QRS complexes as these are closely related. The left and right ventricular depolarization is reflected in this group of waves. After the ST segment, the T wave represents a relatively low, long wave created by ventricular repolarization. If necessary, doctors perform additional tests. The patient may receive medicine, surgery to repair the overstimulating nerves or tool placement, which will correct the irregular heartbeat in the heart. If the heart condition (particularly arrhythmia) is not treated, the heart may not be ready to pump an adequate amount of blood around the body, resulting in injury to the brain, heart or other organs within the body.

Everyone has a different healthy resting heart rate. But the AHA (American Heart Association) recommends that a person should have 60–100 bpm (beats per minute). Fitter people will have lower resting heart rates. For example, the resting heart rate of Olympic athletes is often less than 60 bpm because their hearts are very effective. Likewise, depending on the situation, people's heartbeats vary and should be monitored carefully.

AI is making machines process the tasks done by humans through the simulation of human intelligence. This can be done by developing models with data (labeled or unlabeled). In general, regular heartbeats can be identified easily as they are periodic, but irregular heartbeats require careful scrutinization of EKG signals by medical practitioners. It is a requirement to train the models to perform the same scrutinization for the identification of irregular heartbeat by machines. Machine Learning (ML) and deep learning models are being developed for heartbeat classification based on EKG using different techniques. These current learned models are extensively trained on huge datasets and follow typical learning methods.

There are also assistant systems, which can track regular and irregular heartbeats without physical contact. Depending on the way the sounds reflect back to the speaker, the smart systems can identify and predict heartbeats individually. These systems work when a person sits 1–2 feet away from the smart speaker. Similarly, smartwatches are also now capable of recording real-time heartbeats. Specifically, deep learning models look for patterns in the data and whenever the networks see complex relationships, they may be weakened or strengthened. However, it depends on the sets of data we are using for training, testing and validation. This work is focused on developing a heart rate monitoring device to collect and store the data on the cloud with continuous monitoring, and developing an AI model to predict a different kind of irregular heartbeat. This collected data will be used by the model to predict the irregular heartbeats of an individual.

This research aims to develop an initial prototype system to collect continuous heart rate/EKG signals and store them in the cloud under various conditions. Later, the plans are to analyze and infer heart rate conditions from the collected data. Several factors can affect heart rate, such as stress, diabetes, health problems, disorders, structural changes of the heart, daily food intake, smoking and different kind of medications.

8.2. Literature survey

Abba and Garba (2019) proposed the implementation and design of an intelligent framework based on the IoT for cardiac rate control and the monitoring system. The design consists of a breadboard, liquid crystal display, heart rate sensor, Wi-Fi module, and other electronic components to detect and control the heart rate from any place remotely. This sensor records the heart rate and sends it to the cloud for analysis and visualization. The heart rate is captured as data signals and processed before it is sent to the webserver. Devi and Kalaivani (2020) developed an ML and IoT-enabled EKG telemonitoring system for the diagnosis of cardiac arrhythmia disease that can notably diminish the scale of the current EKG systems. The ML classifier model has been developed with different kinds of features. This enabled system analyzes the dynamic and statistical features of a raw EKG signal using the Pan Tompkins QRS detection algorithm, which has great potential to improve the classifier accuracy. To capture the variable features of the cardiac signal, the proposed system uses the RR interval of the wave group. Raut et al. (2021) proposed a Real-Time Heart Examining System supported by IoT. It can predict cardiac abnormalities in patients and the level of oxygen in the blood. The focus is to identify the main components required for heart rate monitoring and develop a low power communication between the intelligent IoT system and mobile app. This system is capable of storing the data, and patients can communicate with the doctor via Wi-Fi and retrieve data through the same system. Valsalan et al. (2020) proposed a Health Examining System supported by IoT that examines the patients' cardiac rate, room humidity, body temperature and room temperature. The sensors record the basic parameters of the room and the aforementioned patients' parameters. All of this information is sent to the person's smartphone via IoT and is also stored on medical servers based on the values received. The authorized personal access system was developed so that doctors could access the information from a distance, and predict and diagnose diseases. Banerjee et al. (2019) developed and proposed heartbeat monitoring using IoT. This system has certain remote detecting elements to monitor various health parameters, such as a person's cardiac rate and temperature. In addition, the proposed system measures particular proteins that the body secrets excessively before specific cardiac operations, known as a fatty acid-binding proteins, so that cardiac attacks can be detected. The health parameters collected by the sensors transmit the data over the Internet through the microcontroller that is connected to the sensor. For analysis purposes, the database stores the collected data. This data will be compared with the standard statistical data to identify the irregularities in the health parameters and suggest potential measures in an emergency to ensure a higher chance of survival. Islam et al. (2020) and Murugan et al. (2021c) developed an intelligent healthcare monitoring system using the IoT. This system has five sensors that are used to measure the patients' health parameters, such as temperature, cardiac rate, room conditions (for instance, room temperature), levels of CO and CO_2. The error percentage was calculated by comparing the real values and sensor collected values and it was less than 5%. Based on the effectiveness of the developed system, it could be used by doctors to monitor patients remotely during the Covid-19 pandemic and normally. Sekhar Babu et al. (2019) proposed a multiple regression model for the prediction of cardiac attacks supported by ML and the IoT. They tried to design an ML model for the prediction of heart attacks using the previous cardiac rate of the person and usage of IoT devices for the location of a heart attack. This system tries the perfect detection of coronary diseases and relapses for heart diseases. These will be monitored and communicated with the person via the IoT, which also stores the data on the webserver. Agliari et al. (2020) developed statistical algorithms to identify potential cardiac pathologies through time series ML of heartbeat variability and related markers. They have collected a huge amount of data by marking whether the patients have cardiac disease. A total of 49 markers were created to obtain a detailed description of heart variabilities. All of these markers are used as inputs to train the ML models such as multi-layer feed-forward networks, and are intended to identify the features that can distinguish the networks built over healthy patients or patients with heart disease. The overall analysis proves that ML in the classification of cardiac pathologies using heart rate variability (HRV) time series is possible and can also bring benefits in terms of social costs. It also concluded that this approach could be extended to other pathologies, provided that adequate experimental datasets are available.

Authors	Algorithm used	Parameters measured	Device
Abba and Garba (2019)	Cloud Computing	Heart Rate Sensor	Wi-Fi
Devi and Kalaivani (2020)	Pan Tompkins QRS detection algorithm	Electrocardiogram telemonitoring	IoT
Raut et al. (2021)	-	Real-Time Heart Examination	IoT
Valsalan et al. (2020)	-	Patients' cardiac rate, room humidity, body temperature, room temperature	Authorized personal access system with IoT
Banerjee et al. (2019)	-	Humans' cardiac rate and human temperature	Heartbeat Monitoring Using IoT
Islam et al. (2020)	-	Temperature, cardiac rate, room temperature, levels of CO, CO_2	IoT
Sekhar Babu et al. (2019)	Machine Learning	Cardiac rate	IoT
Agliari et al. (2020)	Statistical algorithms	Cardiac rate	-
Yeh et al. (2021)	Deep Neural Networks (DNN)	Electrocardiogram (EKG)	-
Murugan et al. (2021a)	-	Fall Detection	GSM
Murugan et al. (2021b)	Tracking algorithm	Monitor medications	IoT

Table 8.1. *Comparison of literature review*

Yeh et al. (2021) have developed a Deep Neural Network (DNN) model to interpret EKG signals during anesthesia evaluation. This study uses CNNs (Convolutional Neural Networks) to categorize the EKG images and the IoT to develop prototypes for measuring EKG. It also uses DNNs to classify the types of EKG signals, which are separated into ST depression, sinus rhythm, ST elevation and QRS widening. They have used three CNN architectures such as AlexNet, SqueezeNet and Residual Networks (ResNet), with half of the data (50%) used for testing and training. It is concluded that ResNet performs better based on the accuracy and kappa statistics. This study concludes that real-time EKG can be measured via the IoT, while DNN can differentiate between the given types of EKG. Murugan et al. (2021a) proposed a fall detection and avoidance system for the patients and aged humans in case of emergencies and also sends an alert message to the caretaker. Murugan et al. (2021b) proposed and designed a programmed microcontroller and semi-autonomous robot that uses the so-called line tracking or following robot method that reminds patients to take medication at the right time. It is a kind of robot that advises patients and elderly people on when and what kind of medicine to take.

8.3. Heart rate monitoring system

The proposed Heart Rate Monitoring System aims to develop a standard prototype system to collect the continuous heart rate/EKG signals and store them in the cloud under various conditions. The early prototype system was designed using the Arduino UNO development board (see Figure 8.1), ESP8266 Wi-Fi module, ATMEGA 328p controller, Thermistor, heart rate sensor and other required electronic components.

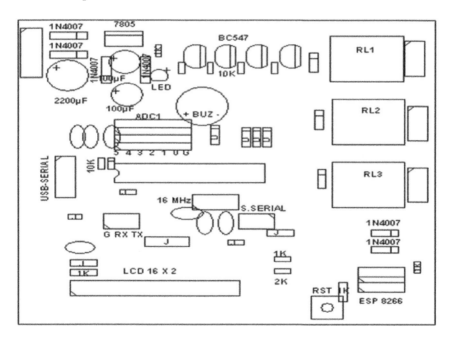

Figure 8.1. *The layout of the Arduino UNO development board*

Figure 8.1 depicts the Arduino UNO development board which has all the annotations of required electronic components, holes and connections on the board to make a potential circuit board. This development board is used to make all of the circuit connections with the potentiometer, ATMEGA 328p, ESP8266 Wi-Fi module, 16x2 LCD and also the required diodes, resistors, capacitors, transistors with the required values.

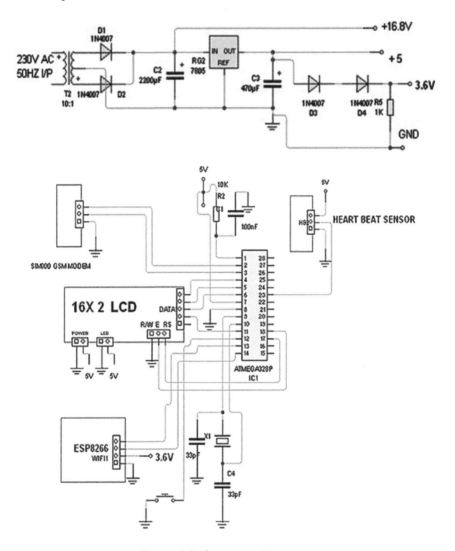

Figure 8.2. *System architecture*

This Arduino UNO with required electronic components on top of it acts as a microcontroller with required digital input/output pins and also contains everything needed from collecting and processing the sensor information (signals) to send them to the cloud for analysis and visualization. The AC supply can be provided for this

UNO as it is connected with a step-down transformer, AC to DC converter, and regulator.

Figure 8.2 shows the architecture of the proposed system with all required components and their connections. It also shows how the AC power supply is converted into DC voltage required for the Arduino board with necessary electronic components. The ATMEGA 328p controller is the main component of the system, which is placed in the center of the architecture and controls all of the sensors and electronic components. Pins 23, 24 of the controllers are connected to the heartbeat sensor and temperature sensor. The heartbeat sensor and temperature sensor require 5V input and the other terminal is grounded. Pins 13, 14 of the controllers are connected to the ESP8266 Wi-Fi module, which requires an input of 3.6V. This powerful Wi-Fi module has adequate onboard processing power and storage capability for storing the data from the integrated sensors and other particular devices connected to it. This module is built with an onboard system-on-chip integrated with the standard protocols such as TCP/IP, which can give the microcontroller connected to it access to the Wi-Fi network. This helps to communicate and store the sensor collected data in the cloud. Pins 2, 3 of the controller are connected to the Arduino GSM shield to send messages in case of emergency. Pins 4, 5, 6, 11, 17, 18 of the controllers are connected to the 16 × 2 LED display to show the heart rate and temperature. Finally, the panic switch is connected to pin 12 of the controller.

The prototype design's flow chart is shown in Figure 8.3. Arduino UNO is equipped with a heartbeat sensor, a thermistor, an emergency button and an Arduino GSM module to collect required health parameters information and send warning messages in case of an emergency. The heartbeat sensor works on a simple principle with a pair of the Light Dependent Resistors (LDRs) or photodiodes and Light Emitting Diodes (LEDs). We can usually feel our pulse in our fingers as the heart pumps the oxygenated blood to all of the organs in a human body. This sensor needs to be kept or held between the two fingers. As the LED emits light onto the finger and the LDR detects the intensity of the light received, the signal passes through the controller and is converted into digital values. When light falls on the finger, some of the light is absorbed by blood and the remaining reflects onto the detector. A thermistor is a resistance thermometer in which the internal resistance depends on the outside temperature. The emergency button can be clicked in emergencies. When a person's heartbeat and temperature readings reach the maximum limit (i.e. 100), a text will be sent to the caretaker's smartphone using the GSM Arduino module.

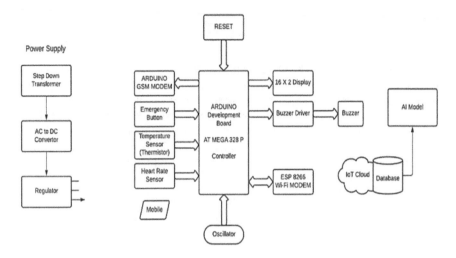

Figure 8.3. *System flow chart*

The GSM Arduino shield enables an Arduino board to send and receive SMS, connect to the Internet, and with the use of the GSM library in the shield, one can make voice calls. To do all these with the Arduino shield and an Arduino, a SIM card is needed to insert into the holder given on the shield. On the shield, slide the metal bracket away from the edge and lift the base.

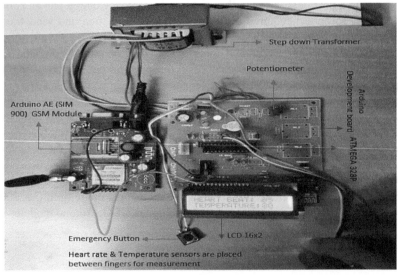

a)

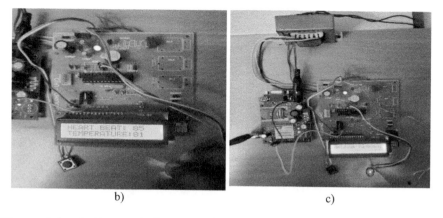

b)   c)

Figure 8.4. *a) Proposed Prototype System with entire setup and electronic components annotation; b) displays the recorded values of heartrate and temperature on 16 × 2 LED; c) depicts the Arduino GSM shield and displays "message sending" text on the 16 × 2 LED screen in emergencies (when the recorded values reach the limit). For a color version of this figure, see www.iste.co.uk/mehta/tools.zip*

Place the SIM card into the plastic holder, so that the metal contact points toward the shield. Push the SIM to the board and lock it. The values of heart rate, temperature and panic rate values will be stored in the cloud. These parameters can be visualized on mobiles and laptops at ThingSpeak. Figure 8.4 depicts the connections of all of the components required for the initial prototype design. All of the components in Figure 8.4(a) are annotated and as aforementioned, the heart rate and temperature sensors are placed between fingers for measurement. Figure 8.4 also shows the step-down transformer which is powered by an AC power supply and an LCD screen that displays the values recorded by sensors. A SIM card has been inserted into the GSM shield for communication between the system and caretaker or nurse.

8.4. Results and discussion

The proposed early prototype can collect information from the heart rate sensor and temperature sensor and store it in the cloud. From Figure 8.5, the visualizations of the heartbeat versus time can be observed, where the heart rate sensor collects the information and converts it into a digital value before sending it to the cloud, and temperature versus time and also the panic versus time, where the red dots on the plot show that the person has clicked the emergency button (see Figure 8.5(c)).

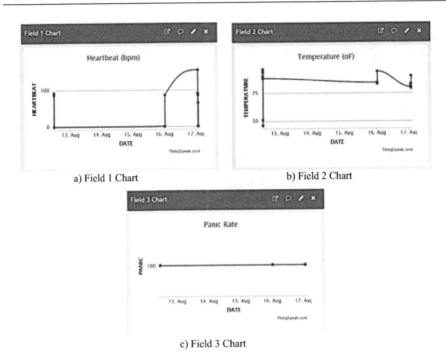

a) Field 1 Chart

b) Field 2 Chart

c) Field 3 Chart

Figure 8.5. *Visualizations and storage of a) recorded heartbeat, b) temperature and c) panic rate in the cloud. For a color version of this figure, see www.iste.co.uk/mehta/tools.zip*

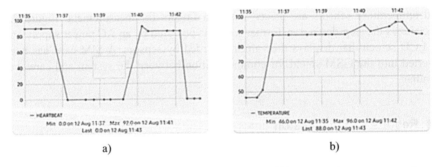

a)

b)

Figure 8.6. *Case – 1: Recorded a) heartrate and b) temperature are normal. For a color version of this figure, see www.iste.co.uk/mehta/tools.zip*

In case 1, the graphs show the recordings of the normal heart rate and temperature of a healthy person (see Figure 8.6). The red dots in the graph represent inputs that were recorded in the cloud at different periods. Both the values of heart rate and temperature are below 100, so no SMS is sent to the caretaker's cell phone, but all values are monitored and saved in the cloud. In case 2, if one of the recorded values (temperature and heart rate) exceeds the limit value set to 100, an SMS is sent to the caretaker's mobile phone, and the entries are shown in Figure 8.7 (the black circles represent the exceeded recorded values). In case of emergencies, the person can click the emergency button.

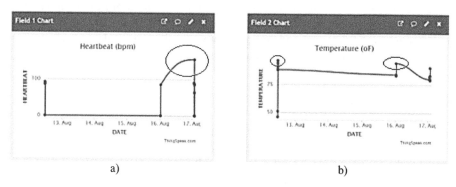

Figure 8.7. *Case – 2: Recorded a) heartrate and b) temperature are high (not normal). For a color version of this figure, see www.iste.co.uk/mehta/tools.zip*

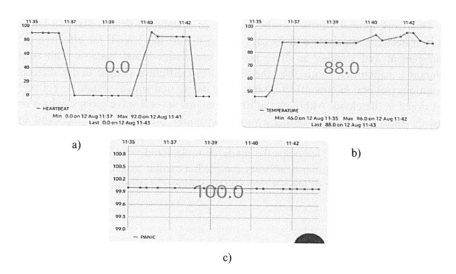

Figure 8.8. *Visualizations (in mobile) of recorded a) heartbeat, b) temperature and c) panic rate. For a color version of this figure, see www.iste.co.uk/mehta/tools.zip*

This system is capable of collecting heart rate and temperature in different situations, which helps to collect and save data in the cloud server where, in turn, the data can be used to train the ML model. The prototype has limitations. Whenever the person's temperature and heart rate are above 100, a message will be sent to the caretaker who helps to take immediate action. These limitations can be customized in the code during data collection. The sensors that collect the data are not as accurate. To design a standard system for the data acquisition of health parameters, proper validation of collected data is necessary with real data. The system architecture can be designed and equipped into a small chip for data acquisition of the continuous heart rate and health parameters of a person.

8.5. Conclusion and future works

This study develops the heart rate monitoring system with basic electronic components, IoT, cloud server and with all requirements so that patients can contact the caretaker or nurse in case of emergency. It also plans to develop a standard design to collect health parameters accurately at all times by conducting experiments with available components on the proposed system, and develop the smart model for collecting and categorizing data based on the state of the situation in which the person lives.

This work extends further to the drafting of a standard design that can collect data on health parameters and focuses on the use of the SWoT for effective data management and storage, as these provide knowledge-based systems with better autonomic capability. With this, the EKG from different people under different conditions (several factors affecting heart rate mentioned above) should be collected and stored in the cloud. Although the EKG contains several wave groups, which can provide information about cardiac entire functioning, the goal is to understand and find patterns or insights into a person's heart rate and its functioning over a lifetime in different conditions. This helps the model to understand the patterns in-depth and can be used to infer irregular heartbeats and predict cardiac arrest. The AI model can also be extended further to predict the state of emotion or condition the person is in, based on the heart rate.

8.6. References

Abba, S. and Garba, A.M. (2019). An IoT-based smart framework for a human heartbeat rate monitoring and control system. *Proceedings of the 6th International Electronic Conference on Sensors and Applications*, 42(1), 36.

Agliari, E., Barra, A., Barra, O.A., Fachechi, A., Vento, L.F., Moretti, L. (2020). Detecting cardiac pathologies via machine learning on heart-rate variability time series and related markers. *Scientific Reports*, 10(1), 1–18.

Arduino (2018). Arduino GSM shield guide [Online]. Available at: www.arduino.cc [Accessed 16 August 2021].

Banerjee, S., Paul, S., Sharma, R., Brahma, A. (2019). Heartbeat monitoring using IoT. *IEEE 9th Annual Information Technology, Electronics and Mobile Communication Conference, IEMCON 2018.* doi: 10.1109/IEMCON.2018.8614921.

Devi, R.L. and Kalaivani, V. (2020). Machine learning and IoT-based cardiac arrhythmia diagnosis using statistical and dynamic features of ECG. *Journal of Supercomputing*, 76(9), 6533–6544.

ELPROCUS (n.d.). Heart beat sensor, working and application [Online]. Available at: www.elprocus.com/heartbeat-sensor-working-application/ [Accessed 16 August 2021].

Islam, M.M., Rahaman, A., Islam, M.R. (2020). Development of smart healthcare monitoring system in IoT environment. *SN Computer Science*, 1(3). Springer, Singapore. doi: 10.1007/s42979-020-00195-y.

Jain, S.K. and Bhaumik, B. (2017). An energy efficient ECG signal processor detecting cardiovascular diseases on smartphone. *IEEE Transactions on Biomedical Circuits and Systems*, 11(2), 314–323.

Koshti, M., Ganorkar, S., Student, M.E. (2016). IoT based health monitoring system by using Raspberry Pi and ECG signal. *International Journal of Innovative Research in Science, Engineering and Technology (An ISO Certified Organization)*, 3297(5), 8977–8985.

Medical News Today (2020). What to know about arrythmia. Medically reviewed by Deborah Weatherspoon Ph.D, R.N., CRNA, Written by Tim Newman.

Muneeswaran, V., Murugan, K., Pavithra, E., Bhuvaneswari, B., Joshna, K. (2021). Automatic injection system for healthcare applications. *The Patent Office Journal*, 25(2021), 27393.

Murugan, K., Muneeswaran, V., Reddy, S.A., Dharmendra, R., Imran, S., (2021a). Fall detection and avoidance system for oldsters. *The Patent Office Journal*, 24(2021), 26323.

Murugan, K., Khan, M.A.A., Kylash, M.R., Muralidharan, M. (2021b). Medicine distribution robot and humanless intervention for Covid-19 affected people (AKM MED ASSISTIVE BOT). *IOP Conference Series: Materials Science and Engineering*, 1049(1), 012013. doi: 10.1088/1757-899X/1049/1/012013.

Murugan, K., Muneeswaran, V., Murugeswari, S., Kumar Reddy, A.R., Kumar, T.M., Ammaar, P. (2021c). Real time patient health monitoring and indication to doctors using IoT. *The Patent Office Journal*, 24(2021), 26308.

Murugan, K., Murugeswari, S., Reddy, J.P., Chandra, M.H., Reddy, P.V. (2021d). Smart medical telemetry acquisition system. *2nd International Conference on Electronics and Sustainable Communication Systems (ICESC).* doi: 10.1109/ICESC51422.2021.9532775.

NIH – National Heart, Lung, Blood Institute (2021). Arrhythmia. Health Topic. NIH-NHLBI.

Raut, S., Vahora, S., Shah, V., Ranka, R., Reddy, M. (2021). IOT based real-time heart monitoring system. *International Research Journal of Engineering and Technology (IRJET)*, 8(4), 3902–3909 [Online]. Available at: https://www.irjet.net/volume8-issue4 [Accessed 2 August 2021].

Sekhar Babu, B., Likhitha, V., Narendra, I., Harika, G. (2019). Prediction and detection of heart attack using machine learning and Internet of Things. *International Journal of Engineering and Advanced Technology*, 8(4), 105–108.

ThingSpeak (2022). ThingSpeak for IoT Projects [Online]. Available at: www.thingspeak.com [Accessed 16 August 2021].

Valsalan, P., Baomar, T.A.B., Baabood, A.H.O. (2020). IoT based health monitoring system. *Journal of Critical Reviews*, 7(4), 739–743.

Wikipedia (2021a). Internet of Things. *Wikipedia, The Free Encyclopedia* [Online]. Available at: https://en.wikipedia.org/w/index.php?title=Internet_of_things&oldid=1084983822 [Accessed 14 April 2021].

Wikipedia (2021b). Machine learning. *Wikipedia, The Free Encyclopedia* [Online]. Available at: https://en.wikipedia.org/w/index.php?title=Machine_learning&oldid=1084622324 [Accessed 14 August 2021].

Wikipedia (2021c). Semantic Web. *Wikipedia, The Free Encyclopedia* [Online]. Available at: https://en.wikipedia.org/w/index.php?title=Semantic_Web&oldid=1080931954 [Accessed 16 April 2022].

World Health Organization (2021). INDIA. *Health-topics, Cardiovascular-diseases*. WHO.

Yeh, L.-R., Chen, W.-C., Chan, H.-Y., Lu, N.-H., Wang, C.-Y., Twan, W.-H., Du, W.-C., Huang, Y.-H., Hsu, S.-Y., Chen, T.-B. (2021). Integrating ECG monitoring and classification via IoT and deep neural networks. *Biosensors*, 11(188), 1–12 [Online]. Available at: https://doi.org/10.3390/bios11060188.

IoT Security Issues and Its Defensive Methods

The Internet of Things, which is abbreviated as IoT, refers to the network of physical objects that are connected or embedded with sensors and software to perform the desired task by connecting and interchanging data over the Internet. In this scenario, every object is provided with a unique identifier and the ability to exchange data automatically, which is openly subjected to vulnerabilities if it is not secured properly, especially when connected to the Internet, providing a large attack surface. Moreover, numerous high-profile incidents were reported, where commonly used IoT devices were used for cyber-attacks, which have been a great concern and have drawn attention toward IoT security. IoT security is one of the crucial steps in developing and implementing IoT devices. It refers to the technology segment which is engrossed in safeguarding the networks and devices associated with the IoT. IoT security focuses on the methods that tend to establish a secured Internet connection and the network to which the devices or objects are connected. It engages with a wide range of technologies, such as the Application Program Interface, Public Key Infrastructure (PKI) and Authentication. It also focuses on the methodologies, such as Network Access Control (NAC), Segmentation, security gateways, patch management, regular software updates, team integration and consumer education. Moreover, IoT security methods provide an efficient solution for security challenges, such as remote exposure, lack of industry foresight and resource constraints.

9.1. Introduction

The IoT is one of the key technologies of the 21st century, with a wide range of applications in various sectors. The IoT is a network of items or things that operate together with sensors, actuators, software and other technologies to connect and exchange data across linked devices and systems over the Internet. The IoT is one of

Chapter written by Keshavi NALLA and Seshu VARDHAN POTHABATHULA.

the widely accompanied global technologies that create the webwork of various devices that communicate effectively. It enables the devices to exchange information among them and work relevantly. The IoT involves the extension of the Internet beyond mobile devices and personal computers. This technology provides a platform for users to connect and control devices remotely. Therefore, it promotes efficiency in the performance, economic benefits, and also decreases human interference and high risk while handling any tedious tasks. The IoT facilitates users to control devices and monitor tasks from the comfort of their homes from the tips of their fingers. Although there are multiple benefits in implementing the IoT, it is also prone to various vulnerabilities and challenges that should be addressed appropriately. Cyber security and privacy are the major risks posing a considerable predicament for users, industries and business organizations. Moreover, many highly prevalent cyber-attacks perfectly demonstrated the vulnerabilities of the IoT and made security and privacy a primary concern where immediate measures should be implemented. Now, security has become an important segment of implementing IoT technology. The IoT is much more diverse when compared to other traditional computing devices, which makes it more vulnerable to cyber-attacks in different ways. Most of the devices involved in IoT applications are comprised of nearly identical components with similar characteristics, which amplifies the extent of vulnerability (Zhang et al. 2014). It has also been found that the number of links that are interconnected is probably unprecedented, which makes it clear that most of the devices and components involved in IoT applications could easily establish connections and communicate with other devices in an irregular way. This creates a necessity to consider tools, tactics and other techniques that can be used to improve security. Due to the continuous involvement of smart gadgets and appliances in daily life, this technology is becoming more passive. However, implementing devices that are weakly protected increases the risk of loss of data and puts the user's privacy at stake (Tawalbeh et al. 2020). The vulnerabilities of any gadgets or appliances make security experts investigate major challenges and solutions, in order to solve them at the industry level. Some of the security issues that are financially challenging the industrial and business organizations are mentioned in Figure 9.1.

The IoT is a technology that provides a large surface for cyber-attacks due to the availability of several access points. This technology uses an Internet-supported connectivity platform to create a network of devices, which makes it much more vulnerable to malicious threats. Since accessibility is considered to be most important to control or monitor devices, it creates an opportunity for hackers to interact and control devices remotely. Though most business organizations have been undergoing the digital transformation to improve business strategy and deliver a better product to their customers, the automotive and healthcare sectors have been expanding their selections and opting for accessible IoT devices for better productivity and cost-efficiency (Mahmoud et al. 2015). This led to a great digital revolution, creating much more dependency on emerging technologies than ever before. An increase in technological reliance may amplify the magnitude of successful data breaches and industries being dependent on a single technology that is quite vulnerable has been a primary concern. Despite this dependency, most of the companies who are paying much more attention to the digital revolution are not ready to invest a sum of money and resources in securing the devices or appliances used. This shows that the manufacturers and organizations in industry lack foresight, which makes them a premier target for cybersecurity threats and attacks. Moreover, not every device is inculcated with better computing power to integrate sophisticated antivirus software and firewalls, where some devices are barely integrated with the capability to connect with other devices. Therefore, resource constraints are considered to be one of the major security challenges in terms of IoT devices. However, by adopting various IoT security measures, organizations could also improve their protection strategies and protocols to defend their data and systems from cyber threats, such as tampering and spoofing. The security protocol starts with designing the IoT security architecture with high protection strategies, such as threat modeling in the design phase of an IoT system. Identifying the trust zones and boundaries over a security architecture or model plays a very important role in defending our devices from malicious attacks. The use of PKI digital certificates and enabling network and Application Programming Interface (API) security are considered to be some of the key measures in implementing IoT security. Some of the other methodologies, such as NAC and Segmentation, can also be used to safeguard devices (Husamuddin et al. 2007).

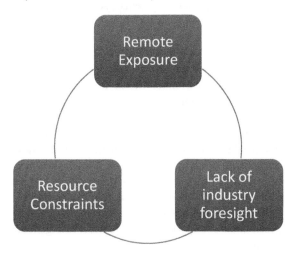

Figure 9.1. *Basic security issues (Shea 2021)*

9.2. IoT security architecture

9.2.1. *Typical IoT architecture*

Whether it is the current service-oriented IoT design or the four- or five-layer IoT architecture that further divides the application layer, its essence can be divided into three logical layers (Zhang et al. 2019). The perception layer, network layer and application layer are the layers from bottom to top. Each section first presents the IoT architecture at a high standard, then moves on to security challenges and research status at various levels.

9.2.1.1. *Security issues with perception layer*

The perception layer's principal purpose is to perceive external data in its entirety. Its equipment mostly consists of ultrasonic, infrared and humidity sensors, as well as picture capturing systems. The data collected by these devices will be analyzed and utilized immediately. Security issues may arise at the perception layer. An example of smart IoT security architecture includes: protocol security, base station security, tag forging and tag encryption security, which are all concerns. Routing protocol security, cryptographic techniques and trusted node management are all concerns with wireless sensors. Some microelectromechanical system (MEMs) and nanoelectromechanical system (NEMs) safety, among other things, are also provided. By examining a huge number of embedded device system firmware, Costin et al. (2014) uncovered multiple exploitable high-risk system vulnerabilities. To secure embedded systems' security, some researchers have proposed establishing a lightweight trusted execution environment, although this solution has a computational complexity and a relatively limited scope. Researchers have indeed created a test architecture for small embedded electronic systems, although static testing and vulnerability detection approaches cannot defend embedded device security in real time. Based on the device's unique physical properties and key generation technique (Sachidananda et al. 2016), this strategy not only saves device resources by separating keys, but also successfully protects against side-channel assaults. To establish device authentication, some researchers use features of the user's human body obtained by the wearable device, such as gait, sliding screen strength and so on. This approach allows for device and user dual authentication while conserving resources. In conclusion, the perception layer's security requirements are intertwined. For example, a researcher can restore the user's heart rate information and obtain the communication key by analyzing the electrical signal information entropy based on the heart rate generation key through the side channel. As a result, to create an efficient security defense strategy, it is a requirement that the security requirements of various components of the perception layer's devices, as well as their mutual effects, are properly evaluated (Rostami et al. 2014).

9.2.1.2. *Security issues at the network layer*

The network layer is primarily responsible for safely and efficiently sending the information obtained by the perception layer to the application layer. The network layer is primarily responsible for network infrastructures, such as the Internet, mobile networks and some professional networks (such as broadcast television networks and national power private networks). A local area network, a core network and an access network are the three types of network layers. GPRS security and WIFI connection security are two that must be considered when accessing the network (Burhan et al. 2018). Many researchers have used lightweight algorithms and protocols to fight against sensor network assaults. However, the applicability of most of these lightweight algorithms and protocols has to be improved due to a lack of testing for device power and network bandwidth usage. Traditional network assaults continue to dominate the attack on the network layer's communication channel at this time (such as replay, middleman and spoofing attacks). However, defending against classic cyber-attacks is insufficient. The network layer communication protocols have evolved with the growth of the IoT. A comparison of centralized and distributed approaches has increased. Identity authentication, key agreement, data secrecy and integrity protection are all difficulties that arise when data are transmitted from one network to another. As a result, the security dangers that will be confronted will grow more significant, necessitating increased study and attention.

9.2.1.3. *Security issues with application layer*

The application layer is also an essential value of the IoT. Mobile payment, smart grid, smart home and other common applications to examine the application layer, can be divided into two levels: IoT application and application support platform. Smart grid security, telemedicine security, smart traffic security and other IoT applications are examples of security concerns. There is also platform security for service support, middleware technology security, information development platform security and so on. It is worth studying how Thomas and Ned use blockchain technology to achieve anonymous sharing of IoT devices. Furthermore, as the number of IoT devices grows, DDoS attacks will grow in size, and the cloud server's capacity to endure DDoS attacks will need to improve. Because application services have the most direct contact with consumers, protecting private user information, while providing services is the most critical security responsibility. According to a review of program source code, more than half of the applications on Samsung's home automation platform have excessive permissions, which could lead to user-sensitive data leakage or malicious home device control. Multiple access control models for sensitive operations and privacy data in the protection program have been developed by existing researchers, but their applicability and security must be enhanced (Sethi and Sarangi 2017). Although the preceding talk focuses on security challenges in the IoT architecture, the security concerns for each stage are interrelated. Its most critical feature is data privacy protection. Any link failure may result in the leakage of the user's personal information. The security architecture of all IoT layers should be included in the deployment of IoT security. Figure 9.2 demonstrates the typical IoT architecture in a better way.

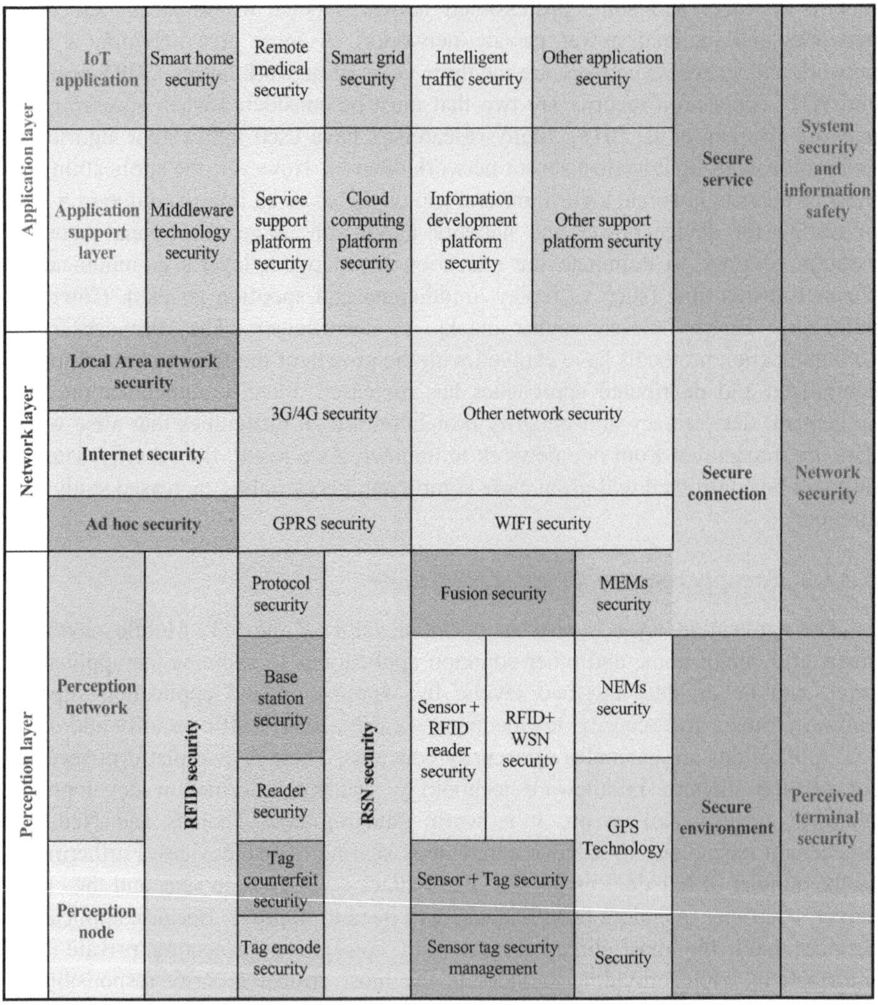

Application layer	IoT application	Smart home security	Remote medical security	Smart grid security	Intelligent traffic security	Other application security	Secure service	System security and information safety
	Application support layer	Middleware technology security	Service support platform security	Cloud computing platform security	Information development platform security	Other support platform security		
Network layer	Local Area network security		3G/4G security		Other network security		Secure connection	Network security
	Internet security							
	Ad hoc security		GPRS security		WIFI security			
Perception layer	Perception network	RFID security	Protocol security	RSN security	Fusion security	MEMs security	Secure environment	Perceived terminal security
			Base station security		Sensor + RFID reader security	RFID+ WSN security	NEMs security		
			Reader security				GPS Technology		
	Perception node		Tag counterfeit security		Sensor + Tag security			
			Tag encode security		Sensor tag security management	Security		

Figure 9.2. *Typical IoT security architecture (Zhang et al. 2019).*
For a color version of this figure, see www.iste.co.uk/mehta/tools.zip

9.2.2. *Centralized and distributed approaches over the IoT security architecture*

The Taxonomy of the Vision Dispersed IoT is governed by two key concepts in general:

1) Intelligent location and services offered at the network's edge.

2) Work collaboratively with several entities to attain a common goal.

9.2.2.1. *Centralized Internet of Things architecture*

In this architecture, the data-collecting network is a passive component whose sole purpose is to deliver data. A central entity will collect all data and transform it into information, while combining it for its consumers. If a user wishes to obtain this information, they must first connect to the Internet interface offered by this central body.

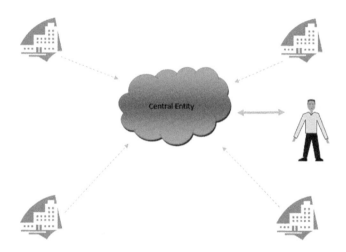

Figure 9.3. *Centralized IoT architecture (Aggarwal et al. 2021). For a color version of this figure, see www.iste.co.uk/mehta/tools.zip*

9.2.2.2. *Distributed Internet of Things architecture*

In this scenario, all entities can obtain, process, integrate and transmit data and services to other entities. Not only will you be able to provide services locally, but you will also be able to collaborate with other IoT systems to achieve common goals. The IoT of a hospital can communicate with the IoT placed in the residence of a patient, or even with the PANs of the workers stationed inside the facilities, and according to electronic health. Furthermore, all hospitals can easily work together to achieve the entire bed occupancy. The house represents the intelligent family, which can generate data; the hospital bed represents the hospital, which can supply and process data; the cloud represents cloud computing, which can provide and process data. Table 9.1 illustrates the properties and characteristics of the IoT security architecture (Aggarwal et al. 2021).

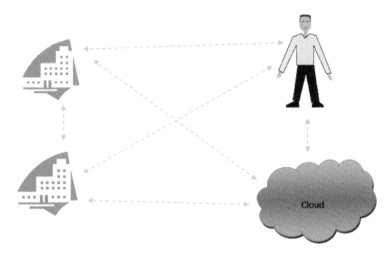

Figure 9.4. *Distributed IoT architecture (Aggarwal et al. 2021). For a color version of this figure, see www.iste.co.uk/mehta/tools.zip*

Table 9.1 explains the properties of both the centralized and distributed IoT architectures.

Property	Parameters	Centralized IoT	Distributed IoT
Openness		High	High
Viability	Business Model	Already in market	Already in market
	Vendor lock-in	Possible	Limited
Reliability	Availability	Zero if failure	Depends on resources
	Performance	Service level + latency	Service level
Scalability		Limited to cloud resources	Superior
Interoperability		Simple	High
Data management		Pull, data at cloud	Follows the push

Table 9.1. *Properties and requirements of centralized and distributed approaches (Aggarwal et al. 2021)*

9.2.3. *IoT security architecture based on blockchain*

In the last two years, blockchain has been applied to the IoT. The IoT is now utilizing blockchains. These projects make use of the benefits of blockchain centralization to provide a fair and trustworthy management platform or key distribution platform that does not rely on a third party. It overcomes the restrictions of third-party centered processing and achieves great processing efficiency. These studies, on the other hand, do not take into account the threat traceability of IoT terminal lifecycles. Furthermore, the lifecycle of IoT terminal devices (e.g. various sensors or mobile devices) varies. Developing efficient threat traceability on terminals can assist in preventing unnecessary security and privacy issues in the real deployment of IoT devices. However, because of the diverse terminal lifecycles, centralization is frequently utilized to trace the source, resulting in resource waste. As a result, figuring out how to deal with it via blockchain is a difficult problem. Blockchain can be used to improve IoT security. We can see how blockchain is being used for IoT device threat tracing, which involves interactions between IoT devices and network transmission, as well as between IoT devices and the cloud (Alphand et al. 2018). The challenges with IoT devices and network transmission include detecting malicious hot spots, malicious terminal access, anomalous traffic monitoring and so on. The issues with IoT devices and the cloud include how to achieve identity identification, among other things. Traditional security methods normally necessitate the use of a trusted third party, which consumes resources. As a result, blockchain technology can be used to achieve the aforementioned security policy without the involvement of a third party. The identity authentication mechanism between the IoT device and the cloud, for example, may necessitate the distribution of the key by third parties. As the number of IoT devices grows, so does the number of IoT terminals. As a result, traditional blockchain technology would necessitate a large amount of computational power at terminals. In the case of the IoT, issues like computational efficiency, privacy protection and supervision for distributed node data management in blockchain must be addressed. As a result, depending on distributed cloud computing, the establishment of a blockchain-based cloud platform for IoT device management in the whole lifecycle may be explored. Through a high-speed network, IoT devices, application software, platform providers and union nodes link to each other. A more efficient cryptographic technique will be used with this blockchain platform, ensuring that the standards for low latency and high throughput in managing data for the IoT are met. In terms of connections between IoT devices and the blockchain database, a device identification-based key method will be used to ensure security and dependability (Lee et al. 2020).

9.2.4. *Internet of Things security architecture: trust zones and boundaries*

Designing and building the architecture of an IoT security solution is very important and necessary without being compromised. Maintaining the security and safeguarding the devices must be the primary goal and is an important detail that should be covered from the beginning of the design phase, from implementation to production. Many aspects should be considered and reviewed while designing a security solution, regardless of what it is being used for. One such important aspect that plays a vital role in security solution design is the identification of trust boundaries among the different parts of the system. This carries major weight in both the physical and software system involved in that particular IoT solution (Cannaday et al. 2019). The basic IoT architecture is divided into various components to optimize the security aspects of a system namely

1) devices;

2) field gateways;

3) cloud gateways;

4) services.

9.2.4.1. *Devices*

These are the IoT devices that are connected to the actuators, sensors, network and other components of a system. They are practically physical objects that are either connected or used for connections in the context of the IoT to perform a desired task. They are either designed or used for the exchange of data in between things. The term "things" in the Internet of Things is related to these devices. They may be the actual sensory equipment or the gadgets used to make a network of connections.

9.2.4.2. *Field gateways*

A field gateway is a software component that acts as a connective gateway in between the devices and cloud or cloud and any other field gateway. They offer a single point connection among the devices or any other components that are running on the premises of the gateway, or in the local network. The field gateways offer various types of functions, namely event/message communication aggregation, message or protocol translation etc., within the solution. The components like edge gateways are also a kind of field gateway that provide much more advanced functions than the field gateway. It possesses the ability to reduce the latency in the real-time data processing loop. It can also run the cloud capabilities locally closer to the devices. This edge gateway is also known as the edge device. These edge devices possess the feasibility to run some of the cloud capabilities, such as machine learning and event stream processing.

9.2.4.3. *Cloud gateway*

The cloud gateway is also one of the important components that have functionalities similar to the field gateway. But field gateways are mostly focused on running the capabilities and functions on the premises closer or local to the devices, whereas cloud gateways prefer running the functionalities over the cloud. It operates on the cloud rather than on the local premises of the devices.

9.2.4.4. *Services*

This is a component that comprises all other backend components of an IoT system, such as databases and API. Services are designed to run in the cloud, local or even in the hybrid manner when it is necessary, to improve the functioning of the overall IoT security solution.

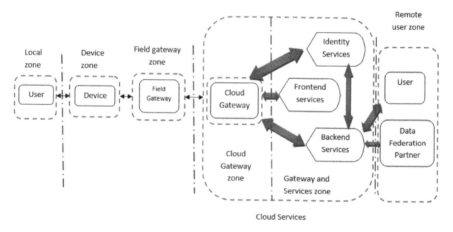

Figure 9.5. *IoT security architecture showing trust zones and boundaries (Cannaday et al. 2019). For a color version of this figure, see www.iste.co.uk/mehta/tools.zip*

The IoT security architecture comprises various components mentioned earlier and they are segregated as trust zones separated by trust boundaries to ensure the functionality of the security practices in a better way. The trust zones are one of the broad ways to fragment a solution, where each zone has its own data, authentication and related requirements. These zones are mainly used for insulating the damage and also help the systems to regulate the impact of the low-trust zones over the high-trust zones. In the IoT security architecture, each zone is segregated using a trust boundary, which is shown in Figure 9.5. The trust boundary is used to illustrate the transition of the data from one device or source to another. However, chances of malicious attacks such as spoofing, tampering or denial of service could be expected during the state of transition. Figure 9.5 illustrates the trust zones and boundaries of an IoT architecture.

Six trust zones should be considered while designing a security architecture, namely:

1) local zone;

2) device zone;

3) field gateway zone;

4) cloud gateway zone;

5) gateway and services zone;

6) remote user zone.

In general, there should be a boundary between each zone. This helps in protecting and safeguarding each layer by creating a new level of isolation in between each zone, which improves security. This creates the validity of safeguarding the communications from the lower zone to the higher zone (Pietschmann et al. 2018).

9.2.4.5. *Local zone*

This zone consists of the local users and acts as a local network consisting of client computers. This may be located in closer physical proximity to the devices and field gateways. The users could connect and interact with the system securely in both physical and virtual platforms by safeguarding this zone. In the context of the virtual space, the end-user systems could be defended from attacks by improving the security practices toward this zone. One of the security practices is to provide the specific access privilege, which facilitates the user to perform their responsibilities, but no more than that. In the scenario of physical space security, the area where the local zone is located could be secured with biometric access or any simple locked doors with locks and keys.

9.2.4.6. *Device zone*

This zone consists of all the IoT devices encompassing the physical space occupied and also a local network to which they are connected. The local network facilitates the device with one-to-one connectivity and establishes communication with the system where Internet connectivity also comes into the picture. The security architecture of the devices must be secured and should comprise both physical and virtual protection, as the IoT has a large surface in both physical and virtual standpoints. Since the scope of access and the connectivity is high, the design of the security architecture must ensure protection in both physical and virtual standpoints. In the virtual context, the security of the device warrants the protection of the devices and the on-premise network to which they are connected, either wired or wirelessly. This security practice includes the use of encryption keys such as SSL or TLS to establish a secure connection, and many encryptions and validation techniques can also be followed. Physically, the devices may be located in different locations which need security architecture depending on the location. To ensure device security from a physical standpoint, they are enclosed in a secure box, or rooms or facilities with a strict access system.

9.2.4.7. *Field gateway zone*

This gateway zone consists of all field gateways that are integrated with the system. This field gateway may be segregated with the same trust boundary or may consist of a separate trust boundary. Since the system consists of different devices located in different locations, there may be a possibility for the use of multiple field gateways at these locations. These multiple field gateways will also be present in the security architecture, establishing communication between the devices and cloud services of a solution. In the virtual stand, the field gateways can be secured by using the encryption keys such as SSL/TLS for communications and other security validations. In the physical stand, the field gateway zone can be secured similarly with the protective techniques implanted in the device zone. They are secured in locked boxes/rooms/facilities. Since the gateways may be located in different areas, all of the multiple field gateways must be secured at all the facilities, depending on their location.

9.2.4.8. *Cloud gateway zone*

This gateway zone consists of the message broker or message queue, which establishes communication between the IoT devices and the backend, service components. This gateway zone is used to facilitate the to and fro data transmission between the backend services and devices by establishing different devices. It is not a database or storage system. The gateway zone could be located in the public cloud or a separate network and location from other devices. The cloud is elucidated as the practice of various measures to prevent physical access. The entire operation takes place with cloud components. The connectivity over a virtual stand should be secured and this is a primary security surface to secure this particular zone. Most of these gateways rely on cloud providers such as Microsoft Azure or Amazon web services to facilitate the message broker services. The use of communication encryption and identity validation for devices is a primary stand that should be taking place to ensure the security of this zone, depending on the requirements of the message broker. In the context of the physical space, this zone is offloaded over the cloud providers, and securing this zone encompasses the datacenter or includes the device in the security architecture.

9.2.4.9. *Gateway and services zone*

This zone comprises the backend services, such as databases, REST API and other backend components of the system. This also facilitates the hybrid connectivity to on-premises. There would be several gateway and service zones depending on the architecture of the backend architecture over the cloud providers and the local networks. Although it consists of all services, it does not include the message brokers or related gateways in the architecture. The security of this zone depends on the services and components that are integrated with the system, where each has its own requirements for protection. This results in the existence of multiple boundaries refereeing to the gateway and service zone to ensure the security of all components.

9.2.4.10. *Remote user zone*

This zone consists of fragments of the IoT security solution, which provide remote access to the user or any third parties. This possesses the integration of the IoT solution with third-party services to improve the ability and performance of the IoT architecture. The remote user connection includes the use of the remote desktop connection to a Windows Virtual Machine, using encryption keys such as SSL or TLS to access the end-user application. This makes the security of this zone less predefined. The remote user zone facilitates the backend zone for communication and the mere integration of other systems, such as third-party APIs and end-user access to the web applications, into the IoT solutions.

9.2.5. *Threat modeling in IoT security architecture*

In the process of designing a system, it is necessary to understand the potential threats and add significant defense measures. The design should start from the security of the product by assuming the possible attacks from a third party. We should make sure that certain mitigations are held in place from the initial state, as the attacker tries to compromise the defense system of a device as their primary move. The main intent behind the implementation of threat modeling in the IoT architecture is to understand the possibilities for the attacker to compromise the system. The application of this model forces the design experts to consider all the threats and mitigations as the designing of the system is performed after the system is deployed. This means that reassembling the security defenses after the deployment is difficult, which in turn makes the system error-prone and may put customers at risk. Microsoft is the company that implemented the threat models for its products and also made the process available publicly (Laorden et al. 2010).

Threat modeling helps in effective security design and improves the performance of the device. It is a structured process that adds great value when assimilated into the design phase. The addition of threat modeling in the design phase makes it feasible to make the necessary alterations to reduce threats. It makes the work more flexible so that appropriate mitigation can be added to improve the effect of IoT security solutions. However, it is harder to eliminate the threats when the product is deployed. Certain aspects should be considered while assimilating the threat model into the design phase and they are mentioned below:

1) the features related to security and privacy;

2) the features where its failures are related to security;

3) the features that touch the trust boundaries.

The threat model should also be considered as a key component and get validated. There are four steps involved in the process of threat modeling:

1) Model the application.

2) Enumerate the possible threats.

3) Mitigate according to the threats.

4) Validation.

Three rules should be considered while designing a threat model:

1) Initially, create the diagram out of the reference architecture.

2) Get an overview of the system and understand it before learning the concept. Then the lengths of the important ones can be understood elaborately.

3) The entire process should be driven by the designer. If any issues were found in the design phase, then they should be explored immediately.

Four core elements are considered as the heart of the threat model. They are as follows:

1) processes (such as web services etc.);

2) datastores;

3) data flow;

4) external entities.

Most of the elements are subject to threats, namely spoofing, tampering, repudiation, information disclosure, denial of service and elevation of service. As previously mentioned, Microsoft uses threat modeling for its products and cloud services, especially Azure IoT. Figure 9.6 shows us the Azure IoT security architecture. This security architecture has four main areas, namely devices and data sources, data transport, device and event processing and presentation.

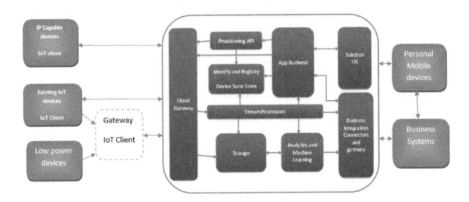

Figure 9.6. *Azure IoT security architecture using threat modeling (Shahan et al. 2018). For a color version of this figure, see www.iste.co.uk/mehta/tools.zip*

9.3. Specific security challenges and approaches

9.3.1. *Identity and authentication*

Managing identity and authentication is considered to be an important aspect of the IoT due to the involvement of multiple entities, such as service providers and data sources etc. All of these entities need to authenticate each other to improve the trusted services. In the process of security mechanisms, certain inherent characteristics of the systems should be considered. The network components could not predict the adjacent entities that are used to create a service, due to dynamic interactions. For example, consider the scenario of the IoT where smart cars share data to roadside equipment and also to other cars present at that instant (Guinard et al. 2010). In the context of centralized IoT, the data provider has its own identity provider, which results in the isolation of the scalability issue. This is due to the ability of the service provider to establish a good relationship with the central entity. In distributed IoT, the entities meet the principles of collaboration, as well as the edge intelligence where the N-to-N condition takes place when the data provider is ready to acquire the information which makes it more passive. The mere consideration of the above mentioned suggests that it is crucial to keep track of things' identities in a scalable way. As a result, gadgets should be able to use their own qualities to identify themselves in the environment they inhabit. The local identity provider can manage the identification of these devices in a given context, as well as build trust connections with associated external resource providers (e.g. patients and hospitals). Users can leverage their social networks to retrieve data from local sensors utilizing an intelligent gateway infrastructure (social access controller or SAC) (e.g. Facebook). It should be noted that if humans do not communicate directly with the IoT object, this strategy may not function. In this instance, creating an agent system that can represent human users is required. Digital shadows are another example, in which users can outsource their credentials (and access control credentials) to various virtual entities (Sarma et al. 2009).

9.3.2. *Access control*

Certain services are built by the agglomeration of several data sources and services from various entities, locations and contexts. The data providers have their control policies and the execution and translation of every task should be managed properly. Some IoT models such as centralized IoT architecture provide access to the control policies that are stored and managed by a central entity with proper authentication. In this context, the data provider and consumer must trust the central entity completely without any choice, which makes it challenging. In addition, the distributed IoT architecture also addresses the same issues, especially the management of numerous implementations and heterogeneous policies. The management of the distributed IoT access control method has been slow. The existing access control approaches are difficult to deploy in a completely dispersed context. When keeping user lists and their associated access privileges in an access control list, for example, there are consistency and scalability difficulties. Various simple tactics can be utilized when things belong to a specific category. For instance, the access control logic can be shifted to a specific legitimate source, and RBAC rules that use attribute certificates must provide cross-domain verification of certain certificates. However, certain elements may be included as part of the access control paradigm due to the unique nature of the IoT. Certain policies (for illustration, only authenticated people who are close to me during work hours can see today's reports) can be simply implemented if there is appropriate technological support. Furthermore, access control logic could be moved to certain trusted entities that will operate as Kerberos token granting services (something will be permitted access with a valid signature provided by a trustworthy organization) (Lutkevich et al. 2020).

9.3.3. *Protocol and network security*

The successful authentication, that is either server or mutual authentication, results in a secure communication channel. In addition, multiple challenges are associated with computative resources. In the process of creating a secure communication channel, the gadgets and devices integrated with the system must have the ability to negotiate the required parameters, such as algorithms, strength and confidentiality and integrity. However, the devices that are constrained may not have the ability to implement specific configurations. Some devices may not need to be implemented with strong protection mechanisms to the data flow, depending on the different factors. In addition, analyzing the number of protocols that should be implemented in the constrained device is very challenging. The security of IoT-designed web transport protocols, notably CoAP, is primarily reliant on these security protocols' implementation, and some protocols can be deployed with no significant developments. Other prototypes, however, will need to be altered due to the complexity of their design (Raza et al. 2012). A protocol like this must strike a balance between convenience and portability. The dissemination of certifications, as well as any items pertaining to a specific local group, may be managed and distributed by one or more individuals. These protocols can give useful characteristics such as high threat resilience. Several scientists are working on innovating hash functions and symmetric algorithms, as well as optimizing current blocks to enforce fast and efficient cryptographic algorithms.

9.3.4. *Privacy*

The distributed IoT architectures instantly benefit from data management and privacy, as they require highly sophisticated security models and mechanisms. In the context of centralized IoT architecture, the data provider decides whether to share a specific data stream even though it follows the idea of collaboration. Here, the data providers and recipients can communicate in a direct path, which increases the chance to negotiate a different set of keys to protect the information. Even the centralized architecture follows the edge intelligence principle. But in this regard, the central entity becomes a storage device if it does not get integrated with the advanced encrypted mechanism that can manipulate the data that is encrypted. Since all entities may control their data directly, the distributed IoT method makes it easier to adopt privacy design principles. Factors including the accessibility of the interface (like what could be accessed or to what extent) should indeed be examined in terms of people (Gusmeroli et al. 2013). The application of existing securing cloud data mining algorithms must also be investigated. For instance, multi-party computing and other privacy improvement technologies (PETs) can be utilized to secure eco-operational protocols. Rogue devices and viruses that could compromise user privacy must be scanned in both input and output items. In this case, architecture such as TRUST could be useful. Furthermore, existing studies on surveillance systems such as CCTVs may reveal special legal difficulties that our society will confront once the IoT becomes an actuality (Oleshchuk et al. 2009).

9.3.5. *Trust and governance*

In the context of centralized IoT, the interactions are undetermined where the overall credibility of all the other components can be calculated by the central entity. However, there will be an exchange of trust data between different central entities if collaborated. This helps in fixing the volatility in the reputation values. The distributed IoT architecture possesses uncertainty in its interaction with the data provider and service provider and also makes trust management more complex and challenging (Mohammadi et al. 2019). The establishment of a circle of user-managed trusts in the shopping lens system is a promising method. By adding trustworthy metadata in the flow of information, the system promotes user trust in the IoT. Patterns (such as QR codes) in an environment (such as a retail mall) can be digitally authenticated and owned by a user-defined specific group. This group's members can also add ratings to a default standard mode. Under this approach, when a user trusts a certain group, information from the mode or a trusted rating from other users can be retrieved.

9.3.6. *Fault tolerance*

The IoT is a webwork of various physical objects, sensors etc. So, there will be a chance of damage, objects may stop working or there may be transmission of fake or manipulated data. Fault tolerance is one of the key parameters in the case of the IoT. In the context of centralized IoT architectures, this task is much simpler due to the ability of the central entity to access the data streams. In distributed IoT architecture, a discovery mechanism that is used to locate the data streams accurately should be developed. The prospect and differences between these methods increase the complexity in implementing the security mechanisms. A group of theoretical platforms are designed for discovery, service discovery and synthesis in the IoT. When entities are aggregated in a local group, a cluster can include mechanisms that not only give push information on local objects, but also support through different specialized middleware (Teixeir et al. 2011). In addition, many of these applications can benefit from the functionality provided by conventional security measures, including trust management. Develop a novel detection system that accounts for the distributed Web of Things' unique risk paradigm. Additionally, existing distributed intrusion detection systems applied in similar situations, including such smart grids, can be used to gain experience.

9.4. Methodologies used for securing the systems

There are various methodologies to implement or ensure the security of IoT systems namely

1) PKI and digital certificates;

2) network security;

3) API security;

4) network access control;

5) segmentation;

6) security gateways;

7) patch management/software updates.

9.4.1. *PKI and digital certificates*

PKI stands for Public Key Infrastructure and helps in securing the client–server connections between numerous devices connected over a network. PKI is mainly used to encrypt and decrypt private information or messages with the help of two-key asymmetric cryptosystems. It also secures the interactions between the system using valid digital certificates. PKI helps in protecting the text data inputs given by the user to the websites. It also secures the private transactions made by the user. Most of the E-commerce sites operate using PKI to ensure their security.

9.4.2. *Network security*

The devices involved in the IoT are connected over a network. This increases the risk factor for the use and becomes an opportunity for hackers to control the devices. Since the network encompasses both the digital and physical components, the local security mechanism should address all of the access points related to the network. The security practices for securing the network include ensuring port security, disabling port forwarding, using anti-malware, firewalls and intrusion detection software, using intrusion prevention systems, restricting unauthorized IP addresses, keeping systems up to date etc.

9.4.3. *API security*

API stands for Application Programming Interface. It acts as the key component in building sophisticated websites. This helps travel agencies to aggregate the flight details and related information from multiple airlines to a single location. The API has vulnerabilities and the hackers could easily compromise the communication channels. This makes the API security necessary to protect user data. Securing API ensures the protection of data transmission between the devices and backend systems, authorized devices, users and app access to the API.

9.4.4. *Network access control*

Network Access Control (NAC) helps in the identification of IoT devices that are connected to the network. This acts as a service line for tracking and monitoring devices. NAC denies access to the non-competent devices or provides limited or constrained access to the requester, in order to secure the network from cyber-attacks. The capabilities of the NAC involve policy lifecycle management, proofing and visibility, guest networking access, security posture check, incident response and bidirectional integration. This protects the network and the connected devices from malicious threats (Gilia et al. 2018).

9.4.5. *Segmentation*

The devices connected over the Internet should be segregated into their own networks and have restricted access to the enterprise network. The segmented networks are monitored and any malicious attacks are detected.

9.4.6. *Security gateways*

Security gateways act as an intermediate zone between the devices and the network. They have more processing power and capabilities than other IoT devices. They facilitate the devices with the ability to implement firewalls, ensuring security.

9.4.7. *Patch management and software updates*

Updating devices plays a crucial role in ensuring security over the devices and network. It reduces the number of vulnerabilities which compromise the devices to attackers. The coordinated disclosure of vulnerabilities is quite important in updating the devices. End of life strategies work well.

9.5. Conclusion

In this chapter we discussed the insights of IoT security and its various segments. This research seeks to better comprehend the IoT's role in the future Internet by examining its characteristics and security issues. Determining business models and managing devices for authentication and authorization require several hurdles to be resolved. Distributed entities manage data and implement privacy standards. You may also design altruistic fault tolerance techniques for this strategy. These and other benefits show that this strategy works in the actual world. A blockchain-based IoT security system was then introduced. One of the design considerations of these security-addressing systems is asset management for devices over their lifetimes. We look at IoT device management and use blockchain technology to tackle the issue. When IoT devices connect to the blockchain database, they will be protected by a device identification-based key mechanism. The three-layer design will require future recommendations on distributed and centralized IoT patterns, challenges and solutions.

9.6. References

Aggarwal, S. and Kumar, N. (2021). Basics of blockchain. *Advances in Computers*, 129–146. doi: 10.1016/bs.adcom.2020.08.007.

Alphand, O., Amoretti, M., Claeys, T., Dall'Asta, S., Duda, A., Ferrari, G., Rousseau, F., Tourancheau, B., Veltri, L., Zanichelli, F. (2018). IoTChain: A blockchain security architecture for the Internet of Things. *IEEE Wireless Communications and Networking Conference (WCNC)*, 15–18 April.

Burhan, M., Rehman, R., Khan, B., Kim, B. (2018). IoT elements, layered architectures and security issues: A comprehensive survey. *Sensors*, 18(9), 2796.

Cannaday, B. (2019). The fundamental IoT architecture. Losant Blog [Online]. Available at: https://www.losant.com/blog/the-fundamental-iot-architecture.

Guinard, D., Fischer, M., Trifa, V. (2010). Sharing using social networks in a composable Web of Things. *8th IEEE International Conference On Pervasive Computing And Communications Workshops (PERCOM Workshops)*. doi: 10.1109/percomw.2010.5470524.

Gulia, N., Solanki, K., Dalal, S. (2018). Security techniques in the Internet of Things (IoT). *SSRN Electronic Journal*. doi: 10.2139/ssrn.3170187.

Gusmeroli, S., Piccione, S., Rotondi, D. (2013). A capability-based security approach to manage access control in the Internet of Things. *Mathematical and Computer Modelling*, 58(5/6), 1189–1205.

Husamuddin, M. and Qayyum, M. (2017). Internet of Things: A study on security and privacy threats. *IEEE 2nd International Conference on Anti-Cyber Crimes (ICACC)*.

Laorden, C., Sanz, B., Alvarez, G., Bringas, P. (2010). A threat model approach to threats and vulnerabilities in online social networks. *Computational Intelligence in Security for Information Systems*, 135–142.

Lee, Y., Rathore, S., Park, J., Park, J. (2020). A blockchain-based smart home gateway architecture for preventing data forgery. *Human-centric Computing and Information Sciences*, 10(1). doi: 10.1186/s13673-020-0214-5.

Lutkevich, B. (2020). What is access control? Search Security, TechTarget [Online]. Available at: https://www.techtarget.com/searchsecurity/definition/access-control.

Mahmoud, R., Yousuf, T., Aloul, F., Zualkernan, I. (2015). Internet of Things (IoT) security: Current status, challenges and prospective measures. *10th International Conference for Internet Technology and Secured Transactions (ICITST)*.

Mohammadi, V., Rahmani, A., Darwesh, A., Sahafi, A. (2019). Trust-based recommendation systems in the Internet of Things: A systematic literature review. *Human-centric Computing and Information Sciences*, 9(1).

Oleshchuk, V. (2009). Internet of Things and privacy-preserving technologies. *1st International Conference on Wireless Communication, Vehicular Technology, Information Theory and Aerospace & Electronic Systems Technology*.

Pietschmann, C. (2018). IoT security architecture: Trust zones and boundaries. Build5Nines [Online]. Available at: https://build5nines.com/iot-security-architecture-trust-zones-and-boundaries/.

Raza, S., Duquennoy, S., Höglund, J., Roedig, U., Voigt, T. (2012). Secure communication for the Internet of Things: A comparison of link-layer security and IPsec for 6LoWPAN. *Security and Communication Networks*, 7(12), 2654–2668.

Rostami, M., Majzoobi, M., Koushanfar, F., Wallach, D., Devadas, S. (2014). Robust and reverse-engineering resilient PUF authentication and key-exchange by substring matching. *IEEE Transaction on Emerging Topics in Computing*, 2(1), 37–49.

Sachidananda, V., Toh, J., Siboni, S., Shabtai, A., Elovici, Y. (2016). POSTER. *Proceedings of the 2016 ACM SIGSAC Conference on Computer and Communications Security*.

Sarma, A. and Girão, J. (2009). Identities in the future Internet of Things. *Wireless Personal Communications*, 49(3), 353–363.

Sethi, P. and Sarangi, S. (2017). Internet of Things: Architectures, protocols, and applications. *Journal of Electrical and Computer Engineering*, 1–25.

Shahan, R. (2018). IoT security architecture [Online]. Available at: docs.microsoft.com.

Shea, S. (2021). What is IoT security? IoT Agenda, TechTarget [Online]. Available at: https://www.techtarget.com/iotagenda/definition/IoT-security-Internet-of-Things-security.

Tawalbeh, L., Muheidat, F., Tawalbeh, M., Quwaider, M. (2020). IoT privacy and security: Challenges and solutions. *Applied Sciences*, 10(12), 4102.

Teixeira, T., Hachem, S., Issarny, V., Georgantas, N. (2011). Service-oriented middleware for the Internet of Things: A perspective. *Towards a Service-Based Internet*, 220–229.

Zhang, Z., Cho, M., Wang, C., Hsu, C., Chen, C., Shieh, S. (2014). IoT security: Ongoing challenges and research opportunities. *IEEE 7th International Conference on Service-Oriented Computing and Applications*.

Zhang, J., Jin, H., Gong, L., Cao, J., Gu, Z. (2019). Overview of IoT security architecture. *IEEE 4th International Conference on Data Science in Cyberspace (DSC)*.

Elucidating the Semantic Web of Things for Making the Industry 4.0 Revolution a Success

Indeed, the Fourth Industrial Revolution (IR4.0) is focusing in the direction of automating various manufacturing technologies which include Cyber-Physical Systems (CPS), Cloud Computing, Artificial Intelligence, Industrial Internet of Things and Internet of Things (IoT). The Semantic Web and the Web of Things known together as the Semantic Web of Things (SWoT) have a very bright future in addressing the plethora of problems in realizing the vision of IR4.0. This chapter aims to compile the various advancements that significantly contribute to the area of SWoT in the realization of IR4.0. The outcome of this study would be an aggregation of different progressions that essentially add to the space of SWoT in the acknowledgement of IR4.0.

10.1. Introduction

Industry 4.0 was first discussed at the Hanover Fair. It was in 2012 that the team responsible for the attainment of the IR4.0 vision met the German Government and laid out a proposal for the computerization of the manufacturing business. It is an amalgamation of various technologies such as the IoT, CPS, smart factories and big data. As coined by Um (2019), Industry 4.0 is a integration of multiple technologies not limited to machines, field gadgets and CPS that are controlling each other freely. As per the Information and Communication Technologies (ICT) at present, we are in the fourth revolution where the vision is to integrate the data originating from mechanical devices. Its innovative premise is the computerization of digital actual frameworks with decentralized control and progressive availability (IoT functionalities). This new paradigm is the modernization and redesigning of earlier existing frameworks, used to integrate the data and thus creating systems that are

Chapter written by Deepika CHAUDHARY and Jaiteg SINGH.

adaptable and self-coordinating. Industry 4.0 (IR4.0) is a revolution in the current industry aspects. The inception of various terms, IoT, CPS, and interactions between human and machine and machine to machine have reformed the Industry 4.0 experience (Zhou et al. 2015). Different kinds of cyber-physical devices, which include sensors, self-governed robots and embedded systems, have intensified the production in the IR4.0 revolution.

Undoubtedly, the IR4.0 is directed towards robotizing different assembling innovations which incorporate digital actual frameworks (CPS), IoT, Cloud Computing, Industrial Internet of Things and Artificial Intelligence.

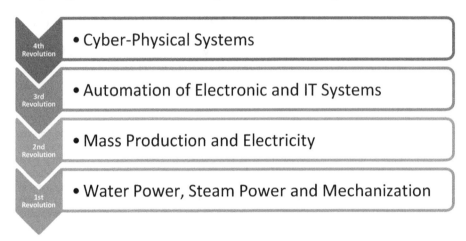

Figure 10.1. *Versions of the Industrial Revolution. For a color version of this figure, see www.iste.co.uk/mehta/tools.zip*

10.2. Correlation of the Semantic Web of Things with IR4.0

The Semantic Web and the Web of Things, known together as the Semantic Web of Things (SWoT), has an exceptionally splendid future in tending to the plenty of issues in understanding the vision of IR4.0. We are currently are in the Fourth Industrial Revolution. In this phase, the transformation is shifted from the automation of mechanical devices to Big Data Analytics. The success of IR4.0 majorly depends on the Big Data Analytics. The beginning in this direction will not just be the creation of knowledge by mining the data coming from CPS, but it also depends on the installation of items with advanced components and how the discovered knowledge is utilized to channel the supply chain cycle. The IR4.0 vision is an umbrella term for providing a unified view to a bunch of mechanical terms for improvement in the area of CPS, the Internet of Services (IoS), the IoT, Big Data, Robotics, Cloud Manufacturing and Augmented Reality and SWoT (Faheem et al. 2018; Mishra and Jain 2018).

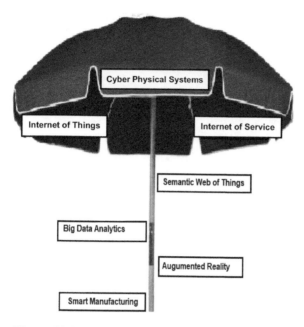

Figure 10.2. *Industrial Revolution 4.0 and its related technologies. For a color version of this figure, see www.iste.co.uk/mehta/tools.zip*

To enable these advancements, improvement in assembling measures is required, which includes incorporating new gadgets to empower smart assembly and manufacturing units. To gain an in-depth understanding of the term Industry 4.0, it is essential to understand the full value chain from the gathering of raw materials to delivery of the end product to the customer. The key components of the full value chain for Industry 4.0 can be categorized into Smart Machines, Smart Products and the Augmented Operators (Hoppe et al. 2017). These key components are discussed in the following sections.

10.2.1. *Smart machines*

These are the devices or the machines which can learn from their own experience and can guide themselves on how to solve a complex problem. This can also be referred to as "Machine Learning" and is a sub-domain of Artificial Intelligence and robotics. Figure 10.3 highlights a few key features of smart machines as given by Gartner[1].

---

1 See: https://blog.capterra.com/what-are-smart-machines/.

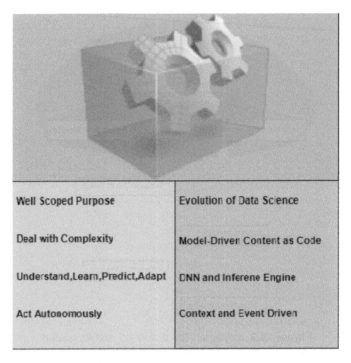

Well Scoped Purpose	Evolution of Data Science
Deal with Complexity	Model-Driven Content as Code
Understand,Learn,Predict,Adapt	DNN and Inferene Engine
Act Autonomously	Context and Event Driven

Figure 10.3. *Key components of smart machines. For a color version of this figure, see www.iste.co.uk/mehta/tools.zip*

10.2.2. *Smart products*

Smart products are the outcome of the integration of ICT into simple products in order to make them smart. A few characteristics of any smart products are that they can be personalized (customized as per customer needs), location aware, proactive, adaptive and network capable. In their study, Raff et al. (2020) defined the framework for smart products as they are digital, they are connected, are responsive and also intelligent.

10.2.3. *Augmented operators*

Gyroscope, Augmented Reality, Google Cardboard and mixed reality are few of the major operators. These operators have the capability of covering both virtual modes in the real world. This way the end user can get real-time data. It also means someone can wear a set of smart glasses and can follow step-by-step instructions in order to display the right side of the product, right in front of their eyes. The other main components of IR4.0 are described below.

10.2.4. *The Web of Things*

The other technology that is swiftly progressing toward the attainment of the vision of IR4.0 is the IoT. This technology focuses on the presence of things around us, for example sensors, radio recurrence ID (RFID) labels, cells and actuators. These devices can collaborate with one another to achieve some shared objectives. The model depicted in Figure 10.4 shows the collaboration of real-world objects, industrialist, homemakers, policymakers, doctors and other responsible entities who can share data anytime, anywhere and anything.

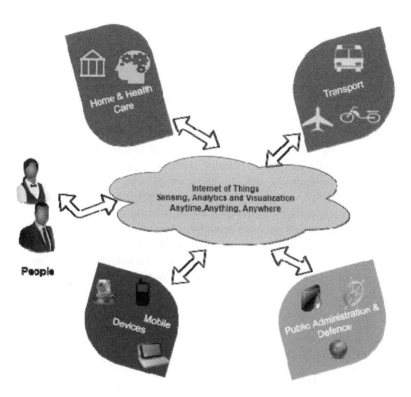

Figure 10.4. *Semantic Web of Things schematic showing the end users and application areas based on data (Chen et al. 2008). For a color version of this figure, see www.iste.co.uk/mehta/tools.zip*

Figure 10.4 describes the five major areas of IoT which include personal, home, enterprise, public administration and mobile devices. The entities in this scenario collaborate and communicate with each other with the help of heterogeneous field devices in real time which thereby generates a huge amount of valuable data. The generated data can be mined and the generated knowledge can be used to enhance the user experience, on time and on-demand production of smart devices, personalization of products, resource optimizations, product customization, maintenance of machines and logistic styles (Chen et al. 2008). However, this is not as simple as it seems as the major challenges in this scenario arise when it comes to the integration of data which is sourced from the heterogeneous devices, their velocity, their variety and their interoperability.

10.2.5. *Semantic Web of Things*

With the origin of the IoT it has become necessary to connect objects which are designed and manufactured by different manufacturers, whether it be Google, IBM or Nokia. The data generated by these devices are heterogeneous in nature and follow different coding formats which makes data complex during integration. Not only is the variety an issue, but the volume and the velocity are all factors that need to be taken care of as well. For instance, temperature can be measured in Celsius, Kelvin and Fahrenheit and to integrate this data from multiple objects generates the need for a common vocabulary, which leads to the origin of the concept SWoT. Furthermore, SWoT can also handle certain other challenges including interoperability, heterogeneity and interpretation of data. This assertion was also proved by claims that integrating semantic technologies to the IoT leads to promoting the interoperability of the data which is being generated through various objects, information models and data providers. According to Staab et al. (2010), the term ontology is defined as an explicit and formal specification of a shared conceptualization. The ontologies are used to express knowledge in the related fields (Mishra and Jain 2020). The ontologies mainly consist of the definitions given in Figure 10.5.

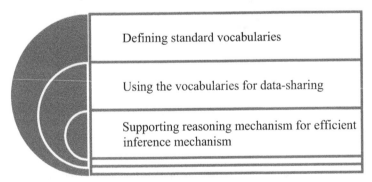

Figure 10.5. *Definition of ontology*

The next section focuses on various ontologies applicable in IR4.0 and certain use cases and describes the application of ontologies in smart manufacturing systems.

10.3. Smart manufacturing system and ontologies

Ontologies can be defined as a formulation of the knowledge expressions for formal representation of the concepts and relationship thereof. Ontologies can also capture domain knowledge in an interoperable way (Wang et al. 2010). As stated in Figure 10.7, there are nine pillars of IR4.0, and out of these nine pillars the most important pillar when considered from a Semantic Web point of view is system integration. As far as system integration is concerned, the devices in smart factories need to be integrated in three dimensions.

10.3.1. *Vertical level integration*

This type of integration takes place when the smart objects are placed hierarchically and at different levels. One of the possible solutions for this kind of integration is to move from the production shop floor to the business floor, means from CPS to Enterprise Resource Planning (ERP).

10.3.2. *Horizontal level of integration*

This type of integration takes place when we integrate various processes at the same level, meaning integration between the resources and information networks within the supply chain. In another words, we can say that CPSs are to be integrated within processes to optimize production.

10.3.3. *End-to-end integration*

This refers to the integration of various activities of the product development lifecycle, that is ideation, design, production, application and closure. To integrate factories around the globe, integration is required between end-to-end resources. To solve this requires the integration of heterogeneous devices, which is very critical and poses a challenge in the attainment of the vision of IR4.0. One of the possible solutions to this problem is presented in Figure 10.6.

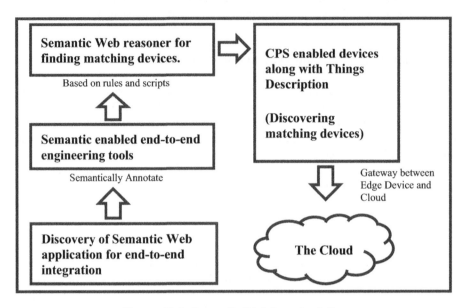

Figure 10.6. *Semantic Web-based solution*
for end-to-end integration

For the proposed architecture we require a Semantic Web-based application with a very user-friendly interface to integrate the data which is coming from end-to-end engineering tools. As these engineering tools would be simple with limited processing capabilities and power, we therefore require an inference engine to infer and hence will be able to find matching devices for system integration over the cloud. The success of IR4.0 is based on nine pillars. Figure 10.7 shows the nine main pillars of IR4.0 (Ismail et al. 2020).

10.3.3.1. *Big Data analytics*

Data analytics were once the concern of the IT department, but they are now entering into the manufacturing and supply chain industry as well. The power of data analytics and data mining can be utilized to reduce industry downtime and also the related wastages.

10.3.3.2. *Autonomous robots*

Robots can transfer goods in a much easier and efficient way. The robots are designed using complex algorithms and do not require any predefined path to work. They make the manufacturing process very smart and efficient.

10.3.3.3. *Simulations and augmented reality*

Instead of manufacturing the components directly, in Industry 4.0 a virtual environment can be used to simulate the components before actually changing anything.

10.3.3.4. *Horizontal and vertical system integration*

As already discussed above, this pillar focuses on the integration of various components placed at various hierarchical levels of manufacturing.

10.3.3.5. *The cloud*

A remote system that can be accessed from anywhere, anytime for obtaining services, that is IaaS, SaaS and PaaS. These services can help both humans and machines to establish communication.

10.3.3.6. *Industrial Internet of Things*

This provides an ecosystem where all the devices can connect together. The connected devices can work in both a separate fashion as well as together. The data collected from these devices can be analyzed to face the harsh environments of the industry.

10.3.3.7. *Additive manufacturing*

Additive manufacturing devices can be used to develop a proof of concept or prototypes, which can reduce the manufacturing time significantly.

10.3.3.8. *Cyber security*

In an environment where data are available with the click of a mouse, it is the responsibility of ethical hackers to secure the data from any kind of vulnerability.

The next section focuses on the year-wise advancements and contribution of SWoT in system integration.

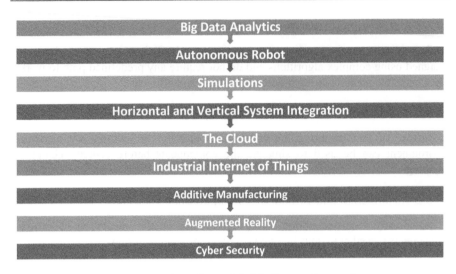

Figure 10.7. *Nine pillars of IR4.0. For a color version of this figure, see www.iste.co.uk/mehta/tools.zip*

10.4. Literature survey

This section highlights various advancements in the area of IR4.0. With the aim of finding existing literature on elucidating the Semantic Web in Industry 4.0, a search was made on Google Scholar, Scopus and dbpedia with different keywords, such as Semantic Web of Things, IoT, Smart Manufacturing and Ontologies. The timeframe for the search was set to 2015–2021. After a careful analysis of the available literature, a good number of research papers were selected and are presented in Table 10.1.

Table 10.1 presents the year-wise advancements and contributions of SWoT for making IR4.0 a success. This review also highlights that there are various domains, that is data exploration, data visualization and big data analysis, which can be digged into and explored further. The next section presents the future scope of research in various domains of IR4.0.

Paper	Ontology	Research focus	Domain
(Nikirofova et al. 2021)	Visualization techniques in biomedical sub-domain	Current visualization techniques for ontology	Biomedical sub-domain
(Tiwari and Abraham 2020)	Smart Healthcare Ontology	To design a smart healthcare ontology for remote monitoring	Healthcare domain
(Kalaycı et al. 2020)	SMT ontology combined with Domain ontologies	To attain interoperability among data set for manufacturing domain	Manufacturing domain
(Ramírez Durán et al. 2020)	ExtruOnt	To describe and integrate spatial data sets and to capture data from different sensors	Manufacturing domain
(Wei et al. 2019)	Design of a new Surface Mounting Process (SMP Ontology)	Bosch Manufacturing Data was integrated and further analyzed	Manufacturing domain
(Lu et al. 2019)	Manuservice Ontology	This ontology was developed for service-oriented data models	Product engineering
(Singh et al. 2019)	Manufacturing System Ontology	Designed to cater for the needs of Inclusive Manufacturing Systems	Manufacturing domain
(Patel et al. 2018)	SWeTI Framework	Authors proposed a framework for the integration of IoT devices using an AI-based approach	Internet of Things
(Santos et al. 2017)	No ontology was designed only an architecture was proposed	Proposed to integrate the data coming from various processes	Process oriented
(Teslya et al. 2018)	Components of Socio-Cyber Physical systems	Creating space to integrate some specific information that is coming from production system	Manufacturing engineering
(Kovalenko et al. 2017)	Automation MLontology	A semantic model for data exchange among various cyber physical systems in IR4.0	Automation system
(Grangel-Gonzalez et al. 2016)	IR4.0 components	Semantically represented the IR4.0 devices in administration shell	Mechanical devices
(Cheng et al. 2016)	IR4.0 Demonstration Production line	Modeled the IR4.0 production line	Product engineering
(Petersen et al. 2016)	Semantic Manufacturing Ontology (SMO)	Modeling of smart factory	Manufacturing engineering
(Fiorini et al. 2015)	Ontology for Agile Manufacturing	Developed an ontology-based knowledge-driven system for planning and verification in agile manufacturing	Agile manufacturing

Table 10.1. *Semantic Web technologies in IR4.0*

10.5. Conclusion and future work

The outgrowth of SWoT has come with a confluence among the various heterogeneous devices to infer certain hidden relationships and has provided a solution to interoperability (Wickens et al. 2021). It is trusted that integration of Semantic Web technologies into industrial technologies can act as a universal model for achieving the vision of IR4.0. In this chapter we have compiled the various advancements that significantly contributed to the area of SWoT in the realization of IR4.0. In this study we have selected papers from the years 2015 to 2021. After going through the literature it has been observed that the most work has been done in the area of manufacturing engineering and product engineering, and there is still a lot of scope for research in other domains of IR4.0.

Future scope of SWoT in achieving the vision of IR4.0		
IR 9 pillars	**Domain/designed ontology**	**Future scope**
Big Data Analytics	Smart Manufacturing – SMT Ontology, ExtruOnt, DFAM Ontology, SMO Ontology Predictive Maintenance – MPMO Ontology	Data exploration, data visualization, data analysis for optimal decision making
Autonomous Robots	Smart Factories – Automation MLOntology (see Figure 10.7)	Data integration from heterogeneous sources and optimization of search algorithms

Table 10.2. *Future scope of SWoT*

10.6. References

Ahmad, S., Badwelan, A., Ghaleb, A.M., Qamhan, A., Sharaf, M., Alatefi, M., Moohialdin, A. (2018). Analyzing critical failures in a production process: Is industrial IoT the solution? *Wireless Communications and Mobile Computing*, 6951318:1–6951318:12.

Bécue, A., Praça, I., Gama, J. (2021). Artificial intelligence, cyber-threats and Industry 4.0: Challenges and opportunities. *Artificial Intelligence Review*, 54(5), 3849–3886.

Berges, I., Ramírez-Durán, V.J., Illarramendi, A. (2021). A semantic approach for big data exploration in Industry 4.0. *Big Data Research*, 25, 100222.

Chen, D., Doumeingts, G., Vernadat, F. (2008). Architectures for enterprise integration and interoperability: Past, present and future. *Computers in Industry*, 59(7), 647–659.

Cheng, H., Zeng, P., Xue, L., Shi, Z., Wang, P., Yu, H. (2016). Manufacturing ontology development based on Industry 4.0 demonstration production line. *2016 3rd International Conference on Trustworthy Systems and their Applications (TSA)*. IEEE.

Dinar, M. and Rosen, D.W. (2017). A design for additive manufacturing ontology. *Journal of Computing and Information Science in Engineering*, 17(2).

Ehrlinger, L. and Wöß, W. (2016). Towards a definition of knowledge graphs. *SEMANTiCS (Posters, Demos, SuCCESS)*, 48(1/4), 2.

Erboz, G. (2017). How to define Industry 4.0: Main pillars of Industry 4.0. *Managerial Trends in the Development of Enterprises in Globalization Era*. Slovak University of Agriculture in Nitra.

Faheem, M., Shah, S.B.H., Butt, R.A., Raza, B., Anwar, M., Ashraf, M.W., Ngadi, M.A., Gungor, V.C. (2018). Smart grid communication and information technologies in the perspective of Industry 4.0: Opportunities and challenges. *Computer Science Review*, 30, 1–30.

Fiorini, S.R., Carbonera, J.L., Gonçalves, P., Jorge, V.A., Rey, V.F., Haidegger, T., Abel, M., Redfield, S.A., Balakirsky, S., Ragavan, V. et al. (2015). Extensions to the core ontology for robotics and automation. *Robotics and Computer-Integrated Manufacturing*, 33, 3–11.

Giustozzi, F., Saunier, J., Zanni-Merk, C. (2018). Context modeling for Industry 4.0: An ontology-based proposal. *Procedia Computer Science*, 126, 675–684.

Grangel-González, I., Baptista, P., Halilaj, L., Lohmann, S., Vidal, M.E., Mader, C., Auer, S. (2017). The Industry 4.0 standards landscape from a semantic integration perspective. *2017 22nd IEEE International Conference on Emerging Technologies and Factory Automation (ETFA)*. IEEE.

Hoppe, T., Eisenmann, H., Viehl, A., Bringmann, O. (2017). Shifting from data handling to knowledge engineering in aerospace industry. *2017 IEEE International Systems Engineering Symposium (ISSE)*. IEEE.

Ismail, N.A., Abd Wahid, N., Yusoff, A.S.M., Wahab, N.A., Abd Rahim, B.H., Abd Majid, N., Din, N.M.N., Ariffin, R.M., Adnan, W.I.W., Zakaria, R. (2020). The challenges of Industrial Revolution (IR) 4.0 towards the teacher's self-efficacy. *Journal of Physics: Conference Series*, 1529(4), 042062.

Kalaycı, E.G., González, I.G., Lösch, F., Xiao, G., Kharlamov, E., Calvanese, D. (2020). Semantic integration of Bosch manufacturing data using virtual knowledge graphs. *International Semantic Web Conference*. Springer, Cham.

Karray, M.H., Chebel-Morello, B., Zerhouni, N. (2012). A formal ontology for industrial maintenance. *Applied Ontology*, 7(3), 269–310.

Kumar, N. and Kumar, J. (2019). Efficiency 4.0 for Industry 4.0. *Human Technology*, 15(1).

Ling, J., Hutchinson, M., Antono, E., Paradiso, S., Meredig, B. (2017). High-dimensional materials and process optimization using data-driven experimental design with well-calibrated uncertainty estimates. *Integrating Materials and Manufacturing Innovation*, 6(3), 207–217.

Lu, Y., Wang, H., Xu, X. (2019). ManuService ontology: A product data model for service-oriented business interactions in a cloud manufacturing environment. *Journal of Intelligent Manufacturing*, 30(1), 317–334.

der Mauer, M.A., Behrens, T., Derakhshanmanesh, M., Hansen, C., Muderack, S. (2019). Applying sound-based analysis at Porsche production: Towards predictive maintenance of production machines using deep learning and Internet-of-Things technology. In *Digitalization Cases*, Urbach, N. and Röglinger, M. (eds). Springer, Cham.

Mishra, S. and Jain, S. (2020). Ontologies as a semantic model in IoT. *International Journal of Computers and Applications*, 42(3), 233–243.

Mishra, S., Jain, S., Rai, C., Gandhi, N. (2018). Security challenges in Semantic Web of Things. *International Conference on Innovations in Bio-Inspired Computing and Applications*. Springer, Cham.

Nikiforova, A., Tiwari, S., Rovite, V., Klovins, J., Kante, N. (2021). Evaluation and visualization of healthcare semantic models. *Evaluation*, 323, 91773–91775.

Nishioka, Y. (2015). Industrial Value Chain Initiative for Smart Manufacturing. Tokyo.

Pal, S.K. (2008). 21st century information technology revolution. *Ubiquity*, June(9) [Online]. Available at: https://dl.acm.org/doi/10.1145/1403922.1399619.

Patel, P., Ali, M.I., Sheth, A. (2018). From raw data to smart manufacturing: AI and Semantic Web of Things for Industry 4.0. *IEEE Intelligent Systems*, 33(4), 79–86.

Pullmann, J., Petersen, N., Mader, C., Lohmann, S., Kemeny, Z. (2017). Ontology-based information modelling in the industrial data space. *2017 22nd IEEE International Conference on Emerging Technologies and Factory Automation (ETFA)*. IEEE.

Raff, S., Wentzel, D., Obwegeser, N. (2020). Smart products: Conceptual review, synthesis, and research directions. *Journal of Product Innovation Management*, 37, 379–404.

Ramírez-Durán, V.J., Berges, I., Illarramendi, A. (2020). ExtruOnt: An ontology for describing a type of manufacturing machine for Industry 4.0 systems. *Semantic Web*, 11(6), 887–909.

Ray, S.R. and Jones, A.T. (2006). Manufacturing interoperability. *Journal of Intelligent Manufacturing*, 17(6), 681–688.

Rivas, A., Grangel-González, I., Collarana, D., Lehmann, J., Vidal, M.E. (2020). Unveiling relations in the Industry 4.0 standards landscape based on knowledge graph embeddings. *International Conference on Database and Expert Systems Applications*. Springer, Cham.

Sabilla, S.I., Sarno, R., Effendi, Y.A. (2018). Optimizing time and cost using goal programming and FMS scheduling. *2018 International Conference on Information and Communications Technology (ICOIACT)*. IEEE.

Sadati, N., Chinnam, R.B., Nezhad, M.Z. (2018). Observational data-driven modeling and optimization of manufacturing processes. *Expert Systems with Applications*, 93, 456–464.

Santos, M.Y., e Sá, J.O., Costa, C., Galvão, J., Andrade, C., Martinho, B., Lima, F.V., Costa, E. (2017). A big data analytics architecture for Industry 4.0. *World Conference on Information Systems and Technologies.* Springer, Cham.

Shekhar, C., Jain, M., Iqbal, J., Raina, A.A. (2017). Threshold control policy for maintainability of manufacturing system with unreliable workstations. *Arabian Journal for Science and Engineering,* 42(11), 4833–4851.

Singh, S., Mahanty, B., Tiwari, M.K. (2019). Framework and modelling of inclusive manufacturing system. *International Journal of Computer Integrated Manufacturing,* 32(2), 105–123.

Staab, S. and Studer, R. (eds) (2010). *Handbook on Ontologies.* Springer Science & Business Media, Berlin.

Teslya, N. and Ryabchikov, I. (2018). Blockchain platforms overview for industrial IoT purposes. *2018 22nd Conference of Open Innovations Association (FRUCT).* IEEE.

Tiwari, S.M. and Abraham, A. (2020). Semantic assessment of smart healthcare ontology. *International Journal of Web Information Systems,* 16, 475–491.

Um, J.S. (2019). *Drones as Cyber-physical Systems.* Springer, Singapore.

Ustundag, A. and Cevikcan, E. (2017). *Industry 4.0: Managing the Digital Transformation.* Springer, Cham.

Wang, S., Wan, J., Zhang, D., Li, D., Zhang, C. (2016). Towards smart factory for Industry 4.0: A self-organized multi-agent system with big data based feedback and coordination. *Computer Networks,* 101, 158–168.

Wei, C., Shao, J., Agrawal, B., Zhu, D., Xie, H. (2019). New surface mount SiC MOSFETs enable high efficiency high power density bi-directional on-board charger with flexible DC-link voltage. *2019 IEEE Applied Power Electronics Conference and Exposition (APEC).* IEEE.

Wickens, C.D. and Carswell, C.M. (2021). Information processing. In *Handbook of Human Factors and Ergonomics,* G. Salvendy and W. Karwowski (eds). Wiley, New York.

Xavier, A. and de Melo Gonzalez, M. (2016). Analysis and improvement of production efficiency in a construction machine assembly line. *Independent Journal of Management & Production,* 7(5), 606–626.

Yahya, M., Breslin, J.G., Ali, M.I. (2021). Semantic Web and knowledge graphs for Industry 4.0. *Applied Sciences,* 11(11), 5110.

Zeid, A., Sundaram, S., Moghaddam, M., Kamarthi, S., Marion, T. (2019). Interoperability in smart manufacturing: Research challenges. *Machines,* 7(2), 21.

Zhou, K., Liu, T., Zhou, L. (2015). Industry 4.0: Towards future industrial opportunities and challenges. *2015 12th International Conference on Fuzzy Systems and Knowledge Discovery (FSKD).* IEEE.

Semantic Web and Internet of Things in e-Health for Covid-19

Healthcare, in simple terms, means the monitoring and care of a person by detecting, diagnosing, treating and creating cures using a given dataset for any type of illness – mental or physical. Due to the outbreak of coronavirus and advancements in various technologies, healthcare systems have moved from traditional to e-health monitoring systems using the Internet of Things (IoT) and Semantic Web (SW). IoT is a collection of devices that are connected with systems and each other via the Internet using sensors, software and exchanging data. These devices perform in sync with the system and with each other to transfer data efficiently and quickly. The SW, otherwise known as Web 3.0, is the updated version of WWW that makes machines understand data present on the web. This data can be handled by creating specific flowcharts or knowledge graphs using various ontologies to extract useful information. Smart devices like wearables, smart TV and smart homes have enabled remote and continuous monitoring of individuals (who require constant medical attention) by collecting data continuously using sensors and transferring and storing it via the Cloud to the central system using IoT framework. These intelligent devices are helpful in managing essential readings of a patient's blood pressure, heart rate, blood oxygen level, sugar level, body temperature and so on. The collected data is shared with medical practitioners and healthcare personnel for analysis and to decide the treatment accordingly. As these recorded data can be analyzed faster and more accurately, healthcare quality and access to care have been increasing while the cost of care has been decreasing. This chapter sheds light on a study on developing an e-health application using SW technologies and the IoT to diagnose and predict Covid-19. The primary aim is the analysis of various e-health applications and estimation of their efficiencies for Covid-19. Finally, how the intermingling of SW technologies with the IoT is done to design an efficient e-health system for the given problem statement is discussed.

Chapter written by ANURAG and Naren JEEVA.

11.1. Introduction

The world was introduced to a new kind of deadly virus when a variant of coronavirus, known as SARS-CoV-2, was found in Wuhan, China, in December 2019. The virus quickly caught WHO's attention when it was found in more than 15 countries. Then, in March 2020, WHO declared coronavirus infection a pandemic (Pagnelli et al. 2021). The virus can spread via mouth or nose droplets and even via air (to some proximity). The situation of Covid has been controlled in most developed countries; however, the fight is still going on in developing countries and underdeveloped nations. Researchers design different architectures of IoT, and numerous applications are developed using SW technologies to fight against the Covid-19 pandemic.

IoT, short for the Internet of Things, includes intelligent devices which are connected via the Internet. These devices can transfer and receive data with low latency (Otoom et al. 2020). These devices also send the recorded data, collected using sensors, to a cloud server which can be accessed by various devices connected with the network. The usage of IoT devices has not been a new concept, as these devices were used way before the coronavirus pandemic shook the world. Various IoT architectures have helped in the remote and real-time monitoring of patients who could not be mentored or monitored in hospitals (Firouzi et al. 2021). IoT has also been utilized for tracking the real-time locations of various pieces of medical equipment such as wheelchairs, defibrillators, nebulizers, oxygen pumps and other monitoring devices. However, the IoT revolution came full force when the coronavirus pandemic started. IoT architectures were extensively used by hospitals, frontline workers, police, etc., to monitor, detect and diagnose patients infected with Covid-19 inside and outside hospitals (Kohler et al. 2020; Dogan et al. 2021).

IoT-based devices collect data of patients from all around the world. Still, this data is applicable only if it can be utilized effectively by researchers and scientists for designing systems and architecture to fight against the ongoing pandemic. The data should be readily available on the Cloud or online for researchers to test the efficiency and accuracy of their designed systems. Researchers are now using SW, otherwise known as Web 3.0, to arrange the data meaningfully (Jayachandran et al. 2020). SW technologies built applications using knowledge graphs and ontologies to make a computer understand the data, process it and classify it into well-defined sub-categories. The data collected from patients (IoT-based devices) can be directly supplied to SW-designed applications, which can be easily accessed by future researchers and scientists, as per their requirements.

Some studies conducted using ontology-based approaches before Covid-19 are as follows: an ontology framework to analyze the performance of a student as per their behavior (Ashokkumar et al. 2020), the amalgamation of web mining and SW technology to improve the molecular biology domain (Kate et al. 2014), an ontology-based agricultural informatics system was proposed for informing farmers with better farming practices (Mohanraj et al. 2016), analyzing the emotions of individuals using opinion mining ontology (Ganesan et al. 2019), and investigating the Information Retrieval system using an Ontology-Based Fuzzy Semantic system (Naren et al. 2019).

The subsequent sections discuss data set information for IoT and SW applications. Different architectures and frameworks are then discussed as regards their applications for Covid-19. Next, the section shows various shortcomings and challenges using IoT and SW technology and how researchers designed models to overcome these limitations. This chapter then includes a discussion about multiple IoT architecture and SW applications and how these technologies can be merged in the future for better performance of models. The chapter ends with a conclusion that discusses the prospects of this chapter.

11.2. Dataset

The primary purpose of designing an IoT architecture is to collect data about various parameters related to human health, which are vital for the problem at hand. State-of-the-art sensors were explicitly designed for collecting information about EKGs, heart rates, sugar levels, blood pressure (Pagnelli et al. 2021), brain signals, temperature (Bolock et al. 2021), face scans and movement of people (Kohler et al. 2020), in order to assist in various applications designed for stopping the spread of Covid-19. Some of these data are collected in real-time to provide telehealth, remote monitoring, e-health, etc. Other data are collected and stored in clouds to analyze the lockdown, quarantine and movement of individuals.

For SW applications, the data are readily available online about a specific topic, like biomedical and coronavirus, and can be used anywhere and by anyone to be accessed readily and without much effort. The primary focus of building SW applications is for providing meaning to the plethora of information about a particular topic using web ontology language (OWL), knowledge graphs, etc. Moreover, it establishes a relationship between various ontologies present for the same domain, like Covid-19. Many standard databases like gene ontology (GO) (Jayachandran et al. 2020), Infectious Disease Ontology (IDO) and Covid Infectious Disease Ontology (CIDO) (He et al. 2020) were utilized for designing various ontology-based applications, which are going to be discussed in later sections of the chapter.

11.3. Application of IoT for Covid-19

Due to the sudden increase of Covid cases, the poor infrastructure of hospitals in developing countries has posed a severe problem. The non-availability of proper medication and proper monitoring of infected patients have caused more deaths than estimated.

11.3.1. *Continuous real-time remote monitoring*

Firouzi et al. (2021) discusses the fact that the need for constant real-time remote monitoring has risen in this pandemic situation to help patients and healthcare workers. Hospitals have utilized wearable-IoT devices to monitor and track patients' records effectively and identify the symptoms of Covid in non-infected people. Various studies defining a different architecture to overcome this problem have been discussed.

11.3.2. *Remote monitoring using W-kit*

Pagnelli et al. (2021) designed a three-layer IoT-based architecture, IoT-HMS, to monitor patients from home and hospitals. They developed a wearable kit (W-kit) to collect various data from the patients. This architecture could also collect info from third-party wearable devices like Apple watches with the patient's consent.

11.3.3. *Early identification and monitoring*

Otoom et al. (2020) developed an IoT-based architecture to detect Covid-infected people and monitor recovered patients in real time. The framework is applied to five main components to detect the presence of coronavirus in people early. These data were supplied to eight machine learning algorithms, five of which showed more than 90% accuracy. The primary purpose of this architecture is to monitor the treatment response of patients who have recovered from Covid-19.

11.3.4. *Continuous and reliable health monitoring*

Filho et al. (2021) extended the above-proposed model for continuous health monitoring by integrating wearables devices with better sensors. They applied this framework to patients infected with Covid in Brazil. The proposed framework was deployed for ICU patients and expanded the approach to critical patient monitoring. Researchers also proposed a fog-based and Machine Learning-based system to improve their future proposed models.

11.3.5. *ANN-assisted patient monitoring*

Rathee et al. (2021) designed an IoT-based Artificial Neural Network (ANN) architecture to detect and monitor the Covid-infected individuals. This ANN architecture classified the patients into infected, non-infected, susceptible and exposed, quickly identifying infected patients and sending them for further treatment. The data were tested using five different machine learning algorithms, which were evaluated using two factors: classification time and accuracy. This architecture can be improved when a large amount of data is provided.

11.3.6. *City lockdown monitoring*

Kohler et al. (2020) proposed a three-layer decentralized IoT-based biometric architecture to monitor the movement of people during the lockdown. The proposed framework utilizes the state-of-the-art FDDB and WIDER FACE datasets for face detection. Face detection using the CNN-based model showed a better response than the above face detection model. The primary purpose of this proposed three-layer edge architecture is to restrict the movement of people. This system outperforms the previously defined cloud-based system.

11.3.7. *Technologies for tracking and tracing*

Firouzi et al. (2021) discuss how different technologies are used to track and trace the movement of people. These technologies include Bluetooth, GPS and ultrasonic-enabled applications for contact tracing. Contact tracing helps identify individuals who have had contact with infected people, places or objects. Governments have utilized various mobile applications like TraceTogether (Singapore), Aarogya Setu (India) and many others to track and curb the spread of coronavirus. The study also discusses different architectures designed by various researchers and scientists to help track and trace the movement of people.

11.3.8. *Tracking and tracing suspected cases*

Rajasekar (2021) designed an IoT-based architecture to automatically track and trace the movement of people using RFID and their mobile phones and to identify various points of contact. This framework would allow individuals who contact exposed people (knowingly or unknowingly) to follow quarantine or treatment procedures for both parties (if infected). The proposed system would help the government to curb the spread of infection during this pandemic. This model will help concerned authorities take necessary actions on the ignored suspected cases to prevent further transmission of Covid-19.

11.3.9. *Anonymity preserving contact tracing model*

Garg et al. (2020) proposed a novel IoT-based privacy contact tracing architecture. The framework utilized RFID proof-of-concept for moving contacts to identify flagged peoples, places or objects. The proposed model presented three blockchain contact tracing prototypes and delivered notifications to help achieve mass isolation while preserving individual privacy. This model helped understand human connectivity to enable policymakers to develop effective policies for future pandemics.

11.3.10. *Cognitive radio-based IoT architecture*

Chandrasekaran et al. (2020) proposed a cognitive-based IoT architecture to monitor and track patients, for better treatment and control, without spreading the infection to others. The proposed model could help governments devise better policies and provide online consultations based on a systematic database that predicts disease activity. This proposed technology is promising for rapid diagnosis and dynamic monitoring.

11.3.11. *Analyzing reasons for the outbreak*

Ramallo-González et al. (2021) designed a four-layer IoT-based architecture to help analyze reasons for the outbreak of Covid-19. IoT sensors collected patients' body parameters and analyzed them using the CIoTVID model proposed in this study. The study helped policymakers, individuals and hospitals to fight against the propagation of Covid-19.

11.3.12. *Analyzing Covid-19 cases using disruptive technology*

Abdel-Basset et al. (2020) proposed an intelligent framework using IoT and IoMT based technology to diagnose and prevent the spread of Covid-19, especially in healthcare facilities like hospitals, isolation wards and Covid centers. The architecture utilized effective medical sensors in hospitals and at home to monitor the health of and diagnose disease severity in a person showing symptoms, using data collected from sensors. This proposed framework utilizes the most disruptive technologies currently available to limit the spread of Covid-19.

11.3.13. *Post-Covid applications*

The ongoing pandemic has made us realize that the world is not equipped to fight this situation. The architectures, as mentioned earlier, are designed to fight the current condition of Covid-19, but what about post-Covid? What steps can be taken to ensure our safety in the future?

11.3.13.1. *Automated health monitoring and surveillance*

Vedaei et al. (2020) and Tiwari and Abraham (2020) proposed an IoT-based healthcare and monitoring system for future pandemic situations. The three-layer framework designed allowed individuals to track their health parameters and monitor them through the designed mobile application. The COVID-SAFE framework, developed by researchers, could minimize the risk of coronavirus exposure.

11.3.13.2. *Extensive use of IoT technology*

Nasajpour et al. (2020) discuss IoT devices for early diagnosis, quarantine time and recovery. The study mentions the use of wearables, robots, drones, IoT buttons and smartphone applications. For early diagnosis, wearables like smart helmets, thermometers and glasses, along with mobile applications such as ncapp, stopcorona and mobiledetect, are used. For quarantine time, disinfectant drones, medical delivery drones with robots such as telerobots, collaborative robots and social robots were employed. Many mobile apps, namely social monitoring, selfie app, the stayhomesafe and civitas apps, were used. Lastly, wearables like the easy band, proximity band, surveillance, announcement and multipurpose drones after the recovery period were used. Various smartphone apps such as Aarogya Setu, TraceTogether and Hamagon were used by governments to track the movement of the general public.

11.4. Semantic Web applications for Covid-19

SW technologies are still under development, but with these technologies' help, categorizing available patients' data (present online) has been done effectively (Jayachandran et al. 2020; Nikiforova et al. 2022; Tiwari et al. 2022). SW applications try to make sense of a vast amount of data on the Cloud or Internet. It tries to define connections or relationships between various data and make it meaningful for machines and humans. SW technologies consist of knowledge graphs and ontology-based applications to divide data into proper categories and sub-categories based on the relationship or connection defined as per the requirements. SW, otherwise known as Web 3.0, is extensively used by researchers and scientists to design a link between previous research and ongoing research. The ontology-based approach has helped scientists to discover treatments, vaccines, repurpose drugs, etc., and even find cures for diseases that were thought untreatable, using the data present from previous clinical trials. How SW technology can be proved helpful for fighting against current and future pandemics is discussed below.

11.4.1. *Ontological approach for drug development*

Jayachandran et al. (2020) discuss how various research related to drug development at the time of outbreak of Covid could be made valid using ontological approaches. These ontology-based applications can help in assisting pharmacology, designing vaccines, medicine preparation, etc., using databases such as Gene Ontology (GO), Infectious Disease Ontology (IDO) and Vaccine Ontology (VO). These databases are readily available for all, accelerate drug development, target new drugs and vaccine development and are more reliable, faster and cheaper than traditional techniques. These ontological approaches focus more on gene and protein interaction in hosts and pathogens, which has also turned out to be superior to traditional techniques.

11.4.2. *Early detection and diagnosis*

Oyelade et al. (2020) proposed a Case-Based Reasoning (CBR) ontological approach to overcome the limitations of previous models. The feature extraction ontology and mapping, semantic and feature-based mathematical similarity computation and CBR framework for detection and classification of suspected cases were achieved effectively using the proposed model. The data used in this study focus on using data from recovered or infected cases rather than assuming parameter values. After testing 71 patients (67 adults and four children) and comparing them using the fuzzy-based approach, the result shows a significant improvement in classification and detection.

11.4.3. *Knowledge-based pre-diagnosis system*

Çelik Ertuğrul and Çelik Ulusoy (2021) proposed a rule-based expert system for monitoring and diagnosing cases using smartphones. When tested with 169 positive patients, this knowledge-based system showed similar results as the RT-PCR test for symptomatic cases. For asymptomatic cases, suggestions given by the proposed system showed a similar result as a healthcare expert, validating its effectiveness. This ontology-based system, OntCov19, can be used in places where experts are not readily available to diagnose the patient. Pre-diagnosis can be done using an individual's phone without the assistance of an expert. This diagnosis is made online, and with expert data and data entered by a user, the system predicts the Covid status of the user.

11.4.4. *Semantic-based searching for online learning resources*

The necessity of online learning was realized during times such as those we are facing right now. Online learning went from just an alternative source to a mainstream learning solution for students and industries. Hence the need for a standard database system arose. Dien et al. (2020) proposed a semantic-based searching in learning resources. The proposed application included an ontology-based representation of learning resources. The searched queries were pre-processed using Support Vector Machine (SVM) to narrow down the search space, and the resultant questions sent to the appropriate ontology showed the required lectures. When tested with IT lectures, the proposed model showed a consistent and better solution than traditional search solutions.

11.4.5. *Ontology-based physiological monitoring of students*

Bolock et al. (2021) proposed an ontological framework for psychological monitoring of education during the ongoing pandemic. The proposed framework extends standard psychology-driven ontology, CCOnto, ascribing human behavior based on a situation to psychological states. Based on psychological theories and concepts, the CCOnto ontology automatically categorizes university students according to learning, worrying, mental health and much more. This framework targets the psychological aspects of Covid-19 on students.

11.4.6. *Analysis of clinical trials*

The exponential spread of Covid-19 forced scientists and researchers to conduct clinical trials at an unprecedented rate to curb the spread as soon as possible. This left scientists with repeated trials, which led to wastage of resources, which posed a big problem. Id (2020) proposed an ontology-based application interface that showed all the research related to Covid-19 be present on ClinicalTrials.gov. The study used Medical Subject Heading (MeSH) and Human Phenology Ontology (HPO) terms to categorize data and make them available on covidresearchtrials.com. Another study (Visweswaran et al. 2021) proposed an ontology-based Covid-19 application in the National Accrual to Clinical Trials (ACT) network using Electronic Health Records (EHR) of 14.5 million patients. This ontology uses the data harmonization technique and contains over 50,000 concepts related to Covid-19 trails.

11.4.7. *Data annotation of EHRs*

Keloth et al. (2020) proposed an ontology-based application, Initial Covid Interface Terminology (ICIT) and CIT_v0 – an extension of CIDO – to annotate a large amount of patient data. They designed a concatenation and anchoring approach to extract or mine essential data from clinical texts. The organized database helped extract data about signs and symptoms of Covid-19, and using concept mining with ML techniques opens the door for future research. Fries et al. (2021) proposed a framework, Trove, for weekly supervised entity classification of EHRs. The system uses medical ontologies and expert-generated rules to outperform the traditional method of creating manually-labeled training data. Trove analyzed the record of patients infected from Covid-19 presenting symptoms and risk factors.

11.4.8. *Disease pattern study*

Rawal et al. (2020) proposed a description logic-based ontology to study the disease patterns of Covid-19. The system removes ambiguity around the spread of Covid-19 and provides proper reasoning to facts. Description Logic (DL) is used to understand the spread, treatment and diagnosis, related to the family of viruses. A SW application is designed by converting the above information into ontological-based entities. The system proposes a solution to investigate the current pandemic to study the root cause of the spread and find disease patterns to help policymakers and governments effectively fight this situation.

11.4.9. *Surveillance in primary care*

To ensure transparency and consistency, de Lusignan et al. (2020) proposed an ontology application for surveillance of Covid-19 patients. The study is an extension of the RCGP Research and Surveillance Center (RSC) to monitor the situation of the ongoing pandemic. The proposed application studied the course of the current pandemic and showed the spread and effects of measures. The ontology application was developed using a three-step method, and a Covid identification algorithm was developed. The resultant application was able to identify 19,115 definite, 5226 probable and 74,293 possible cases in the RCGP sentinel network. The proposed system can be implemented for primary care, public health, virology, clinical research and informatics.

11.4.10. *Performance assessment of healthcare services*

Sayeb et al. (2021) proposed a unique semantic-based application to assess the performance of healthcare services provided in the wake of Covid-19. The study implemented an ontology called the Covid-19 Crisis Health Care Ontology Information System (C3-HIS) to support healthcare service management. The ontology responds quickly and effectively by providing a clear definition of healthcare services available. Patients were directed to specific healthcare services as per the competence and performance of the service available. For Covid-19 patients, the proposed system helped monitor a patient's condition and provide healthcare services accordingly. Researchers proposed a web-based software solution to illustrate the effectiveness of the designed system and gather the appropriate healthcare workers for critical situations.

11.4.11. *Vaccination drives and rollout strategies*

Sreeganga et al. (2021) proposed an ontological-based approach to tackle the limitations of vaccine rollout strategies after looking at the system of the USA and India. Many roadblocks, such as large population, the health infrastructure, vaccine hesitancy, adequate supply, distribution, variation in demand, production capacity, regulatory issues, labor, decentralization for administrating the vaccine and science communication, have posed severe problems. The proposed system tries to solve these problems by implementing a supportive framework for vaccine rollout strategies. The study focuses on the vaccine rollout strategies of two countries to visualize the similarities and barriers in developing and developed countries. The unique design was mapped onto ontology and various monad maps and theme maps were generated for comparison. The study visualizes the gaps and barriers in their approach and proposes solutions to overcome them and make them more effective.

11.5. Limitations and challenges of IoT and SW models

Both IoT and SW models have some shortcomings when implemented for Covid-19. When it comes to IoT architecture, the most critical challenges for the current pandemic are as follows: security, privacy concerns, system integrity, sensors for wearables, unobstructed sensing and continuous sharing of information, data connection and transfer issues (Vedaei et al. 2020). The IoT frameworks proposed by researchers and scientists tried to overcome some of the issues but still need a lot of iterations for their work to improve the models. Researchers designed various IoT architectures, either by ignoring the problems entirely or by assuming some of the initial parameters to enhance the performance of the models with limitations. These models can be improved using more advanced algorithms and better accuracy devices in future implementations. SW technology is still a very new area of study. However, it has received serious attention from researchers and scientists due to its capabilities. The studies have shown that the use of SW technologies in various studies has increased exponentially in the last decade. The SW applications are limited in number and are still under development, but they are not immune to shortcomings and challenges. The interoperability issues, absence of generalized and standard databases, capturing data in a standard form and a connection between various databases (Bauer et al. 2021) are significant limitations of these models. Various researchers tried to decrease the effect of these shortcomings by utilizing standard ontology models designed explicitly for Covid-19, which included other related information from previous ontologies (on a need basis). Researchers also tried to give solutions for challenges related to efficiency, cost, largescale usage, availability, distribution and many more in order to tackle this pandemic situation as early as possible.

11.6. Discussion

IoT and SW applications have provided a big push for the fight against the new coronavirus (Covid-19) and have given people a chance to fight head-on. IoT architecture has provided the necessary help to save countless lives by providing continuous real-time monitoring, early identification, diagnosis, classification, tracking and tracing suspected cases and providing the appropriate solutions to post-pandemic situations. The models mentioned above helped governments to devise necessary guidelines and rules for people to cope with prolonged lockdown situations, stress created from the professional environment, work-from-home setups and have allowed better availability of healthcare solutions in their own homes. SW applications have helped researchers to recognize disease patterns and pre-diagnosis, early detection and treatment of Covid-19 (measures taken in the case of early detection) and people's psychological monitoring. Moreover, they are utilizing the data from previous clinical trials, data annotation, drug discovery, surveillance and vaccine rollout strategies to assist in developing new and more efficient models to fight the current pandemic. The proposed frameworks helped policymakers to regulate effective procedures to minimize the spread of Covid-19 and navigate through the lockdown procedures, quarantine periods, global panic and distribution of vaccines.

11.7. Conclusion

This chapter sheds light on frameworks and architecture designed with the help of IoT and SW applications against the biggest fight of this century: the fight against Covid-19. The ongoing pandemic has made humans realize the extent of the loopholes present in our healthcare systems and how poorly our healthcare institutions can handle this situation. Nevertheless, scientists and researchers have learned a lot from this ongoing pandemic and have utilized state-of-the-art architectures to ensure our survival and make us ready for any future pandemic (although it may not be as vast as Covid-19 turned out to be). However, looking at the positive side, the revolution in IoT has been a boom in this challenging time, as Covid-19 forced scientists and healthcare management to implement innovative architectures to provide essential healthcare services to people. In addition, SW technologies are now on the right path to become the application technologies for tomorrow and assist humans and machines in understanding data better than before. Furthermore, the amalgamation of IoT and SW in future architecture would provide a more robust and secure model to handle this pandemic situation. Finally, this chapter could be referred to by young researchers and scientists who would like to contribute to this fight against an invisible force – Covid-19.

11.8. References

Abdel-Basset, M., Chang, V., Nabeeh, N.A. (2020). An intelligent framework using disruptive technologies for COVID-19 analysis. *Technological Forecasting and Social Change*, 163. Available at: https://doi.org/10.1016/j.techfore.2020.120431.

Ashokkumar, K., Naren, J., Rakshanasri, S.L., Ganesan, V. (2020). Ontological framework for analyzing student's emotional behavior performance enhancement using Fuzzy Logic. *International Journal of Psychosocial Rehabilitation*, 24, 155–164.

Bauer, D.C., Metke-Jimenez, A., Maurer-Stroh, S., Tiruvayipati, S., Wilson, L.O.W., Jain, Y., Perrin, A., Ebrill, K., Hansen, D.P., Vasan, S.S. (2021). Interoperable medical data: The missing link for understanding COVID-19. *Transbound and Emerging Diseases*, 68(4), 1753–1760.

Bolock, A.E., Abdennadher, S., Herbert, C. (2021). An ontology-based framework for psychological monitoring in education during the COVID-19 pandemic. *Frontiers in Psychology*, 12(July), 1–16.

Çelik Ertuğrul, D. and Çelik Ulusoy, D. (2021). A knowledge-based self-pre-diagnosis system to predict Covid-19 in smartphone users using personal data and observed symptoms. *Expert Systems*. Available at: https://doi.org/10.1111/exsy.12716.

Chandrasekaran, B. and Fernandes, S. (2020). Since January 2020 Elsevier has created a COVID-19 resource centre with free information in English and Mandarin on the novel coronavirus. The COVID-19 resource centre is hosted on Elsevier Connect, the company's public news and information website. *Diabetes & Metabolic Syndrome*, 14(4), 337–339.

Dien, T.T., Van Trung, L., Thai-Nghe, N. (2020). An approach for semantic-based searching in learning resources. *Proceedings of the 2020 12th International Conference on Knowledge and Systems Engineering, KSE 2020*. Available at: https://doi.org/10.1109/KSE50997.2020.9287798.

Dogan, O., Tiwari, S., Jabbar, M.A., Guggari, S. (2021). A systematic review on AI/ML approaches against COVID-19 outbreak. *Complex & Intelligent Systems*, 7(5), 2655–2678.

Filho, I.D.M.B., Aquino, G., Malaquias, R.S., Girao, G., Melo, S.R.M. (2021). An IoT-based healthcare platform for patients in ICU beds during the COVID-19 outbreak. *IEEE Access*, 9, 27262–27277.

Firouzi, F., Farahani, B., Daneshmand, M., Grise, K., Song, J., Saracco, R., Wang, L.L., Lo, K., Angelov, P., Soares, E. et al. (2021). Harnessing the power of smart and connected health to tackle COVID-19: IoT, AI, robotics, and blockchain for a better world. *IEEE Internet of Things Journal*, 8(16), 12826–12846. Available at: https://doi.org/10.1109/JIOT.2021.3073904.

Fries, J.A., Steinberg, E., Khattar, S., Fleming, S.L., Posada, J., Callahan, A., Shah, N.H. (2021). Ontology-driven weak supervision for clinical entity classification in electronic health records. *Nature Communications*, 12(1). Available at: https://doi.org/10.1038/s41467-021-22328-4.

Ganesan, V., Naren, J., Varun, V. (2019). Opinion mining with real time ontology streaming data. *International Journal of Psychosocial Rehabilitation*, 23, 346–357.

Garg, L., Chukwu, E., Nasser, N., Chakraborty, C., Garg, G. (2020). Anonymity preserving IoT-based COVID-19 and other infectious disease contact tracing model. *IEEE Access*, 8, 159402–159414.

He, Y., Yu, H., Ong, E., Wang, Y., Liu, Y., Huffman, A., Huang, H.-H., Beverley, J., Hur, J., Yang, X. et al. (2020). CIDO, a community-based ontology for coronavirus disease knowledge and data integration, sharing, and analysis. *Scientific Data*, 7(1), 1–5. Available at: https://doi.org/10.1038/s41597-020-0523-6.

Id, S.A. (2020). Analysis of COVID-19 clinical trials: A data-driven, ontology-based, and natural language [Online]. Available at: https://doi.org/10.1371/journal.pone.0239694.

Jayachandran, S.K. and Anusuyadevi, M. (2020). Decoding information on COVID–19: Ontological approach towards design possible therapeutics. *Informatics in Medicine Unlocked*, 22, 100486.

Kate, A.V., Balakrishnan, H., Naren, J. (2014). Ontology mining in Molecular Biology domain (Lac Operon problem). *Proceedings of IEEE International Conference on Computer Communication and Systems ICCCS14*. Available at: 10.1109/ICCCS.2014.7068157.

Keloth, V.K., Zhou, S., Lindemann, L., Elhanan, G., Einstein, A.J., Geller, J., Perl, Y. (2020). Mining concepts for a COVID interface terminology for annotation of EHRs. *Proceedings of the 2020 IEEE International Conference on Big Data, Big Data 2020*. Available at: https://doi.org/10.1109/BigData50022.2020.9377981.

Kolhar, M., Al-Turjman, F., Alameen, A., Abualhaj, M.M. (2020). A three layered decentralized IoT biometric architecture for city lockdown during Covid-19 outbreak. *IEEE Access*, 8, 163608–163617.

de Lusignan, S., Liyanage, H., McGagh, D., Jani, B.D., Bauwens, J., Byford, R., Evans, D., Fahey, T., Greenhalgh, T., Jones, N. et al. (2020). COVID-19 surveillance in a primary care sentinel network: In-pandemic development of an application ontology. *JMIR Public Health and Surveillance*, 6(4). Available at: https://doi.org/10.2196/21434.

Mohanraj, I. and Naren, J. (2016). The application of semantic web on agricultural domain – A state of art survey. *10th INDIACom; 2016 3rd International Conference on Computing for Sustainable Global Development, INDIACom*, New Delhi, 16–18 March.

Naren, J., Raja, R.J., Sannidhi, N., Ganesan, V. (2019). An investigation on ontology based fuzzy semantic information retrieval. *International Journal of Psychosocial Rehabilitation*, 23, 377–384.

Nasajpour, M., Pouriyeh, S., Parizi, R.M., Dorodchi, M., Valero, M., Arabnia, H.R. (2020). Internet of Things for current COVID-19 and future pandemics: An exploratory study. *J. Healthc. Inform.*, 4, 325–364.

Nikiforova, A., Tiwari, S., Rovite, V., Klovins, J., Kante, N. (2022). Evaluation and visualization of healthcare semantic models. *Evaluation*, 323, 91773–91775.

Otoom, M., Otoum, N., Alzubaidi, M.A., Etoom, Y. (2020). An IoT-based framework for early identification and monitoring of COVID-19 cases. *Biomedical Signal Processing and Control*, 62(2020), 102149.

Oyelade, O.N. and Ezugwu, A.E. (2020). A case-based reasoning framework for early detection and diagnosis of novel coronavirus. *Informatics in Medicine Unlocked*, 20(2020), 100395.

Paganelli, A.I., Velmovitsky, P.E., Miranda, P., Branco, A., Alencar, P., Cowan, D., Endler, M., Morita, P.P. (2021). A conceptual IoT-based early-warning architecture for remote monitoring of COVID-19 patients in wards and at home. *Internet of Things*, 40, 100399.

Rajasekar, S.J.S. (2021). An enhanced IoT based tracing and tracking model for COVID-19 cases. *SN Computer Science*, 2(1), 2–5.

Ramallo-González, A.P., González-Vidal, A., Skarmeta, A.F. (2021). Ciotvid: Towards an open IoT-platform for infective pandemic diseases such as COVID-19. *Sensors (Switzerland)*, 21(2), 1–13.

Rathee, G., Garg, S., Kaddoum, G., Wu, Y., Dushantha, D.N., Alamri, A. (2021). ANN assisted-IoT enabled COVID-19 patient monitoring. *IEEE Access*, 9, 42483–42492.

Rawal, R., Goel, K., Gupta, C. (2020). COVID-19: Disease pattern study based on Semantic-Web approach using description logic. *2020 IEEE International Conference for Innovation in Technology, INOCON 2020*, Bangalore, 6–8 November. Available at: https://doi.org/10.1109/INOCON50539.2020.9298278.

Sayeb, Y., Jebri, M., Ghezala, H.B. (2021). Managing COVID-19 crisis using C^3HIS ontology. *Procedia Comput. Sci.*, 181, 1114–1121.

Sreeganga, S.D., Chandra, A., Ramaprasad, A. (2021). Ontological analysis of Covid-19 vaccine roll out strategies: A comparison of India and the United States of America. *International Journal of Environmental Research and Public Health*, 18(14). Available at: https://doi.org/10.3390/ijerph18147483.

Swayamsiddha, S. and Mohanty, C. (2020). Application of cognitive Internet of Medical Things for COVID-19 pandemic. *Diabetes Metab. Syndr.*, 214(5), 911–915.

Tiwari, S. and Abraham, A. (2020). Semantic assessment of smart healthcare ontology. *International Journal of Web Information Systems*, 16(4), 475–491. Available at: https://doi.org/10.1108/IJWIS-05-2020-0027.

Tiwari, S., Ortiz-Rodriguez, O., Jabbar, M.A. (2022). Semantic models in IoT and eHealth applications. *Elsevier*, 380, 91773–91775.

Vedaei, S.S., Fotovvat, A., Mohebbian, M.R., Rahman, G.M.E., Wahid, K.A., Babyn, P., Marateb, H.R., Mansourian, M., Sami, R. (2020). COVID-SAFE: An IoT-based system for automated health monitoring and surveillance in post-pandemic life. *IEEE Access*, 8, 188538–188551.

Visweswaran, S., Samayamuthu, M.J., Morris, M., Weber, G.M., MacFadden, D., Trevvett, P., Klann, J.G., Gainer, V.S., Benoit, B., Murphy, S.N. et al. (2021). Development of a Coronavirus Disease 2019 (COVID-19) application ontology for the Accrual to Clinical Trials (ACT) network. *JAMIA Open*, 4(2), 1–6.

Development of a Semantic Web Enabled Job_Search Ontology System

Classical process recruitment portals on the Internet depend on keyword searching to discover jobs. However, this approach results in excessive recall, low precision and low semantic similarity among the keywords. Many researchers have proposed semantic matching strategies through growing ontologies, but those strategies now no longer quantify how carefully matched candidates and employers are, primarily based totally on middle skills (Kumar and Ramu 2021).

Today, ontologies serve as a conceptual knowledge model. Semantic Web and semantic search have promoted meaning-based web searching. This chapter proposes a "SearchAJob" system enabling companies to find the right candidate, and jobseekers to find the right job. The ontology has been developed using the Protégé editor and SPARQL queries are written to execute the user's queries and retrieve more meaningful information. A PHP Interface is developed serving as a search medium for the company and jobseeker. The "SearchAJob" ontology will serve as a database to the PHP interface, using the Apache Jena Fuseki server, which is a recommended SPARQL server, enabling the SPARQL queries to be executed. The basic aim of research is to create a single Decentralized Job Ontology portal from scratch, integrating different job recruitment domains, enabling the search for a job through a single query executed on multiple domains. The proposed ontology can be easily integrated by creating the required Application Programming Interface (API) using current recruitment websites.

12.1. Introduction

The challenging aspect of the World Wide Web is to provide users with the right information at the right time when searched for. Information becomes meaningful if it is provided by understanding the context (meaning) in which it is required. The

Chapter written by Hina J. CHOKSHI, Dhaval VYAS and Ronak PANCHAL.

answer to the issue faced by the WWW is an extended version of it, known as the Web 4.0, also referred to as the Semantic Web and ontology development. The proposed chapter discusses the creation of ontology for job searching, which provides meaning-specific search, that is based on semantics, which is much more efficient compared to the traditional searching techniques. The chapter explains the concepts related to understanding ontology and its importance, traditional job searching techniques, syntactic web comparison with the Semantic Web, design of ontology structure, querying it using SPARQL queries, developing it using ontology development tools like Protégé and integrating it using the Apache Jena Fuseki server to enable job searching using the PHP interface.

Unemployed people can search for the jobs on the web grounded on their qualifications. They can determine what specializations are required in their field of work. Unemployed people can learn these specializations and get jobs. Youths can choose their career path by hunting for available jobs on this website for that particular study (Hasan et al. 2013).

A customized concept comparison matching algorithm was deployed to CV ontology in order to match the core skills of applicants to employers more accurately (Kumar et al. 2021).

12.1.1. *Ontology*

"An ontology is a formal specification of shared conceptualization" (Gruber 1993). Ontology uses a specific language. This language consists of symbols and expressions with a particular importance. Based on the semantics, class clusters and symbols are created. As per Stuckenschmidt and Harmelen (2005), ontologies are also known as "information sharing".

Specific to a particular domain, ontologies are created. It is also termed as an iterative process. It consists of the following steps:

– find the ontology scope;

– for the given ontology, define entities/classes and relationships between them;

– reusability of concepts is the main aim of forming an ontology;

– concepts, that is, a sub class-super class hierarchy is formed;

– for each defined class, find the attributes and properties;

– for each class, define instances and fill the slot values.

12.1.2. *Importance of ontology*

Proper analysis of domain knowledge and information structure should be carried out.

– Domain knowledge should be made reusable.

– Domain assumptions should be made explicit.

– Operational knowledge should be separated from domain knowledge.

12.1.2.1. *Challenges of World Wide Web*

People search for any information across the WWW, and get multiple links as an answer to their search. Computers can be said to be a mere source of presenting things, whereas the actual linking and interpretation of data is only carried out by people. The World Wide Web faces many challenges, namely:

– searching for data and information in big data pools;

– answering various real-time complex inquires;

– managing rates of goods and services;

– executing queries requiring background details and related information.

Tim Berners Lee, the inventor of the World Wide Web, strongly believed that for sharing data in future:

– a URL should point to data;

– accessing the URL should retrieve the data.

The link between other URLs and the data retrieved should be shown. There are many limitations faced by WWW, namely:

– Online searching retrieves data of low precision along with irrelevant data.

– Retrieved results are web pages which are vocabulary sensitive.

– The unstructured format of the contents to be published makes querying difficult.

– On WWW, data is defined with its syntax and not semantics.

12.1.3. *Semantic Web and its solutions*

Using the Semantic Web, data can be easily published in different languages, namely RDF (Resource Description Framework), Web Ontology Language (OWL) and Extensible Markup Language (XML).

RDF, OWL and XML are combined while searching for data in the Semantic Web to enable the machine to process the data with reasoning and inference and the corresponding results with meaningful information. Data on the web are searched for using metadata, enabling data searching on the basis of the meaning of the word. Data exchange and the representation of metadata is done using the RDF. RDF also has the property of merging data while working with different schema.

When working with Web 2.0, a webpage search is represented as:

<item>newsblog</item>

When working with Web 4.0, that is the Semantic Web, the webpage is represented as:

<item rdf:about="http://example.org/semantic-web/">Semantic web</item>

12.1.4. *Online recruitment scenarios*

The WWW has made the online job search and recruitment process very easy and efficient. The main aim of recruitment is to find an appropriate candidate to match the desired job. Online recruitment encompasses the process of job searching, posting job offers, uploading resumes, conducting online interviews and selecting a candidate. Rather than manually going to various offices and applying for a job, with online recruitment a candidate can easily search for a job, upload their resume and apply for a job in a very simple and efficient manner. This way of recruitment has simplified the entire job search and recruitment process.

The major issue faced by online recruitment scenarios is difficulty in finding the right candidate for the right job. While working online, multiple users may access the same webpage at the same time, which in turn leads the website to give results at a lower rate, consuming more time. There may be certain technical issues that also affect the functionality of the website. Searching for a particular term related to recruitment fetches multiple pages, which may or may not be the exact match for the search, as the data are linked across the web through keyword matching and not by their semantics. Today, with the click of a button, the need has risen for online recruitment, enabling a candidate to search for a job online and get semantic-specific search results. Semantic Web enabled job searching is an answer to this issue.

12.2. Review of the related work done for online recruitment

The review of the work done in this field focuses on the different findings, reviews and limitations related to the work done in the field of Semantic Web, ontology development, data mining and ontology development tools.

Yi et al. (2007) proposed SRM (Structured Relevance Models) as a solution for blank value fields filled by the jobseeker while applying for a job offer online. Furthermore, they emphasized how an empty value field can be generalized on the basis of other fields which are provided with some value. SRM is a considered example of the Collaborative Filtering approach. Paparrizos et al. (2011) proposed an automated recommendation system based on supervised machine learning techniques using the Content-Based Filtering approach. For the process of selecting a new job based on the jobseekers past experience, the main intention was to infer jobs to the jobseekers using different job transition patterns to extract features. A system for job search and recruitment sites was given by Lu et al. (2013), which basically collects data from different sources. A multi-relational, heavy and directed graph is used to model the collected data. To rank features on the basis of relevance from a group of target users, it used the 3A ranking algorithm. The data model collected is based on the entity connections. On the basis of content-based and interaction-based relations, these entity collections were developed.

A content-based system gathers the relations between the candidates who are looking for a job in two ways. In the first relation, the profile of the candidates are matched. The suitable candidates with an equivalent option are identified within the job offer. In the second relation, the similarity of the profile is checked. The jobseekers and employers are matched from the given group.

The relationships based on interactions express the aggregation of the system details, with reference to the previous interaction of the candidate with the company, which is hiring. Similarly, Dooms (2013) describes a complex skilled worker system that supports the co-operative filtering principle, combining completely opposite algorithms dynamically. This helps to match the jobseekers profile with the job role offered by a company. The previously used algorithms specified in the paper are classified into various classes that support the exploited data. Algorithms use the behavior of community ratings, content-based algorithms are used to extract the options and data-based algorithms are used to analyze the final knowledge on the market within the system. The authors have used the hybrid recommendation approach, as they believe that each user in the system is different and has individual characteristics. As mentioned by Faliagka et al. (2014, 2015), more recent studies focus on the adjustment in the achievement system and claim that already existing e-recruitment platforms fall back in assessing the attribute traits. In the paper by

Faliagka et al. (2014), a position of applicant matching is represented, with the system performing humanistic discipline matching techniques using the machine learning techniques algorithms, which means that a ranking can be given to the jobseekers. To include human input in the evaluation process, a journal universal resource locator on the registration process needs to be produced. Later on in the completion process, linguistic analysis is applied to the blog post to derive the features of personal traits. According to Faliagka et al. (2015), suggestions for applying the techniques were proposed. These techniques use internet data for data mining and extracting a candidate's personality, which depends on the candidate's social media activities, such as Twitter, Instagram, Facebook and LinkedIn.

Similarly, some studies (for example, Fazel-Zarandi (2009) and Gómez-Pérez et al. (2007)) describe the subject from a distinct linear perspective and present metaphysics research, which is managed within the achievement domain. As defined by Sicilia (2014, p. 95): "An ontology is an explicit, formal specification of a shared conceptualization". In addition, "ontology in the field of computer technology and science are bestowed as 'a model that describes the globe that consists of building a group of topics, properties and relationships'. A likeness is established between the real world and the model created by ontologies". Fazel-Zarandi (2009) proposed a way to outline the jobseeker and job post. They applied a deductive model to form a match between two outlined entities. Finally, the candidate was ranked with their parallel degree.

The interested candidate who is seeking a job is considered against a collection of expert statements and the job advertisement with a set of requirements, all drawn from the utilization of description logic. Gómez-Pérez et al. (2007) proposed that the employer should describe their support of prevailing HR (Human Resource) standards like NACE and FOET in the small print of the job offer. The reference ontology in all consisted of total 13 ontologies, namely proficiency, rectification, driving legal document, economical activity, education, Earth science, job offer, jobseeker, labor restrictive, language, occupation, talent, skill and time. Moreover, other national researches, as mentioned by Niculescu et al. (2009), show the interest in this field of the ontology and their planned exploitation for information technology companies. Some other domain ontologies are also designed for domain-specific tasks, such as the Military_Resource_Ontology (MRO) (Mishra and Jain 2019; Mishra and Jain 2021) and Smart Health Care ontology (SHCO) (Tiwari and Abraham 2021). Panchal et al. (2021) have created an ontology for higher education (AISHE-Onto) as a domain-specific ontology.

12.3. Design of "SearchAJob" ontology for the IT domain

The proposed job ontology includes the identification of the different subdomains of the application, such as knowledge, experience, programming skills and many more. The identification of four basic steps of the recruitment process is carried out, namely:

– recruitment analysis;

– publishing the various job posts;

– receiving and selecting the applications;

– final recruitment decisions.

The skill set of a jobseeker in the various IT domains can be described as shown in Figure 12.1.

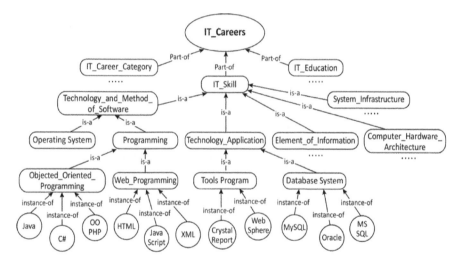

Figure 12.1. *IT jobs hierarchy*

The proposed e-recruitment system shall encompass designing the ontology from the scratch, querying it and creating the user interface. The basic step of ontology development is the identification of various functionalities and requirements of an online recruitment system.

The technologies used for the development and execution of the ontology include the following:

– for ontology designing – Protégé;

– for query writing – SPARQL;

– for interface linking – Apache Jena Fuseki Server;

– for creating a user interface – PHP.

Company details	Information related to the company needs to be identified so that jobseekers can see it.
Job offers	The company should be able to post different job offers with various options to match jobseeker applications.
Jobseekers profile generation	Jobseekers have to provide all of the job-related information so that they can apply for jobs posted by the company.
Matching job offers with jobseekers profile	Appropriate matching of job offers with jobseekers should be provided so that a company can find a suitable candidate.
Displaying job offers matching jobseekers profile	The jobseeker should also be able to search for a required job from the given list of jobs posted by the recruiter company.
Company posted jobs list	Each company should get the list of all jobs posted by it.
Updating company's profile	The ontology should provide enough options to update the company's profile.
Updating jobseeker's profile	The ontology should provide enough options to update the candidate's profile.

Table 12.1. *Requirement of online recruitment system*

12.3.1. *Ontology structure*

A structure of ontology is designed, mentioning the various classes, data properties, object properties and axioms. A proposed flow of the entire system is designed as shown in Figure 12.2.

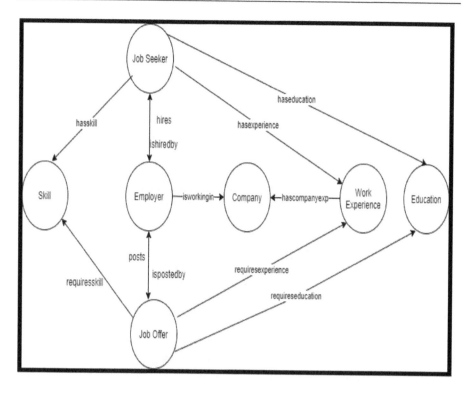

Figure 12.2. *Data flow diagram of the job search process*

On the basis of the proposed requirements as mentioned in the Table 12.1, the ontology is developed in order to provide a proper structured interface to connect jobseekers with companies and vice-versa. The classes created and the relationships established between the classes are shown below.

Class name	*Class and relationship*
Company :	Company_hasEmployer_Employer
Education:	JobSeeker_hasExperience_Company
Person:	Employee n JobSeeker can be inherited from the Person
CityEmployer:	Employer_hired_JobSeeker, Employer_posted_JobOffer Employer_WorksIn_Company

JobOffer:	JobOffer_ispostedBy_Employer,
	JobOffer_requires_Education,
	JobOffer_requireSkill,
	JobOffer_requires_WorkExperience
	JobOffer_requiresminqual_Company
JobSeeker:	JobSeeker_ishiredby_Employer,
	JobSeeker_haseducation_Education,
	JobSeeker_hasskills_Skill,
	JobSeeker_hasugdegree_Education,
	JobSeeker_haspgdegree_Education,
	JobSeeker_hasotherdegree_Education,
	JobSeeker_isofferedsalary_JobOffer,
	JobSeeker_worksin_Company,
	JobOffer_isofcompany_Company
Skill:	JobSeeker_hasSkills_Skill
WorkExperience:	Work_Experience_hascompanyexp_Company

The ontology is created consisting of nine basic classes/entities and few more, namely Company, Education, Person, City, State, Employer, JobOffer, JobSeeker, Skill, WorkExperience and Education. Each entity has its own properties, as mentioned below.

The Company entity is defined with attributes, namely company name, location, city, state and number of employees.

The Education entity is defined using the datatype properties, namely graduate degree, post-graduate degree, UG university name, PG university name, passing year, city and country.

The Person entity is linked with the Education entity because every human will have their education qualification, and it is identified using attribute fields such as gender, birthdate, person's first name, last name and address.

WorkExperience is represented using an object property: Company (because work experience must be linked with a company that the individual worked for), and a set of data type properties, such as position, start date, end date, city, country and skill (multiple skills can be also assigned).

The Employer posts the JobOffer and it has datatype attributes or properties, namely the name of employer, their username and corresponding password, along with the salary offered.

The JobSeeker entity has the datatype properties, namely jobseekername, jobseekercity, qualification and experience.

The Skill entity has the datatype property, namely skillno and languagename.

Finally, the last entity, JobOffer, is posted by an employer requiring fields such as Skill, Language, Education and WorkExperience, and has a paid salary.

To obtain higher accuracy when matching a given job description with the profile of the jobseekers, instead of the knowledge level, the jobseekers position can be chosen. For example, a person with Java as a skill and work experience in a "Data Analyst" position means that the person is more likely to have advanced Java knowledge compared to any other jobseeker that possesses advanced Java skills, having the designation of "Junior Java Developer".

Concept-based ontologies share many structured similarities despite the language in which they are created. Ontologies depict instances, classes, attributes and relations. Class/Entity description and instance description of the "SearchAJob" Ontology in Protégée are shown in Figure 12.3.

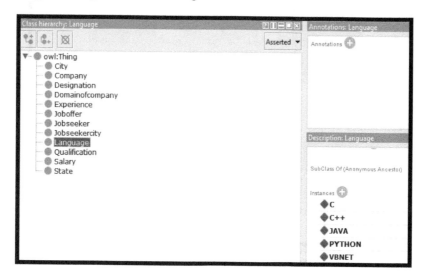

Figure 12.3. *Class – instance description of ontology in Protégé.*
For a color version of this figure, see www.iste.co.uk/mehta/tools.zip

In Figure 12.3, the entities forming the ontology are represented through the basic characteristics of object property. An open-source ontology editor, named Protégé, is used to design and develop the ontology. Here, the object property "posts" represents the inverse of the "isPostedBy" object property. Indicating the object property in this way describes triplets, like an Employer posted a Job. The different classes or entities used in the proposed SearchAJob ontology describe company data, employers data, job offers posted and jobseekers data in a RDF format so that it can be stored on the server. With regard to the representation of layers, the proposed ontology also represents the application's data layer.

12.4. Implementing the proposed ontology

The company's online recruitment process will be classified into a sequence of steps, namely:

– analyzing the requirements;

– job posting done by the employers;

– jobseekers application retrieval;

– interviewing and allocation of job.

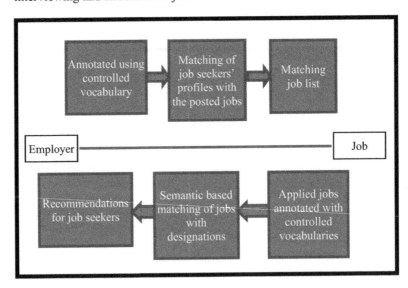

Figure 12.4. *IT job ontology proposed structure*

The chapter describes the various steps in which online recruitment is done using semantic technology supported by linguistic web technologies. Using RDF and the controlled vocabularies to annotate various jobs and applications received, are the main building blocks of the entire process. Figure 12.4 represents the entire process flow.

12.4.1. *Architecture of semantics-based job ontology*

The proposed architecture depicts the way in which the proposed ontology will be implemented for online recruitment platform development. As defined in Table 12.1, all of the functionalities are implemented to enable the creation of a user interface. The main goal behind creating the application is to provide aid to the candidate in the selection process. The selection process would be manual for the candidate at a later phase. But initially, the system will provide help to match job applications with the posted job offers, where a number of resumes are scrutinized manually and many working hours are spent on it. The chapter proposes a job-searching interface using PHP language, as shown in Figure 12.5.

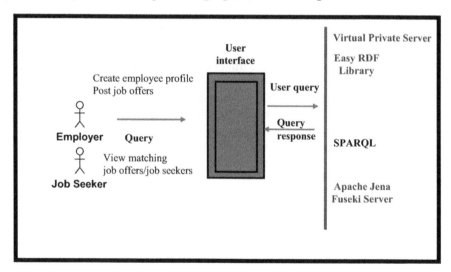

Figure 12.5. *Architecture of ontology*

The online SearchAJob system is a PHP application. Using the interface, the employer, as well as the jobseeker, can easily post, as well as search for a job using the interface. Multiple fields required by the employer related to the job and job posting are also provided. On the user side, a flexible interface for the user to search for a job and post their personal and professional details are provided. For employers, controls for adding new job offers, deleting job offers, as well as updating job offers are provided. For jobseekers, similar controls are also provided for updating their profile.

The input given to the system is fed to the Apache Jena Fuseki server. To overcome the Protégé limitations, the triple are directly executed using this server.

12.4.1.1. *Working of Apache Jena Fuseki server*

The SPARQL server used here is Apache Jena Fuseki. The main functionality of the server is its ability to run as an independent working framework administration and also as a Java web application.

Fuseki comes in two structures, a solitary framework "webapp", joined with a UI for administration and query, as the "main", and a server that is appropriate to run as a larger deployment. Fuseki gives the SPARQL 1.1 conventions to inquiry and update just as the SPARQL Graph Store convention. It is user-friendly and enables the SPARQL queries to be executed. With the installation of Java, it runs as a Java web application as an independent server. A key feature of Semantic Web applications is that the semantic principles of RDF, RDFS and OWL can be utilized to infer information that isn't explicitly mentioned in the graph. Jena's induction API provides a way through which the triples can be shown up in the store, although they had been added explicitly. The collection of standards that define Semantic Web technology includes SPARQL, which is a query language for RDF. It is the responsibility of SPARQL API to handle SPARQL for query, as well as for update. Both OWL and RDFS ontology languages are supported in Jena by SPARQL API. In all, Fuseki is a data publishing server, which can present and update RDF models over the web using HTTP and SPARQL. The steps for installing and working with the Fuseki server are as follows:

– Install Apache Jena Fuseki Server on the C drive of your system.

– Run Apache Jena Fuseki on the web browser.

– Uploading the ontology (SearchAJob) dataset in it.

– Upload the required ontology (.owl) file.

The uploaded .owl file is processed by the Fuseki server and displays the total number of extracted triples.

After uploading the SearchAJob data set and the .owl file, the Fuseki server executes the SPARQL queries directly, without using the Protégé tool. The following steps should be followed to execute the SPARQL queries:

– Set up the SPARQL Endpoint.

– Type "http://localhost:3030/SearchAJob/JobOntology" in the browser.

– Write and execute a basic SPARQL query or perform any Create, Read, Update and Delete (CRUD) operation to display the subject, object and predicate for the given SearchAJob ontology.

Examples for SPARQL query execution on the Fuseki server.

Select Query: Query to display the execution of SPARQL query on the dataset.

Figure 12.6. *Select query execution on the server. For a color version of this figure, see www.iste.co.uk/mehta/tools.zip*

Using the IP address of the virtual private server, the GUI of Apache Jena Fuseki is accessed. Different SPARQL queries are executed on the dataset to perform all of the CRUD operations, as shown in Figures 12.7 and 12.8.

Insert Query: Execute Insert SPARQL Query on the SearchAJob Dataset.

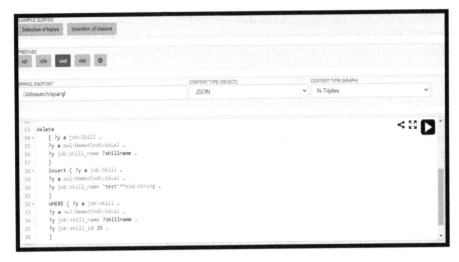

Figure 12.7. *Insert query execution on the server. For a color version of this figure, see www.iste.co.uk/mehta/tools.zip*

Delete Query: Execute Delete Query on the SearchAJob Dataset.

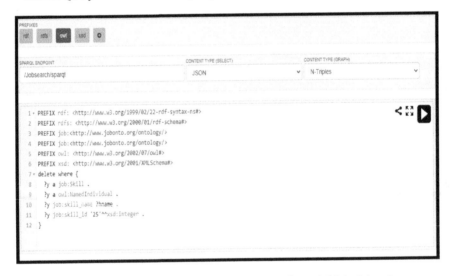

Figure 12.8. *Delete SPARQL query on the SearchAJob dataset. For a color version of this figure, see www.iste.co.uk/mehta/tools.zip*

The importance of the Jena Fuseki Server is that it exposes the triples as a SPARQL end-point that is accessible over HTTP. It has the characteristics to represent RDF data. It answers various SPARQL queries over HTTP. Using RDF data, the Fuseki server provides REST-style interaction. It is generally used as a mediator to execute federated queries.

12.4.1.2. Implementation and result of SearchAJob ontology using EasyRdf library

The Semantic Web enabled SearchAJob system is implemented using PHP language and a Java-based server, Apache Jena Fuseki Server. PHP language is selected because it supports the EasyRdf library with easy programming and responsive features. Another benefit of PHP is it is a platform-independent language that is required to implement a distributed system on the WWW with a heterogeneous type of computational resource. To implement the ontology structure, the EasyRdf library is used.

```php
<?php
set_include_path(get_include_path() . PATH_SEPARATOR . '../lib/');
    require_once "EasyRdf.php";
    require_once "html_tag_helpers.php";

    // Setup some additional prefixes for DBpedia
    EasyRdf_Namespace::set('rdf', 'http://www.w3.org/1999/02/22-rdf-syntax-ns#');
    EasyRdf_Namespace::set('owl', 'http://www.w3.org/2002/07/owl#');
    EasyRdf_Namespace::set('job', 'http://www.jobonto.org/ontology/');
```

Figure 12.9. *Including EasyRdf library in PHP. For a color version of this figure, see www.iste.co.uk/mehta/tools.zip*

Below PHP coding, an insert operation of skill class is mentioned. Skill class has two attributes: skillid and skillname. The researcher has implemented the GUI form for entering skillname and skillid, and then both the values are stored in an ontology (.owl) file as triple, as shown in Figure 12.10.

```php
<?php
set_include_path(get_include_path() . PATH_SEPARATOR . '../lib/');
    require_once "EasyRdf.php";
    require_once "html_tag_helpers.php";

    // Setup some additional prefixes for DBpedia
    EasyRdf_Namespace::set('rdf', 'http://www.w3.org/1999/02/22-rdf-syntax-ns#');
    EasyRdf_Namespace::set('owl', 'http://www.w3.org/2002/07/owl#');
    EasyRdf_Namespace::set('job', 'http://www.jobonto.org/ontology/');
    //EasyRdf_Namespace::set('dbp', 'http://dbpedia.org/property/');
$endpoint = new EasyRdf_Sparql_Client('http://localhost:3030/jobonto/sparql', 'http://localhost:3030/jobonto/update');


if(isset($_POST['skilladd']))//Add record
{

    $sid=$_POST['skillid'];
    $sname=strtoupper($_POST['skillname']);


    $result = $endpoint->update("insert data
                {
                    job:Skill$sid rdf:type job:Skill .
                    job:Skill$sid rdf:type owl:NamedIndividual .
                    job:Skill$sid job:skill_id '$sid'^^xsd:integer .
                    job:Skill$sid job:skill_name '$sname'^^xsd:string .
                }");

    //====================================================================
        //display success message
    if($result) {
            echo "<script>alert('Record is inserted successfully!')</script>";
            echo "<script>window.open('skillDetail.php','_self')</script>";
        }
}
```

Figure 12.10. *Execution of insert query using EasyRdf library in PHP.*
For a color version of this figure, see www.iste.co.uk/mehta/tools.zip

The PHP interface developed for employer and jobseeker is shown in Figure 12.11.

Figure 12.11. *SearchAJob system portal developed in PHP.*
For a color version of this figure, see www.iste.co.uk/mehta/tools.zip

The employers and jobseekers dashboard are developed in PHP, as shown in Figures 12.12 and 12.13.

Figure 12.12. *SearchAJob system employer's dashboard.*
For a color version of this figure, see www.iste.co.uk/mehta/tools.zip

Figure 12.13. *SearchAJob system jobseeker's dashboard. For a color version of this figure, see www.iste.co.uk/mehta/tools.zip*

The main goal of developing a Semantic Web enabled job searching system is to provide flexibility to the users. The job searching platform is implemented as a PHP application, with both the employer and jobseeker's interface, as shown in Figure 12.12 and Figure 12.13.

A jobseeker who wants to search for a job and a different job offer in the IT domain can easily search through the system and get the required details. The jobseeker has their own dashboard created once they register and login to the system. They are provided with the various options of updating their profile, filling educational information, skill details, searching a job and will also be able to see the list of jobs that they have applied for with the corresponding interview details. Similarly, at the employers end, multiple companies/employers are allowed to register, login and create their profile. Once the profile is generated, the employer can view their dashboard, update their profile, manage jobs and view the jobs applied for by the candidates.

Figures 12.14 and 12.15 represent the various job offers posted by the employers and various company details viewed by the jobseeker, respectively.

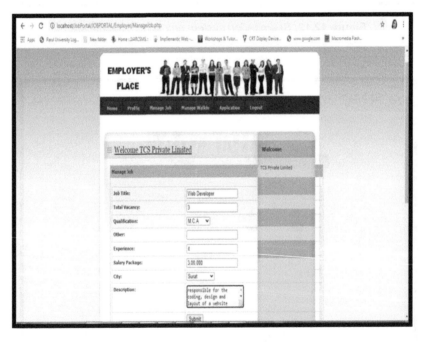

Figure 12.14. *Job offers posting by employer. For a color version of this figure, see www.iste.co.uk/mehta/tools.zip*

The jobseeker searches for a specific job and gets a list of matching jobs, as shown in Figure 12.15.

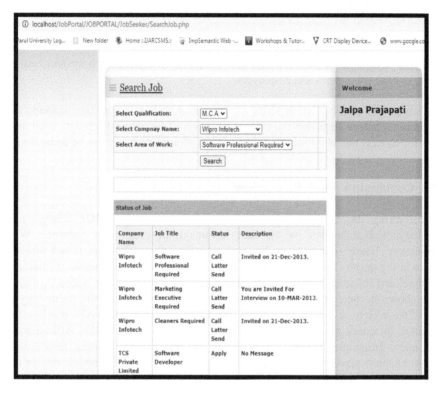

Figure 12.15. *Job searching by jobseeker. For a color version of this figure, see www.iste.co.uk/mehta/tools.zip*

12.5. Benefits of Semantic Web enabled SearchAJob system

The most important benefit observed for the SearchAJob ontology is its extendability and reusability feature through which any other ontology can easily reuse the proposed ontology in the future. The following benefits are gained by the proposed ontology in comparison to the traditional searching techniques.

– The PHP interface provides a user-friendly interface, enabling job searching and posting easily.

– All basic CRUD operations can be easily performed on the ontology.

– The ontology developed is open source and can be easily extended in the future.

– It is not proprietary, compared to a database which is always proprietary.

– Meaning-specific search can be done by removing the word similarity context of the web searching.

– The data retrieved are specific and more relevant.

– The advantage of the semantic technology in this job search system can be availed by the jobseekers and employers.

Despite the number of benefits of the semantic-based ontology system, the limitations observed are that the direct utilization of Semantic Web data used as a basis for context based information retrieval are an important issue to be addressed.

12.6. Conclusion and future scope

Integrating the semantic concepts and RDF relationship, RDF schema and Ontology Web Language is the best advantage of creating a Semantic Web application. These concepts can be used to infer information that is not directly shown in the graph. The Apache Jena Fuseki server provides an interface to link the database, and its programming interface enables the triples that are added explicitly to be shown in the store. One of the standards defining the semantic technology is SPARQL, which is a query language for RDF. The SPARQL API handles the SPARQL for querying, as well as for updates. Moreover, the SPARQL API supports both query languages, namely OWL and RDFS. Finally, the Apache Jena Fuseki data publishing server can help to present and update the RDF models across the web using HTTP and SPARQL.

The chapter proposes a SearchAJob ontology that is created specifying the various classes related to the jobseeker, as well as the employer. The ontology specifies the different specializations such as Area, City, Job, Language and Platform information. The basic scenario describes how employers create different announcements for the job vacancies. The jobseeker, on the other hand, can access the vacancies through the search queries executed on the PHP interface and apply for the corresponding job. The matching of employer requirement and jobseeker qualifications can easily be reflected through Semantic Web enabled searching. Reusing any existing ontology in the proposed ontology is observed.

The contributions of the chapter are as follows:

– an approach for building ontology-based knowledge base, which is able to capture knowledge-relating job postings, including relevant concepts and attributes;

– a justification of the proposed approach with an application in the IT domain;

– an ontology mechanism for data extraction with a semi-automated method based on a rule-based technique. This mechanism is composed of a text processor for text analyzing and natural language processing, and a set of extraction rules to capture concept instances (Kumar et al. 2021).

12.7. References

Ahmed, N., Khan, S., Latif, K. (2017). Job description ontology. *Proceedings of the 14th International Conference on Frontiers of Information Technology, FIT 2016.* doi: 10.1109/FIT.2016.047.

Amdouni, S. and Karaa, W.B.A. (2010). Web-based recruiting: Framework for CV structuring. *ACS/IEEE International Conference on Computer Systems and Applications, AICCSA 2010*, June. doi: 10.1109/AICCSA.2010.5587018.

Dada, O.S. and Kana, A.F.D. (2019). An ontology-based approach for improving job search in online job portals. *The Journal of Computer Science and its Applications*, 25(1).

Dooms, S. (2013). Dynamic generation of personalized hybrid recommender systems. *Proceedings of the 7th ACM Conference on Recommender Systems*, 443–446.

Faliagka, E., Iliadis, L., Karydis, I., Rigou, M., Sioutas, S., Tsakalidis, A., Tzimas, G. (2014). On-line consistent ranking on e-recruitment: Seeking the truth behind a well-formed CV. *Artificial Intelligence Review*, 42(3), 515–528.

Faliagka, E., Rigou, M., Sirmakessis, S. (2015). An e-recruitment system exploiting candidates' social presence. *Lecture Notes in Computer Science*, 9396, 153–162.

Fazel-Zarandi, M. (2009). Semantic matchmaking for job recruitment: An ontology-based hybrid approach. *Proceedings of the 3rd International Workshop on Service Matchmaking and Resource Retrieval.*

Gatteschi, V., Lamberti, F., Sanna, A., Demartini, C. (2011). Using tag clouds to support the comparison of qualifications, résumés and job profiles. *Proceedings of the ICETA 2011 – 9th IEEE International Conference on Emerging eLearning Technologies and Applications.* doi: 10.1109/ICETA.2011.6112585.

Gómez-Pérez, A., Ramírez, J., Villazón-Terrazas, B. (2007). An ontology for modelling human resources. *11th International Conference on Knowledge-Based Intelligent Information & Engineering Systems KES*, 1, 534–541.

Guedj, M. (2017). Levelized taxonomy approach for the job seeking/recruitment problem. *Proceedings of the 15th International Symposium on Distributed Computing and Applications to Business, Engineering and Science, CSE-EUC-DCABES 2016.* doi: 10.1109/CSE-EUC-DCABES.2016.222.

Hao, W., Yang, Y., Lin, C., Zhai, Z. (2006). QoS-aware scheduling algorithm based on complete matching of user jobs and grid services. *Proceedings of the 2006 IEEE Asia-Pacific Conference on Services Computing, APSCC*, 1(90412012), 433–439.

Hasan, R. and Gandon, F. (2013). Predicting SPARQL query execution time and suggesting SPARQL queries based on query history. Research Report RR-8392, Inria. ffhal-00880314f.

Hexin, L. and Bin, Z. (2006). Skill ontology-based semantic model and its matching algorithm. *7th International Conference on Computer-Aided Industrial Design and Conceptual Design, CAIDC*. doi: 10.1109/CAIDCD.2006.329389.

Huang, S.W., Yu, C.-H., Shieh, C.-K., Tsai, M.-F. (2015). Efficient and scalable SPARQL query processing with transformed table. *IEEE Wireless Communications and Networking Conference Workshops, WCNCW 2015*, 103–106. doi: 10.1109/WCNCW.2015.7122537.

Kumar, N.A. and Ramu, K. (2021). Ontology based website for job posting and searching. *IOP Conference Series: Materials Science and Engineering*, 1042, 012006. doi: 10.1088/1757-899X/1042/1/012006.

Liao, G.-D., You, M.-Z., Wang, G.-C. (2015). Experimental economic research for matching job positions. *International Conference on Behavioral, Economic, and Socio-Cultural Computing, BESC 2015*.

Lu, Y., El Helou, S., Gillet, D. (2013). A recommender system for job seeking and recruiting website. *Proceedings of the 22nd International Conference on World Wide Web Companion*. doi: 10.1145/2487788.2488092.

Miller, E. (2004). The Semantic Web: A web of machine processible data. *W3C Semantic Web Activity Lead*.

Mishra, S. and Jain, S. (2019). Towards a semantic knowledge treasure for military intelligence. *International Journal of Web-Based Learning and Teaching Technologies (IJWLTT)*, IGI Global, 14(3), 55–75.

Mishra, S. and Jain, S. (2021). An intelligent knowledge treasure for military decision support. *Research Anthology on Military and Defense Applications, Utilization, Education, and Ethics*. IGI Global.

Mochol, M., Wache, H., Nixon, L. (2006). Improving the recruitment process through ontology-based querying. *CEUR Workshop Proceedings*, 226, 59–73.

Montuschi, P., Gatteschi, V., Lamberti, F., Sanna, A., Demartini, C. (2014). Job recruitment and job seeking processes: How technology can help. *IT Professional*, 16(5), 41–49.

Niculescu, C. and Trausan-Matu, S. (2009). An ontology-centered approach for designing an interactive competence management system for IT companies. *Informatica Economica*, 13(4), 159–167.

Panchal, R., Swaminarayan, P., Tiwari, S., Ortiz-Rodriguez, F. (2021). AISHE-Onto: A semantic model for public higher education universities. *22nd Annual International Conference on Digital Government Research*. doi: 10.1145/3463677.3463750.

Paparrizos, I., Cambazoglu, B.B., Gionis, A. (2011). Machine learned job recommendation. *Proceedings of the 5th ACM Conference on Recommender Systems, RecSys'11*. doi: 10.1145/2043932.2043994.

Paudel, S. and Shakya, A. (2017). Ontology based job-candidate matching using skill sets. *Proceedings of IOE Graduate Conference*, 8914, 251–258.

PHP (n.d.). PHP [Online]. Available at: https://www.php.net/ [Accded 23 October 2021].

Rana, V. and Singh, G. (2015). MBSOM: An agent based semantic ontology matching technique. *1st International Conference on Futuristic Trends in Computational Analysis and Knowledge Management, ABLAZE 2015*. doi: 10.1109/ABLAZE.2015.7155009.

Sarda, À.V., Sakaria, À.P., Nair, À.À.S. (2014). Relevance ranking algorithm for job portals. *International Journal of Current Engineering and Technology*, 31574(5), 3157–3160 [Online]. Available at: http://inpressco.com/category/ijcet.

Sharma, K., Marjit, U., Biswas, U. (2016). Efficient provenance storage for RDF dataset in Semantic Web environment. *Proceedings of the 2015 14th International Conference on Information Technology, ICIT 2015*. doi: 10.1109/ICIT.2015.21.

Sicilia, M. (2014). *Handbook of Metadata, Semantics and Ontologies*. World Scientific Pub. Co, Singapore.

Stuckenschmidt, H. and van Harmelen, F. (2005). Information sharing on the Semantic Web. *Information Sharing on the Semantic Web*, January. doi: 10.1007/b138282.

Tiwari, S. and Abraham, A. (2020). Semantic assessment of smart healthcare ontology. *International Journal of Web Information Systems*.

Tutorials Point (n.d.). PHP Tutorial [Online]. Available at: https://www.tutorialspoint.com/php [Accded 23 October 2021].

W3Schools (n.d.). PHP Tutorial [Online]. Available at: https://www.w3schools.com/php [Accded 23 October 2021].

Yi, X., Allan, J., Croft, W.B. (2007). Matching resumes and jobs based on relevance models. *Proceedings of the 30th Annual International ACM SIGIR Conference on Research and Development in Information Retrieval, SIGIR '07*, 809-810. Association for Computing Machinery, New York [Online]. Available at: https://doi.org/10.1145/1277741.1277920.

List of Authors

Fatima Zahra AMARA
ICOSI Laboratory
University of Abbes Laghrour
Khenchela
Algeria

ANURAG
Independent researcher
India

Deepika CHAUDHARY
Chitkara Institute of Engineering
and Technology (CIET)
Chitkara University
Punjab
India

Hina J. CHOKSHI
HOD-BCA
Parul Institute of Computer Application
Parul University
Gujarat
India

Gaurav CHOUDHARY
DTU Compute
Department of Applied Mathematics
and Computer Science
Technical University of Denmark (DTU)
Kongens Lyngby
Denmark

Gerard DEEPAK
Department of Computer Science
and Engineering
National Institute of Technology
Tiruchirappalli
India

Sangam DEVA KISHORE REDDY
Department of Electronics and
Communication Engineering
Kalasalingam Academy of Research
and Education
Tamil Nadu
India

Meriem DJEZZAR
LIRE Laboratory
University of Abdelhamid Mehri
Constantine
and
University of Abbes Laghrour
Khenchela
Algeria

Raúl García-Castro
Universidad Politécnica de Madrid
Spain

Jinghua Groppe
Institute of Information Systems (IFIS)
University of Lübeck
Germany

Sven Groppe
Institute of Information Systems (IFIS)
University of Lübeck
Germany

Tobias Groth
Institute of Information Systems (IFIS)
University of Lübeck
Germany

Mounir Hemam
ICOSI Laboratory
University of Abbes Laghrour
Khenchela
Algeria

M.A. Jabbar
Head of the Department CSE
(AI and ML)
Vardhaman College of Engineering
Hyderabad
India

Naren Jeeva
iNurture Education Solutions Private Ltd
JAIN (Deemed-to-be University)
Bangalore
India

Ayush A. Kumar
Department of Chemical Engineering
National Institute of Technology
Tiruchirappalli
India

Moufida Maimour
University of Lorraine
CNRS, CRAN
Nancy
France

Shikha Mehta
Department of CSE and IT
Jaypee Institute of Information
Technology
Noida
India

Kalpana Murugan
Department of Electronics and
Communication Engineering
Kalasalingam Academy of Research
and Education
Tamil Nadu
India

Keshavi Nalla
Bionicsol Bharat Private Limited
Tamil Nadu
India

Cherukuri Nikhil Kumar
Department of Electronics and
Communication Engineering
Kalasalingam Academy of Research
and Education
Tamil Nadu
India

Fernando Ortiz-Rodriguez
Universidad Autonoma de Tamaulipas
Mexico

Ronak PANCHAL
Vidyabharti Trust College of BBA
and BCA
Gujarat
India

Sheeba J. PRIYADARSHINI
Data Science Research Group
CHRIST (Deemed-to-be-University)
Bangalore
India

Shishir Kumar SHANDILYA
VIT Bhopal University
India

Shachi SHARMA
Department of Computer Science
South Asian University
Delhi
India

Patrick SIARRY
Lab Signals, Images and Intelligent
Systems
University Paris-Est Créteil
France

Vikas SIHAG
Sardar Patel University of Police
Security and Criminal Justice
Jodhpur
India

Jaiteg SINGH
Chitkara Institute of Engineering
and Technology (CIET)
Chitkara University
Punjab
India

Dhananjay SINGH CHAUHAN
Cybersecurity and Digital Forensic
Division
Department of SCSE
VIT Bhopal University
India

Donthu Sai SUBASH
Department of Electronics and
Communication Engineering
Kalasalingam Academy of Research
and Education
Tamil Nadu
India

Sanju TIWARI
Universidad Autonoma de Tamaulipas
Mexico

Seshu VARDHAN POTHABATHULA
Bionicsol Bharat Private Limited
Tamil Nadu
India

Dhaval VYAS
C.U. Shah University
Gujarat
India

Index

2022

ZAIDOUN Ameur Salem
Computer Science Security: Concepts and Tools

2021

DELHAYE Jean-Loic
Inside the World of Computing: Technologies, Uses, Challenges

DUVAUT Patrick, DALLOZ Xavier, MENGA David, KOEHL François,
CHRIQUI Vidal, BRILL Joerg
*Internet of Augmented Me, I.AM: Empowering Innovation for a New
Sustainable Future*

HARDIN Thérèse, JAUME Mathieu, PESSAUX François,
VIGUIÉ DONZEAU-GOUGE Véronique
*Concepts and Semantics of Programming Languages 1: A Semantical
Approach with OCaml and Python*
*Concepts and Semantics of Programming Languages 2: Modular and
Object-oriented Constructs with OCaml, Python, C++, Ada and Java*

MKADMI Abderrazak
Archives in The Digital Age: Preservation and the Right to be Forgotten
(Digital Tools and Uses Set – Volume 8)

TOKLU Yusuf Cengiz, BEKDAS Gebrail, NIGDELI Sinan Melih
Metaheuristics for Structural Design and Analysis (Optimization Heuristics
Set – Volume 3)

2020

DARCHE Philippe
Microprocessor 1: Prolegomena – Calculation and Storage Functions –
Models of Computation and Computer Architecture
Microprocessor 2: Core Concepts – Communication in a Digital System
Microprocessor 3: Core Concepts – Hardware Aspects
Microprocessor 4: Core Concepts – Software Aspects
Microprocessor 5: Software and Hardware Aspects of Development,
Debugging and Testing – The Microcomputer

LAFFLY Dominique
TORUS 1 – Toward an Open Resource Using Services: Cloud Computing
for Environmental Data
TORUS 2 – Toward an Open Resource Using Services: Cloud Computing
for Environmental Data
TORUS 3 – Toward an Open Resource Using Services: Cloud Computing
for Environmental Data

LAURENT Anne, LAURENT Dominique, MADERA Cédrine
Data Lakes
(Databases and Big Data Set – Volume 2)

OULHADJ Hamouche, DAACHI Boubaker, MENASRI Riad
Metaheuristics for Robotics
(Optimization Heuristics Set – Volume 2)

SADIQUI Ali
Computer Network Security

VENTRE Daniel
Artificial Intelligence, Cybersecurity and Cyber Defense

2019

BESBES Walid, DHOUIB Diala, WASSAN Niaz, MARREKCHI Emna
Solving Transport Problems: Towards Green Logistics

CLERC Maurice
Iterative Optimizers: Difficulty Measures and Benchmarks

GHLALA Riadh
Analytic SQL in SQL Server 2014/2016

TOUNSI Wiem
*Cyber-Vigilance and Digital Trust: Cyber Security in the Era of Cloud
Computing and IoT*

2018

ANDRO Mathieu
*Digital Libraries and Crowdsourcing
(Digital Tools and Uses Set – Volume 5)*

ARNALDI Bruno, GUITTON Pascal, MOREAU Guillaume
Virtual Reality and Augmented Reality: Myths and Realities

BERTHIER Thierry, TEBOUL Bruno
From Digital Traces to Algorithmic Projections

CARDON Alain
*Beyond Artificial Intelligence: From Human Consciousness to Artificial
Consciousness*

HOMAYOUNI S. Mahdi, FONTES Dalila B.M.M.
*Metaheuristics for Maritime Operations
(Optimization Heuristics Set – Volume 1)*

JEANSOULIN Robert
JavaScript and Open Data

PIVERT Olivier
NoSQL Data Models: Trends and Challenges
(Databases and Big Data Set – Volume 1)

SEDKAOUI Soraya
Data Analytics and Big Data

SALEH Imad, AMMI Mehdi, SZONIECKY Samuel
Challenges of the Internet of Things: Technology, Use, Ethics
(Digital Tools and Uses Set – Volume 7)

SZONIECKY Samuel
Ecosystems Knowledge: Modeling and Analysis Method for Information and Communication
(Digital Tools and Uses Set – Volume 6)

2017

BENMAMMAR Badr
Concurrent, Real-Time and Distributed Programming in Java

HÉLIODORE Frédéric, NAKIB Amir, ISMAIL Boussaad, OUCHRAA Salma, SCHMITT Laurent
Metaheuristics for Intelligent Electrical Networks
(Metaheuristics Set – Volume 10)

MA Haiping, SIMON Dan
Evolutionary Computation with Biogeography-based Optimization
(Metaheuristics Set – Volume 8)

PÉTROWSKI Alain, BEN-HAMIDA Sana
Evolutionary Algorithms
(Metaheuristics Set – Volume 9)

PAI G A Vijayalakshmi
Metaheuristics for Portfolio Optimization
(Metaheuristics Set – Volume 11)

2016

BLUM Christian, FESTA Paola
Metaheuristics for String Problems in Bio-informatics
(Metaheuristics Set – Volume 6)

DEROUSSI Laurent
Metaheuristics for Logistics
(Metaheuristics Set – Volume 4)

DHAENENS Clarisse and JOURDAN Laetitia
Metaheuristics for Big Data
(Metaheuristics Set – Volume 5)

LABADIE Nacima, PRINS Christian, PRODHON Caroline
Metaheuristics for Vehicle Routing Problems
(Metaheuristics Set – Volume 3)

LEROY Laure
Eyestrain Reduction in Stereoscopy

LUTTON Evelyne, PERROT Nathalie, TONDA Albert
Evolutionary Algorithms for Food Science and Technology
(Metaheuristics Set – Volume 7)

MAGOULÈS Frédéric, ZHAO Hai-Xiang
Data Mining and Machine Learning in Building Energy Analysis

RIGO Michel
Advanced Graph Theory and Combinatorics

2015

BARBIER Franck, RECOUSSINE Jean-Luc
COBOL Software Modernization: From Principles to Implementation with the BLU AGE® Method

CHEN Ken
Performance Evaluation by Simulation and Analysis with Applications to Computer Networks

2014

PASCHOS Vangelis Th
Combinatorial Optimization – 3-volume series, 2ⁿᵈ Edition
Concepts of Combinatorial Optimization – Volume 1, 2ⁿᵈ Edition
Problems and New Approaches – Volume 2, 2ⁿᵈ Edition
Applications of Combinatorial Optimization – Volume 3, 2ⁿᵈ Edition

QUESNEL Flavien
Scheduling of Large-scale Virtualized Infrastructures: Toward Cooperative Management

RIGO Michel
Formal Languages, Automata and Numeration Systems 1:
Introduction to Combinatorics on Words
Formal Languages, Automata and Numeration Systems 2:
Applications to Recognizability and Decidability

SAINT-DIZIER Patrick
Musical Rhetoric: Foundations and Annotation Schemes

TOUATI Sid, DE DINECHIN Benoit
Advanced Backend Optimization

2013

ANDRÉ Etienne, SOULAT Romain
The Inverse Method: Parametric Verification of Real-time Embedded Systems

BOULANGER Jean-Louis
Safety Management for Software-based Equipment

DELAHAYE Daniel, PUECHMOREL Stéphane
Modeling and Optimization of Air Traffic

FRANCOPOULO Gil
LMF — Lexical Markup Framework

GHÉDIRA Khaled
Constraint Satisfaction Problems

ROCHANGE Christine, UHRIG Sascha, SAINRAT Pascal
Time-Predictable Architectures

WAHBI Mohamed
Algorithms and Ordering Heuristics for Distributed Constraint Satisfaction Problems

ZELM Martin *et al.*
Enterprise Interoperability

2012

ARBOLEDA Hugo, ROYER Jean-Claude
Model-Driven and Software Product Line Engineering

BLANCHET Gérard, DUPOUY Bertrand
Computer Architecture

BOULANGER Jean-Louis
Industrial Use of Formal Methods: Formal Verification

BOULANGER Jean-Louis
Formal Method: Industrial Use from Model to the Code

CALVARY Gaëlle, DELOT Thierry, SÈDES Florence, TIGLI Jean-Yves
Computer Science and Ambient Intelligence

MAHOUT Vincent
Assembly Language Programming: ARM Cortex-M3 2.0: Organization, Innovation and Territory

MARLET Renaud
Program Specialization

SOTO Maria, SEVAUX Marc, ROSSI André, LAURENT Johann
Memory Allocation Problems in Embedded Systems: Optimization Methods

2011

BICHOT Charles-Edmond, SIARRY Patrick
Graph Partitioning

Printed and bound by CPI Group (UK) Ltd, Croydon, CR0 4YY

27/10/2024

14580320-0001